A BLOOMSDAY
POSTCARD

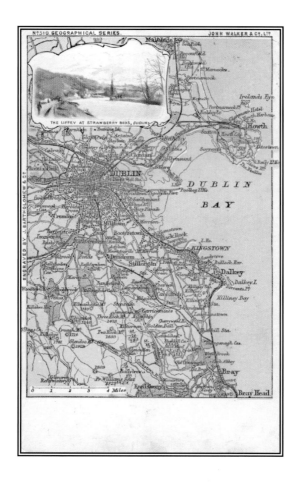

Contained within the delineations of this postcard map of Dublin and environs are most of the places associated with the early life of James Joyce and his most famous book, Ulysses. Many of the seaside locations immortalized in Ulysses are easily identifiable and visible; from north to south these include: Malahide, Howth, Bailey Lighthouse, Pigeon House, Irishtown, Sandymount, Sydney Parade, Kingstown, Sandycove, Bullock Harbour, Dalkey, Killiney, Bray and Bray Head. The photographic cartouche showing the Liffey at the Strawberry Beds was a popular picnic location for Dubliners and the characters of Ulysses.

Niall Murphy

A BLOOMSDAY
POSTCARD

THE LILLIPUT PRESS • DUBLIN

© The Lilliput Press, 2004

First published 2004 by
THE LILLIPUT PRESS LTD
62-63 Sitric Road, Arbour Hill, Dublin 7, Ireland
www.lilliputpress.ie
in association with
The National Library of Ireland

A CIP record for this title is available from the British Library.

ISBN 1 84351 043 X (pbk)
1 84351 050 2 (hbk)

Set in 11 on 14.5 point Garamond
Designed and typeset by Anú Design, Tara
Printed by LEGO of Vicenza

Love and death are
the principle themes of Ulysses.

For my wife Loraine,
and to the memory of deceased family members.

Contents

Acknowledgments

Anthony Byrne, Edward Chandler, Joseph Collins, Neal Duggan, Eileen Griffiths, John Griffiths, Mary Griffiths, Seamus Kearns, Felicity M. Matthews, Rosemarie Mulcahy, Sean Mulcahy, Loraine Murphy, James O'Brien, Brian O'Neill, Lil Scully, LizAnne Stacey and the late Phillip John Whymark.

Special Acknowledgments
Brendan O Donaghue, Former Director, National Library of Ireland.
Antony Farrell, Editor-in-Chief, The Lilliput Press.

Preface

It is said that more books have been published about James Joyce than about any other author in the history of literature. This particular odyssey into his world is, by and large, a glowing tribute to the man himself and to his most famous book, *Ulysses*. Possibly because the opening three chapters of *Ulysses* are difficult, many would-be readers have been discouraged. Some abandon ship with a half-hearted resolve to come back on board at a later date, but never do. Others are left with a vague feeling of inadequacy for not trying. The majority of failed Ulysseans are convinced that the book should be left to students, scholars and devotees of James Joyce.

One of the main objectives of this eulogy is to impart a good working knowledge of the essential background, characters and story of *Ulysses*, which will encourage fresh or renewed attempts to conquer one of the greatest literary masterpieces of the world.

In the third chapter, a short explanation of the Homeric background and schema introduces a further eighteen chapters under the titles that Joyce originally assigned to *Ulysses*. Inasmuch as a few pages will allow, these chapters provide the bare outline of the story and the movements of the characters. The final chapter contains pen-pictures of the leading characters, supported by additional information on captioned postcard illustrations.

Some twenty-five years ago the die was cast when I turned my attention to trading in collectibles for a livelihood. Old postcards were part of the business and putting aside those associated with Joyce and *Ulysses* was an inexpensive way of feeding a habit. The sole qualification for inclusion in the collection, which today numbers over 1600, was that the postmark on each postcard identified it as being posted in Dublin and environs during 1904. The entire collection has now been acquired by the National Library of Ireland.

Many of the messages on the postcards chosen for illustration describe day-to-day life in Edwardian Dublin. At times they eerily mirror events in *Ulysses*. The individuals who wrote and posted these humble records of their existence walked side by side in Dublin with those immortalized by Joyce. It is an honour to muster these postcard characters and march them shoulder to shoulder alongside those of *Ulysses* across the waters of Lethe, to be forever frozen in a time warp of Dublin on 16 June 1904.

Niall Murphy
Dublin, 16 June 2004

Select Bibliography

A full and fair bibliography of books about James Joyce is impossible, for reasons of space. In this instance, ten of the most frequently consulted publications are acknowledged, with sincere apologies to the excluded:

Shari Benstock and Bernard Benstock, *Who's He When He's at Home* (Illinois 1980).

Harry Blamires, *The Bloomsday Book* (London 1985).

Peter Costello, *James Joyce* (Dublin 1980).

Richard Ellmann, *James Joyce* (Oxford 1982).

Don Gifford with Robert J. Seidman, *Ulysses Annotated* (California 1989).

Clive Hart and Leo Knuth, *A Topographical Guide to James Joyce's* Ulysses (Colchester 1975).

Matthew Hodgart, *James Joyce* (London 1978).

James Joyce, *Ulysses* (London 1960).

The National Library of Ireland, *James Joyce* (Dublin 1982).

Robert Nicholson, *The Ulysses Guide* (London 1988).

1

A Short Biography of James Joyce

JAMES AUGUSTINE JOYCE was born on 2 February 1882 at 41 Brighton Square, Rathgar, Dublin. He was the eldest son of ten children born to John and Mary Joyce, both of comfortable, middle-class, Catholic origins. At the time of their marriage John Joyce had a good job as a rate collector, and had inherited both property and cash. However, this lasted only a few years and gradually the Joyces were reduced in circumstances, partly by the loss of John Joyce's job but mainly because of his lifelong propensity for spending beyond his means.

Educated almost exclusively by the Jesuits, Joyce was enrolled as a paying boarder at their Clongowes Wood College at the early age of six. On arrival, he earned the nickname 'half-past six' for the witty reply to an enquiry about his age. Joyce was happy in Clongowes and prospered there in his education, character and knowledge of human behaviour. Not surprisingly, his sojourn at Clongowes is by and large favourably mentioned throughout *Ulysses*, most particularly the kindness of the then rector, Father John Conmee SJ.

However, in 1891 John Joyce's job as a collector of rates was abolished, and the boy was taken from Clongowes. That year was of great political significance in Ireland, seeing the downfall and death of Charles Stewart Parnell. A divorce action taken by the husband of Parnell's mistress, Kitty

Rathgar

O'Shea, had led to a bitter split in the Irish Home Rule Party, followed by a public denunciation of Parnell by the Catholic bishops, who declared him unfit for leadership. Parnell was abandoned by the majority of his hitherto loyal followers. John Joyce and his son remained intensely loyal to 'The Chief' and the nine-year-old Joyce composed a poem attacking Tim Healy, the principal opponent of Parnell. The poem, 'Et Tu Healy', was published in broadsheet form by John Joyce and distributed to his friends. Parnell's downfall, coinciding with the downturn in the family fortunes, deeply affected the life and work of James Joyce.

After his removal from Clongowes, Joyce educated himself and spent a short time under the tutelage of the Christian Brothers at the O'Connell Schools in North Richmond Street. In 1893 he was entered as a so-called free boy with the Jesuits at Belvedere College, Dublin, where he distinguished himself academically, became head boy and won valuable cash prizes in national examinations. In the autumn of 1898 he entered University College Dublin, which was formally under the control of

[3]

Joyce was born in 1882 at 41 Brighton Square, Rathgar, a township united with Rathmines.

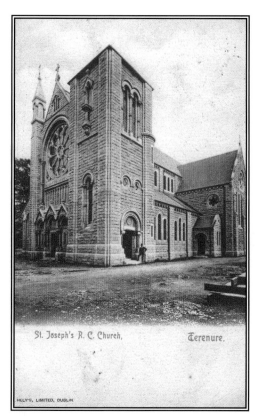

St. Joseph's R. C. Church, Terenure.

HELY'S, LIMITED, DUBLIN

[4]

Three days after his birth, James Augustine
Joyce was baptized at St Joseph's Chapel of
Ease, Roundtown, a short distance from St
Joseph's RC Church, Terenure, opened in 1904.
Roundtown was so called after a circle of houses
in Terenure. In *Ulysses* Joyce honours the place
of his baptism by using the old name of
Roundtown, rather than Terenure, as the location
for Mat Dillon's fondly remembered party. Joyce
liked and was superstitious about his birthday,
so it was no coincidence that, forty years later
to the day, *Ulysses* was formally published by
Shakespeare and Company in Paris.

[5]

In 1884 John Joyce took a lease at 23
Castlewood Avenue, adjoining Rathmines Road,
pictured here.

August. 14. 1904

Rathmines Road

Front Avenue from the Castle, Clongowes Wood College,   Co. KILDARE.

will stay like this till I go home.
Union day is on the 4th June all the past Clongonian
come down and we will have a good day. B

In 1887 the Joyce family moved to 1 Martello Terrace, Bray, County Wicklow. Their fashionable residence was at times subject to flooding caused by dramatic storms battering the Esplanade, such as this captured by local Bray photographer, B. Killick.

On 1 September 1888 Joyce, accompanied by his parents, drove up this avenue to Clongowes Wood College, Sallins, County Kildare, where they were received by the rector, Father John Conmee SJ.

the Jesuits. Joyce soon became well-known in the life of the university and contributed prominently to the debates of the Literary and Historical Society.

In April 1900 his appreciative notice of *When We Dead Awaken* by Henrik Ibsen was published in the *Fortnightly Review*, for which he received payment of twelve guineas. He spent that summer in Mullingar with his father, who was working on the election lists. During this sojourn he wrote a play called *A Brilliant Career*, which he subsequently destroyed after unfavourable comment by William Archer. In 1901 Joyce combined with Francis Skeffington to publish, at their own expense, a pamphlet called 'Two Essays', after their pieces had been rejected by the college magazine, *St Stephens*. Joyce's essay, 'The Day of the Rabblement', attacked the Irish literary establishment.

In 1902 he graduated, without distinction, in modern languages. He had completed about fourteen years under the Jesuits, their influence on his life and character clearly reflected in his writings. Like most of their past pupils, he usually spoke well of them.

After his graduation the Jesuits offered him a teaching post, which he turned down. For a short time he studied medicine at St Cecilia's Medical School in Dublin. On 1 December 1902 he left Dublin for Paris, where he made an abortive attempt to enter a French medical university. Joyce was back in Dublin for Christmas, at his father's expense, in the new year returning to Paris where he became a part of the bohemian life of the city. In April 1903 news of his mother's serious illness was telegrammed by his father and he returned immediately. She died of cancer on 13 August.

By this time Joyce had achieved limited literary success. He had twenty-seven reviews published in the *Daily Express*, had written some poetry and about fifteen short stories. In January 1904 he submitted a story called *A Portrait of the Artist* to the editors of *Dana*, which was rejected. However, he continued writing on the same theme and completed over six hundred pages of a work called *Stephen Hero*. This exercise eventually formed the basis for two of his later novels, *A Portrait of the Artist as a Young Man* and *Ulysses*. Meanwhile he received payments for articles in various literary journals, and had short stories published in the *Irish Homestead*, three of which, 'The Sisters', 'After the Race' and 'Eveline', were later to appear in *Dubliners*. For a time, he had a temporary job as a teacher at a preparatory school in Dalkey.

On 10 June 1904 he met a young Galway girl called Nora Barnacle in Nassau Street, Dublin. He made an appointment to meet her but she failed to appear. Undaunted, he wrote requesting another meeting and, on 16 June 1904, she did turn up and together they walked out to Ringsend. This was the beginning of a relationship that was to last for thirty-seven years. Joyce commemorated the anniversary of their first day together in a most remarkable fashion, by setting the entire events of *Ulysses* on 16 June 1904. This date is now established in the calendar of world literature and celebrated internationally each year as Bloomsday.

On 8 October 1904 Joyce and Nora left Ireland. They were to spend the rest of their lives in permanent exile in Europe except for brief visits to Dublin and Galway. For a short time they stayed in Pula, Croatia, where Joyce taught English to naval officers. In 1905 they moved north to Trieste, Italy, where he secured another job as an English teacher in the Berlitz School. Soon after his arrival he arranged for a printing of fifty copies of 'The Holy Office', a broadside poem written prior to his departure from Dublin, in which he once again attacked and ridiculed the leading figures of the Irish Literary Revival, including Yeats, Synge, Moore, Colum and Russell.

On 27 July 1905 a son, Giorgio, was born and on 26 July 1907 a daughter, Lucia. With the exception of over a year spent in Rome, where Joyce worked as a bank clerk, the family remained in Trieste from 1905 until Italy entered the First World War in 1915. The family then moved to Zurich.

[8]

Throughout their four years in Bray, the Joyce family loved to picnic in the beauty spots of County Wicklow including Powerscourt, Poulaphouca and Glencree, all of which receive special mention in *Ulysses*. The reverse of this postcard contains an interesting racial observation: 'it was simply rotten, cold wet & muddy, enough to kill a black'.

[9]

Joyce's father, John Stanislaus Joyce, was born in 1849, the only son of a prosperous Cork city family. John Joyce inherited extensive properties and cash. In 1894 James Joyce and his father visited Cork city when some of these assets were sold at auction.

Lawrence, Publisher, Dublin.

Sugar Loaf Mountain, (from Terrace, Powerscourt House.)   Co. WICKLOW.

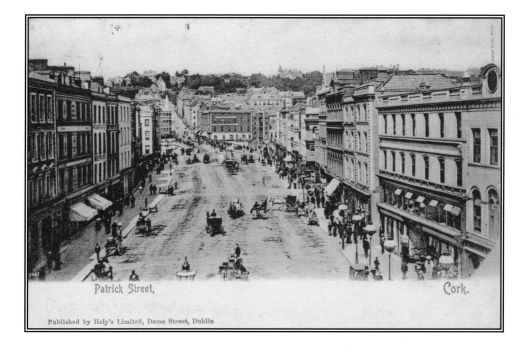

Patrick Street,   Cork.

Published by Hely's Limited, Dame Street, Dublin

A Short Biography of James Joyce   ❧   7

Kingstown Harbour   Valentines Series

Howth.

We have an electric tram service from Dublin to Howth which is a lovely drive & the view from the top of the hill is beautiful O do come & see for yourself I know you would enjoy it

The Wrench Series.

His first major publication, a book of poems called *Chamber Music*, appeared in 1907 and *Dubliners* in 1914. In that year he wrote an account of his relationship with one of his pupils, a young girl named Amalia Popper, under the title 'Giacomo Joyce', which was not published. In 1916 *A Portrait of the Artist as a Young Man* appeared, followed in 1918 by his only play, *Exiles*. His perpetual financial problems were eased considerably by the news, in early 1917, that he was to receive a series of anonymous cash gifts. His benefactor later proved to be Harriet Shaw Weaver, the avant-garde editor of *The Egoist*. Joyce had begun work on *Ulysses* in 1914 and in March 1918 excerpts were first published in an American magazine called *The Little Review*.

In 1919 Harriet Shaw Weaver also serialized *Ulysses* in *The Egoist* and tried, without success, to find a British printer willing to undertake the risk of printing the book. In 1920 an American court injunction halted publication of further episodes in *The Little Review* and, in the following year, a conviction for publishing obscene material was obtained against the editors.

In July 1920 the family moved to Paris for what was intended to be a short visit, but they stayed for twenty years. Shortly after his arrival, Joyce became friendly with Sylvia Beach, a young American bookseller who owned a newly opened bookshop called Shakespeare and Company. It was her firm that finally published *Ulysses*, on the occasion of Joyce's fortieth birthday, 2 February 1922. Its publication reverberated around the world in the succeeding years, and through it Joyce achieved international fame as a writer and recognition among his peers for what was later acclaimed as a masterpiece of artistic innovation.

At the time of the publication of *Ulysses* Paris was the centre of the literary universe and Joyce became its shining star. Among his friends and admirers were many of the great writers of the period including Marcel Proust, Ezra Pound, T.S. Eliot, F. Scott Fitzgerald, Ernest Hemingway and a young Samuel Beckett. Joyce delighted in the role of a Parisian celebrity. He often dined in the fashionable

H.E. CARDINAL VANNUTELLI.

EASON & SON, LTD.   PHOTO. LAFAYETTE.   DUBLIN & BELFAST.

About the turn of the century Joyce abandoned Catholicism and subsequently refused to be party to the practices of a religion in which he did not believe. On this principle he turned down the dying request of his mother to make a good confession and receive communion. Joyce was castigated by the Catholic establishment for *Ulysses*. He would have been greatly amused by the comments on this postcard, which appear to be from one nun to another: 'He was here yesterday executing a graceful & gracious glide for about ten minutes.'

restaurants of the Champs-Élysées, where he drank excessively and tipped lavishly. His reputation was further enhanced by translations of his works into several languages, the most prestigious being the first complete French translation of *Ulysses*, published in 1929 by Adrienne Monnier in Paris.

In 1927 *Pomes Penyeach*, a collection of his later poems, was published. Following the appearance of *Ulysses*, Joyce embarked on *Finnegans Wake*. It took seventeen years to complete and was finally published in 1939. Joyce had partially invented a new language for his last work, but

[13]

In the summer of 1904 Joyce worked as a temporary teacher at Francis Irwin's preparatory school, Dalkey Avenue, Dalkey, a picturesque coastal town between Kingstown and Bray. Some of the events of this sojourn are vividly depicted in the 'Nestor' episode of *Ulysses*.

it was poorly received, even among his family and friends, many of whom found it incomprehensible.

In 1931 Joyce married Nora in a London registry office so that his estate would pass to their children. His daughter, Lucia, had shown early signs of mental ill-health. She was eventually diagnosed as schizophrenic and permanently confined to a sanatorium. This was a source of great distress to Joyce.

In later years he was almost blind and underwent some twenty unsuccessful and painful operations to correct a deteriorating eye condition. His general health also declined at the outbreak of the Second World War, although nothing specific had been diagnosed. When Germany invaded France Joyce moved the family, first to Vichy and then on to Switzerland. Some weeks after his arrival he developed stomach cramps and underwent an operation for a perforated duodenal ulcer. At first it appeared that the operation had been successful but he died on the morning of 13 January 1941. He was buried two days later at the Fluntern Cemetery in Zurich.

Dalkey.

EASON & SON, LTD., DUBLIN & BELFAST

DUBLIN HORSE SHOW, 1904.
MAKING FOR THE ENCLOSURE.

PHOTO. LAFAYETTE

14

Kingstown.
Pavilion.

15

Copyright Chas. Cook, Kingstown.

August 9th 5 04

[14]

On 27 August 1904, the last night of the Dublin Horse Show week, Joyce appeared in an important concert in the Antient Concert Rooms on the same programme as J.C. Doyle and John McCormack. Joyce received a good review for his performance in the *Freeman's Journal*, and a special compliment for his rendering of 'The Croppy Boy'.

[15]

Joyce had a good tenor voice and at one time considered a career as a professional concert singer. He is reputed to have appeared in concert here at the Pavilion, Kingstown. Intriguingly, the sender of this postcard writes: 'Laurie Wylie & his mannikin are here this week. Stratton, Dan Leno & C. Stanley.' Eugene Stratton, the Negro impersonator, features prominently in *Ulysses*.

[16]

If ever a scene encapsulated the ambience of a 1904 Joycean Dublin summer, it is this postcard moment in time taken at the junction of Suffolk Street, Nassau Street and Grafton Street.

16

Stephens Green West   Dublin

Lynch Memorial Stone, Galway   Valentines Series

[17]

In 1904 Joyce was injured in a fight over a young woman in St Stephen's Green. A man called Alfred Hunter came to Joyce's assistance. Hunter was said to be Jewish and married to an unfaithful wife. Hunter may have partly inspired the character of Leopold Bloom in *Ulysses*.

[18]

In July 1912 Joyce and his family visited Ireland and stayed in Galway and Dublin. The main purpose of this visit was the intended publication of *Dubliners*. Maunsel & Co., fearing a libel action, now refused to publish *Dubliners* without changes. On 11 September 1912 they formally destroyed the sheets; fortunately, Joyce had managed to obtain one set of proofs. Angered and disenchanted, he and his family left Dublin that night from North Wall. He was never again to return to Ireland and his beloved city of Dublin.

CATHAIR LUIMNIGHE. Cloch na Síothchána; Droichead Tuath-Mhumhan; Caisleán ríogh
Seaghán; árd-teampall Mhuire; an tSionainn.
(361) This is not Greek : it is the language which no one speaks.

[19]

The Irish Language Revivalists
published this postcard view of the
Treaty Stone, Limerick. The sender
shares Joyce's dispassionate view
of the Irish language. His message
reads: 'This is not Greek: it is the
language which no one speaks.'

[20]

The most famous date in world literature is
16 June 1904, universally celebrated as
Bloomsday. As may be seen on the reverse
of this postcard of actress Dora Barton, the
postcard bears the magic date to all admirers of James Joyce: 'Dublin, 11.45 am, Ju 16,
04.' Interestingly, the stamp is affixed upside
down, which could be by chance or perhaps
it is a deliberate political insult to King Edward
VII and Britain. Alternatively, in the language
of stamps, this means 'I am not free.' The
handwritten message on the picture side
reads: 'Best love to Tim. Hope all at home are
well. I'm sorry I couldn't get a few more like
this, Moll. How is T. Kelly.' The reverse message reads: 'Dear Bridge I received your
P.C. I suppose I will go home the 1st week in
July "D.V.". My brother is coming down
from Belfast so I will wait to see him. I sent
a P.C. to Tim. I suppose he will take my life
for doing it. Yours Mollie.'

1654 B ROTARY PHOTO. E.C.   MISS DORA BARTON.   LANGFIER. GLASGOW

Miss Mai Stewart and James Joyce shared
a common interest in music, particularly
singing. By coincidence, both achieved
limited success in singing examinations
during 1904. Joyce was quite unhappy with
a creditable bronze medal in the Feis Ceoil,
while Miss Stewart was very pleased with
a humble pass in her test. On 16 June 1904
Miss Stewart sent news of her singing
success, by postcard from Blackrock, County
Dublin, to her sister 'Cis' at The Hotel, Cashel,
County Tipperary: 'My dearest Cis, I received
your welcome postcard & I am praying hard
for J.B. since. We got result of singing exams
which were successful. I got a pass. We got
our photos taken today several groups Tennis
Hockey etc. and also the Orchestra & drill
class which turned out splendid. I hope we
will be able to procure some copies
I know you would like them.'

BRAY HEAD AND PARADE.

Dear St. I am sending you particulars of Bagatelle table by this post. This is rather a good view of Bray, only it shld be the Esplanade & not Parade. Mrs Willie

[22]

The Joyce family home commanded this panoramic view of the Esplanade, Bray, County Wicklow. On the front of this postcard the sender, 'Willie', amends the caption of legendary British publisher, Raphael Tuck & Sons, as follows: 'This is rather a good view of Bray, only it should be the Esplanade & not Parade.'

[23]

Rugby football and bullying were part of life at Clongowes Wood College, which may have contributed to Joyce's dislike of violence and physical sports. In any event a six-year-old boy was utterly unsuited to compete with boys at least three or four years his senior. Although he disliked rugby, or perhaps for this reason, Joyce competed, with some success, at cricket and athletics.

After the black & white drawing by S. T. DADD

FOOTBALL INCIDENTS.
NEARLY IN (*Rugby*).

[24]

The young Joyce was fascinated by the excitement of bazaars, mainly charitable fund-raising ventures rather like sales of work today. Two receive special mention in his writings: the Araby Bazaar in *Dubliners*, which he visited in 1894 at the Royal Dublin Society, Ballsbridge, and the Mirus Bazaar in *Ulysses*, actually held in May 1904 at the same venue.

[25]

The sender of this postcard availed of the printed message: 'We had a merry time' to add 'during the holidays. I hope you enjoyed yours. I was glad to hear that you got such good marks at the Inter. You must get a prize this year.' Joyce himself won valuable cash prizes in this examination in 1894 and 1895.

[26]

Howth, the charming fishing village nine miles north of Dublin, was beloved of James Joyce and features prominently and frequently throughout the pages of *Ulysses*.

26

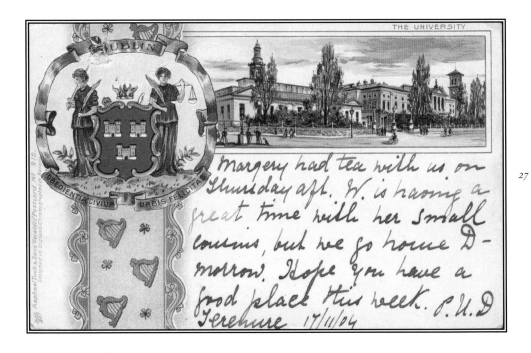

THE UNIVERSITY

Margery had tea with us on Thursday aft. W. is having a great time with her small cousins, but we go home to-morrow. Hope you have a good place this week. P. U. D Terenure 17/11/04

27

The National Library, Dublin.

HELY'S, LIMITED. DUBLIN.

28

[27]

In 1898 Joyce entered University
College, 86 St Stephen's Green
South. The Royal University,
Earlsfort Terrace, pictured here,
was an examining body only, from
whom Joyce received his Bachelor
of Arts degree on 31 October 1902.

[28]

The National Library of Ireland
was a focal point of intellectual
and literary life in Dublin. Joyce
was a frequent visitor to the reading
room and was acquainted with the
director, T.W. Lyster, and librarians
Richard Best and W.K. Magee.
All three appear as themselves
in the 'Scylla and Charybdis'
episode of *Ulysses*.

[29]

The caption in Gaelic, *Bárr na
maidne duit*, is translated as
'The top of the morning to ye.'
The ironic observation at foot, that
two Irish together leads to 'a split',
is a truism more than likely written
with the Irish Home Rule Party split
over the Parnell issue in mind.
In *Ulysses* Joyce returns repeatedly
to the issues of the Parnell split.

[30]

On 10 June 1904 Joyce met Nora
Barnacle in Nassau Street, Dublin,
and six days later they spent their
first day together. Joyce celebrated
the importance of his relationship
with Nora by setting the entire
events of *Ulysses* on 16 June 1904.

29

30

A Galway Girl.

31

32

[31]

Nora Barnacle was born in Galway city in 1884. Following a family row she moved to Dublin, where she worked as a chambermaid in Finn's Hotel in Nassau Street. Not unlike this Galway girl, she was tall, auburn-haired and attractive. Only four months after their first meeting she threw in her lot with the young writer and accompanied him to Europe, for what was to be a relationship that lasted until his death thirty-seven years later.

[32]

In 1906 Joyce found work for a year as a bank clerk in Rome. He was always critical of the wealth and splendour of the Papacy.

[33]

Dubliners reacted badly to *Ulysses* and the portrayal of the seamier side of their city. Joyce was not surprised and observed that his fellow Dubliners would not easily forgive him. He reasoned with his aunt that if his book was not fit to read, as she asserted, then life was not fit to live.

[34]

The City of Dublin Steam Packet Co. operated the Royal Mail Service between Kingstown and Holyhead. In 1909 Joyce and Giorgio sailed into Kingstown for a family reunion.

33

Dear Jennie,
I am just starting
for a shop window stroll to see
the latest Paris fashion; hope
to be home at 8·30 ready for
T.P.   Ta Ta for the present.
Yours &c.   Alf.

34

A Cabin (double) for Mr. R. Shortis reserved with pleasure
on Royal Mail Steamer leaving Kingstown on Friday morning 24/-.
J. M. Burke

Unterwäldneralpen   Sonnenaufgang   Berneralpen

GRUSS vom
PILATUS

Aussicht vom
Tomlishornweg nach Süden

LITHOGR. KUNSTANSTALT FREY & SÖHNE, vorm Frey & Conrad, ZURICH

[35]

At the outbreak of the Second World War Joyce and his family took refuge in Zurich, as they had done during the First World War. Joyce died in Zurich in 1941. Nora lived on there and died in 1951. They are buried in the Fluntern Cemetery, Zurich. A statue of Joyce marks their grave.

2

The Pictorial Postcard

IN 1904 IRISH POSTCARD PUBLISHER, Hely's Limited, Dublin, prophetically proclaimed in their advertising slogan: 'Pictorial Post Cards Have Come to Stay'. The use of the word pictorial was gradually replaced by picture and, in time, the two words 'post' and 'card' were joined as one.

The first postcards were issued by the government of Austria in 1869 and were plain-backed cards with a printed stamp. Shortly afterwards other countries throughout the world, including Britain, produced similar issues. In September 1894 regulations were introduced in Britain and Ireland allowing the use of pictorial postcards, provided that the message and picture were confined to one side and the address only on the other. By the turn of the century pictorial postcards were widely circulating.

In 1902 the British postal authorities allowed the use of a divided back for both message and address. This measure led to an explosion in the number of postcards in production and use and began what is generally recognized as the golden age of the pictorial postcard. The Edwardian era (1902-10) is accepted by many as encompassing the entire golden age, although some will argue it ended in 1914 with the outbreak of the First World War.

By the year 1904 the sending, receiving and collecting of postcards had become a well-established part of Edwardian life in Dublin. A postcard and stamp could be purchased for less than two pence and there were up to six

HELY'S, LIMITED   HIS MAJESTY LEAVING LEINSTER LAWN AFTER LAYING THE FOUNDATION STONE   DUBLIN.
OF THE ROYAL COLLEGE OF SCIENCE.

mail deliveries a day in Dublin and one on Sunday. In the 'Nausicaa' episode of *Ulysses* there is a description of the nine o'clock postman doing the final deliveries of 16 June 1904 to the houses adjacent to Sandymount Strand.

In an age of few private telephones, the postcard provided a popular, easy and reliable method of communication that did not involve the tedium of letter writing. Edwardian Dubliners could reasonably expect – and there are several examples in this book – that a postcard posted in the morning would be delivered to the recipient by the afternoon or evening of the same day.

An entirely new industry arose to meet the enormous demand for postcards to suit all occasions. Publishers recruited the best photographers of the day for views of topographical interest. The best artists were contracted to produce impressions of any subject thought to be of interest to the consumer. Coloured postcards proved extremely popular. Many postcards were laboriously hand-coloured, while much of the colour printing was contracted to specialized German firms. The superb chromo-lithographic process of printing, invented in

[36]

This postcard of His Majesty leaving Leinster Lawn was one of six issued by Hely's Limited, Dublin, to commemorate the King's visit in 1904. The address was handwritten by an employee of Hely's to their customer in Swinford, County Mayo. The perforations on the halfpenny stamp spell out the letters HLD for the company's name. This was a security device utilized by businesses with large stocks of unused stamps. The stamp has been placed upside down on this postcard, due to either carelessness or to the relatively common practice in Edwardian Ireland of making a political statement by turning the King upside down.

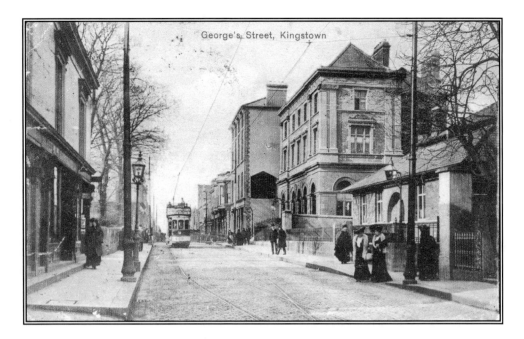

George's Street, Kingstown

[37]

The open-topped electric tram
is on its way from Kingstown to
Nelson's Pillar. The publisher's
name does not appear but it is
probably a splendid example of
local photography and
postcard production by Chas.
Cook, Kingstown.

late nineteenth-century Germany, proved irresistible to
the postcard-buying public, although these postcards were
considerably more expensive to buy.

Among the famous international artists whose works are
illustrated in this book are Louis Wain, C. Dana Gibson,
Lance Thackery and Raphael Kirchner. Cats acting like
humans were a speciality of Louis Wain, although the odd
time he used frogs or other animals. Louis Wain had a
life afflicted by financial difficulties and severe mental
ill-health. Towards the end his cats took on a wild and
mildly unpleasant look compared with those of his early
years.

C. Dana Gibson was world famous for his drawings of
beautiful women, which appeared in magazines and books
entirely devoted to his work. Females of all ages aspired to
what was commonly called the 'Gibson Girl' look.

Lance Thackery took delight in exposing the mores
and foibles of the British upper classes. In 1904 he executed a series of six so-called 'Oilettes' for Raphael Tuck
& Sons showing humorous leap year situations.

Raphael Kirchner was one of the principal postcard

Rathmines, Dublin

proponents of art nouveau, which flourished in Paris at the turn of the nineteenth century. His postcards sometimes depicted beautiful young girls in states of undress beyond the point of prudent despatch through the postal system.

In 1904 the Dublin postcard market traded in a state of irrational exuberance as publishers, large and small, strove to satiate the almost limitless demand. The main British-based publishers competing for market share were Raphael Tuck & Sons, Valentine and Hartmann, while the dominant Irish firms were Lawrence, Eason & Son Limited and Hely's Limited.

However, the postcard business, like any other, was highly competitive. There were many casualties, most notably Wrench Limited who dominated the British and Irish market at the turn of the century. By 1902 Wrench Limited had borrowed heavily to outfit a large number of shops with display stands exclusively devoted to selling their own productions. Although greatly admired contemporaneously, postcards at a penny each could not generate the necessary cash flow to repay their massive

[38]

Hely's Limited published this animated view of Rathmines. A most interesting postcard message reads: 'Look out for Miss Zena Dare in "Catch of Season" on P. Cards.'

[30]

The sender of this lovely soubrette, Miss Gabrielle Ray, is reminded of a girl called 'Nora'. She informs Miss A. Mooney, 43 Londonbridge Road, Sandymount: 'The usual question:– who does this remind you of? especially the right eye', and continued over: 'How are you after Tom-T-S on Saturday.'

borrowings and the company went bankrupt. Whether through leftovers, remainders or bankrupt stock sales, the elegant Wrench Limited postcards, with their tiny fish-like hallmark, were still in common usage in 1904.

Not least among the many publishers who competed for a share of the lucrative Dublin postcard market was the firm of Hely's Limited, Dame Street, the former employer of Leopold Bloom. In common with other publishers, they produced their own standard issues of topographical views, depicting scenes of monuments, historic buildings and streets. The year 1904 proved a

27. 9. 04. When I came down stairs this morning
Your   two very nice Cards, my dear Friend
The Boat Slip   Howth
were waiting to say "good morning" to me.
Thank You so much for them. Millicent.

Malahide   The Beach

The Wrench Series No. 8963

[40]

The Boat Slip at Howth is one of the many illustrations in this book timelessly recording the love affair between Millicent, a Dublin girl, and her French beau, Francisque de Boissieu, Château de la Forêt, Toulon sur Allier, France.

[41]

The charm and style of the Wrench Series is illustrated in this evocative view of The Beach, Malahide, County Dublin.

vintage one for the production of special-event postcards by Hely's Limited. They surpassed all their competitors with extensive coverage of the royal visit of King Edward VII. They also featured the Dublin Horse Show and the rather novel event of motor racing at Portmarnock. One of their main competitors, Eason's, also published a good selection of Dublin Horse Show scenes. Interestingly, both Eason's and Hely's Limited used the services of Lafayette, a well-known firm of photographers.

For more than thirty years, prior to the postcard boom, the firm of Lawrence were prominent in Irish photographic publishing. Through the efforts of their legendary photographer, Robert French, Lawrence accumulated a vast array of more than 50,000 photographic images of Ireland, all of which, fortunately, are preserved today in the National Library of Ireland. Thus the firm of Lawrence was perfectly poised to establish dominance of the Irish market in printed photographic images. Unlike Wrench Limited, Lawrence were astute enough to realize from experience that an animated view of O'Connell Street, Dublin, would sell a thousand times more copies than a fair day on Main Street, Borrisokane, County Tipperary. Accordingly, Lawrence published the popular scenes of large Irish cities and towns and left the more difficult pickings to smaller firms and local publishers. The British publisher Valentine was the main challenger to Lawrence for the popular market, but they could never match the superb photographic imagery of their Irish competitor.

If surviving topographical postcards of Dublin and environs is the criteria for success, it would seem that a number of small publishers were well able to compete with the giants of the trade. They avoided direct competition for the mass market and concentrated on the unusual or local views. Stewart & Woolf, London, produced delicately hand-coloured views of Clyde Road, Howth, the Great Northern Railway Terminus, Palmerston Park, Westland Row, and other interesting

Dublin views. Chas. Cook, a local publisher, carved out a huge niche against fierce competition for the valuable postcard market of Kingstown, the point of arrival and departure to and from Britain.

Many publishers resorted to what only can be described as gimmickry to catch the attention of postcard-buying Dubliners. This novelty genre included midget, miniature, diamond, bookmark, peat and the so-called 'Hold-to-Light' postcards. Surviving examples of these abnormally sized gimmicks are scarce, particularly the 'Diamond Book Postcard', while the normal-sized peat and 'Hold-to-Light' are relatively common.

'Hold-to-Light' postcards were published in two distinctly different series by the same company, W.H. Berlin. They became known in Dublin as 'Hold-to-Lights' from the instruction which appears on the front of the most popular of the two series: 'Pray hold this card up to the light and you shall see a charming sight.' When this instruction is obeyed the black and white view turns to beautiful colour. The other W.H. production involved the tedious and laborious task of cutting out small pieces by hand, mainly windows and a quarter moon, which gave a night-time, moonlit effect to views of central Dublin.

Ireland's sole contribution to postcard gimmickry appears to be the peat postcard. In our examples the publisher's name does not appear but the method of paper production is proudly stated: 'Paper made from Irish Peat at the Celbridge Peat Paper Mills, Co. Kildare.' A further message in verse extols the postcard's origins as part of an Irish bog:

> *I was a sod of turf*
> *But now am Paper brown;*
> *and used for wrapping parcels up*
> *In every house and town.*

Nearly all prominent publishers produced comic postcards. Lawrence garnered a huge share of this market by

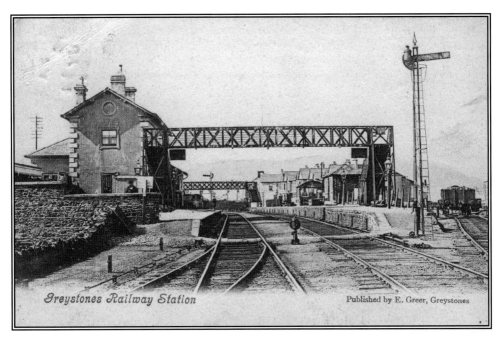

Greystones Railway Station   Published by E. Greer, Greystones

[42]

Local publishers, like E. Greer, Greystones, carved out a profitable niche for themselves by publishing attractive and interesting local views. Employees of Greystones Railway Station obliged Mr Greer by standing to attention on either side of the tracks.

concentrating on the Irish comic genre. They commissioned established Irish artist John Carey, who signed most of his postcards. The vast Lawrence series included Irish dancing, pipers, peasants, illustrated songs and various comic postcards. Some of the supposedly comic postcards portrayed the stage Irishman or 'Paddy' in a poor light, in much the same way as the 'coloured races' were ridiculed and lampooned in foreign postcard publications. Although many publishers produced imitations of John Carey, they all lacked the inimitable style and imagination of Ireland's leading postcard illustrator.

In about 1904 Hely's Limited belatedly attempted to grab a share of the 'write-away' comic market. This term was used to describe an early type of postcard that provided a picture, space for a message and a printed catch-all line, all on the front. It would seem that Hely's Limited were quite unaware of the 1902 regulation permitting message and address on a divided back or perhaps they decided to chance it. In the event they published a series by Irish artist Frank Rigney, which proved relatively unsuccessful. (Rigney's 'write-aways' pale to insignificance

Kate Kearney's Cottage, Killarney

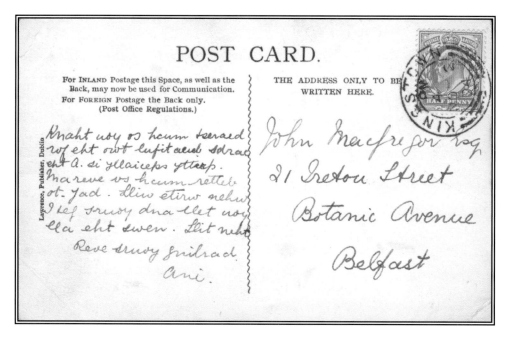

POST CARD.

For INLAND Postage this Space, as well as the
Back, may now be used for Communication.
For FOREIGN Postage the Back only.
(Post Office Regulations.)

THE ADDRESS ONLY TO BE
WRITTEN HERE.

Lawrence, Publisher, Dublin

Knaht uoy os hcum tseraed
rof eht owt lufit ueb sdrac
eht A. si yllaiceps yttærp.
Ma reve os hcum rettet
ot Jad. Lliw etirw nehw
I teg sruoy dna llet uoy
ela eht swen. Ltit neht
Reve sruoy ylidaed.
Ani.

John Macfregor esq
21 Ireton Street
Botanic Avenue
Belfast

The intense love of Ina for John MacGregor is concealed from prying eyes by the simple code of writing the message backwards. The apparently unintelligible writing translates, when the code is broken, as: 'Thank you so much dearest for the two beautiful cards. The A. is specially pretty. I am ever so much better today. Will write when I get yours and tell you all the news. Till then. Ever your darling, Ina.'

when compared with those of Louis Wain.)

B. & N. Limited, Dublin, produced a fine series of evocative 'Dublin Sketches' by an artist who signed in Irish, called Fagan. The proud claim of this firm was that their postcards were 'designed and printed in Ireland'.

As might be expected, there are numerous references to postcards in *Ulysses*. The first mention of a postcard is by an acquaintance of Buck Mulligan towards the end of the opening episode, 'Telemachus'. The young man speaks of a postcard from Mullingar, County Westmeath, in which his friend Alec Bannon mentions his new girl-friend, Milly Bloom, the fifteen-year-old daughter of Leopold Bloom. The next time we hear of a postcard is in the 'Calypso' episode. Mr Leopold Bloom returns home to find that the postman has delivered a postcard and two letters. The postcard is from Milly Bloom to her mother, Molly. It is interesting that Joyce would utilize two postcards from Mullingar to link his characters and establish the blossoming love affair between Milly Bloom and Alec Bannon. There are several stories or subplots in which postcards are central to the narrative.

One of the main subplots in *Ulysses* concerns the sending to Denis Breen of an anonymous postcard bearing an insulting coded message. It is not clear what the message is meant to convey, but Denis Breen, who is half mad anyway, is determined to take an action for libel against the perpetrators of the hoax. He and his wife, Josie, spend most of the day traversing the streets of Dublin in search of a solicitor, and are a source of general amusement and comment.

In the 'Cyclops' episode the Denis Breen postcard hoax is debated at length in Barney Kiernan's public house. An argument develops as to whether Denis Breen had a reasonable case for libel against the hoaxers. J.J. O'Molloy, a down-and-out barrister, pronounces his opinion that anything written on a postcard is publication and that an action could be taken on the grounds that the message implied that Denis Breen was insane.

In support of his argument, O'Molloy cites a famous British test case where writing on a postcard was adjudged to be sufficient evidence of malice.

During the 'Aeolus' episode, set in the offices of the *Evening Telegraph*, an interesting postcard incident is discussed. It concerns Lady Dudley, the wife of the lord lieutenant of Ireland, who decided to buy a postcard view of Dublin from one of the hawkers outside the Viceregal Lodge, her official residence in the Phoenix Park. It turned out to be a postcard commemorating one of the Invincibles who had perpetrated the murders in the Phoenix Park some years previously. As a result, the postcard sellers had to appear before the recorder to answer charges.

Central to the 'Eumaeus' episode is the fact that W.B. Murphy, from Carrigaloe, Queenstown Harbour, is a barefaced liar. In the cabman's shelter Murphy is regaling his audience, which includes Mr Bloom and Stephen Dedalus, with tall tales of his exploits around the world. One particular story concerns the ferocious man-eaters of Peru whom Murphy had seen with his own eyes eating corpses and the raw livers of dead horses. As proof of his integrity, Murphy produces a postcard of these savage cannibals which, he claims, was sent to him by a friend. The postcard features a group of primitive Bolivian Indian women and infants that hold Murphy's audience spellbound for a time. Mr Bloom silently observes that the postcard is addressed to a Mr Boudin in Chile and not, of course, to the liar Murphy, as claimed.

Edwardian Dubliners delighted in sending a postcard, suitable for their collection, to a family member, friend or sweetheart. Postcard albums were specially manufactured in a wide variety of designs to house and display these highly regarded collections. A small proportion of these albums survived and collecting early postcards is a popular hobby today.

The illustrations in this book have been selected from

Do you recognise anybody here? Expect you think we look dangerous. Hope you are pleased with your new career.

[44]

Many photographers automatically printed postcard-sized photographs with a postcard back. This young Dublin girl, Miss N. Mulcahy, could have requested this photograph of herself and her hockey-playing chums to be printed on a postcard, which she then despatched to her gentleman friend in England.

[45]

Dan Leno, the popular music-hall entertainer, passed away in 1904. The sender has left a Joyceanesque epitaph: 'Poor old Dan,' and over, 'Gone but not forgotten.'

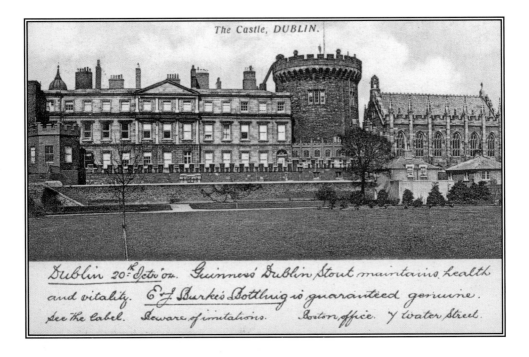

The Castle, DUBLIN.

Dublin 20ᵗʰ Octʳ'o4. Guinness' Dublin Stout maintains health and vitality. E & J Burke's Bottling is guaranteed genuine. See the label. Beware of imitations. Boston office. 7 Water Street.

a collection of about 1600 survivors, painstakingly accumulated over the past twenty-five years. Ten years into the hunt for postcards sent or received in Dublin and environs in the year 1904 a famous postcard dealer and dear friend, the late P.J. Whymark, found the first one bearing the magic and treasured date to all Joyceans and lovers of *Ulysses*: Dublin, 16 June 1904.

One of the most fascinating aspects of the illustrations are the messages of ordinary people who walked the streets of Dublin side by side with the characters of *Ulysses*. They bought their postcards, wrote their lines, affixed their stamps and posted them to friends and loved ones throughout the world. In doing so with love and affection, each person has left behind a small imprint of their individuality, a quality that Joyce so eloquently expresses throughout *Ulysses*.

Sometimes the messages eerily mirror events and situations described in *Ulysses*. There is a rescue from drowning in Kingstown, crime and punishment in Grafton Street, the Great Storm of 1903, King Edward's

[46]

This handwritten printed advertising message was despatched from Dublin to Boston on 20 October 1904. The definitive assertion that 'Guinness' Dublin Stout maintains health and vitality' precedes the later, and more famous slogan, 'Guinness is good for you.'

visit, memories of a 'departed day' spent in Howth and several other accounts of day-to-day life in Joyce's Dublin. Among the many tales of love, three are transacted in varying degrees of intimacy: Millicent and Francisque de Boissieu, Jack Millar and Maude Tighe, and Ina and John MacGregor.

In the mid-1980s postcards from Millicent to Francisque de Boissieu appeared on the London market. In time the Irish-interest postcards found their way into the stocks of Dublin postcard dealers and thereafter into

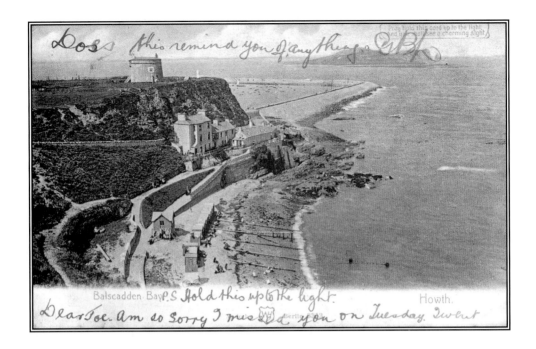

Does this remind you of anything. GHH

Pray hold this card up to the light, and if so shall see a charming sight

Balscadden Bay. P.S Hold this up to the light. Howth.

Dear Joe. Am so sorry I miss you on Tuesday. I went

O'Connell Bridge. Dublin.

Made by W. H. Berlin. 3162.

[48]

This novel series of Dublin views by W.H. Berlin was first published in 1904 and known as 'Hold-to-Light' postcards. When the instruction is obeyed, the black-and-white view turns to colour: 'Pray hold this card up to the light and you shall see a charming sight.'

[49]

W.H. Berlin also produced this different type of 'Hold-to-Light'. The windows and quarter moon were cut out to give a night-time effect in central Dublin when the postcard is held up to the light.

the collection of 1904 postmarks. We may deduce from the messages on the front of her postcards that Millicent appears to be a young, well-educated middle-class Dublin girl who lived 'by the sea', probably in Howth. She calls Francisque her 'dear friend' and on one occasion, rather daringly, signs off with a Freudian misspelling, duly corrected, of the word 'affectionately'. We never learn if the love affair between Millicent and Francisque blossomed to fruition. Self-evidently, the descendants of Francisque sold his collection but Millicent's has yet to appear. Unknown to Millicent, Francisque, in the time-honoured tradition of the archetypal Frenchman, carried on a postcard liaison with another Irish girl called Louie. As will be seen, Millicent was definitely on more intimate terms with Francisque.

The Maude Tighe collection of about 200 postcards turned up at a Dublin auction in the early 1990s. Jack Millar sent Maude a few postcards a week, mainly to confirm visits to her home at 31 Victoria Avenue, Donnybrook. He went out of his way to accumulate interesting postcards for Maude, from places as far away as Egypt and Rome. Jack was highly strung and very much in love, as one recorded message indicates: 'Am mad I can't see you tonight can't get off. Going to have a row in the office and give in resignation.' Presumably they lived happily ever after.

The love of a girl called Ina for John MacGregor of Belfast is intimately recorded on her surviving postcards. Ina used a simple code to hide her words of endearment for John by writing her message backwards. She often calls him 'darling' and 'dearest' and signs off 'ever your darling Ina'. In one particular postcard she combines her code, English and French, to tell John: 'I ma llits, avec tout mon coeur à toi mon cher toujours' (I am still, with all my heart to you my dear always).

The main themes of *Ulysses*, love and death, could not be better mirrored in words and picture on a postcard than by the final illustration of this book. It is titled

'The end of the Journey' and depicts a poignant family meeting. The postcard has been very carefully selected by a young Dublin girl called Effie for despatch to her girlfriend, Miss Rita O'Brian, 7 North Great Georges Street, Dublin. The sad message reads: 'Glad to get your note this morning. But sorry I can not meet you, as Mother is sinking rapidly & I may say there is no hope now. Yours in haste. Effie.'

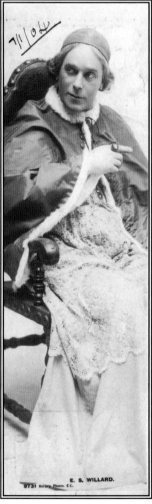

[50]

This bookmark postcard published by Giesen's was described as, 'Book-Post, Giesen's panel-cards'. Here we see the most popular postcard personality of the day, Miss Marie Studholme.

[51]

Rotary printed an instruction on the back of their 'Book Post Card': 'Sender's name and address only allowed here. Signature on Picture Side.'

[52]

Another Giesen, featuring Miss Topsy Sinden in classical pose.

[53]

Rotary relies on the ever-popular felines for one of their 'Book Post Cards'.

54

[54]

Here is a rare 'Diamond Book Post Card' from Rotary, showing the ubiquitous Marie Studholme to good advantage for her many admirers.

[55]

Rotary named this half-size novelty a 'Midget Post Card'.

[56]

The Philco Publishing Company calls this example a 'Miniature Post Card'. Interestingly, the postcard bears a Blackrock postmark dated 17 June 04 and carries the enigmatic message 'B.B.B.E. 16-6-04'.

[57]

The unusual aspects and origins of Peat postcards are fully explained here. They tended to be sentimental, patriotic and appealed to visitors. This example was sent to Springfield, Mass., USA.

[58]

The Irish language message on the right of this Peat post-card is translated immediately underneath. The personal message to Miss Robinson in England reads, 'Hard times come again no more. A.L.R.'

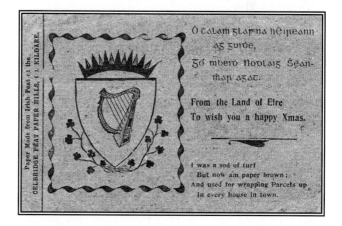

[59]

Postmarked Dublin, 16 February 04, this postcard bears the receiving stamp of St-Jean-de-Monts, Vendée, France, of 18 February 04. Contrary to the sender's opinion, these straw-berry pickers do not appear to be native Irish!

[60]

The Irish Lion Cubs was published by the Zoological
Gardens, Dublin. The 1904 *Thom's Directory* records that
in 1901 there were 154,444 paid admissions to the Dublin
Zoo. This postcard recalls a happy visit to see the three
new cubs and a memorable trip to Killiney.

[61]

On 27 December 1904, as the Royal
Mail Service ship the *Majestic* drew
near the Irish coast, Mr Arthur Bray
sent a postcard to his brother William
in Philadelphia, USA. Along with all the
other mail posted on board this ship,
the postcard was marked with the
maritime cancellation, 'PAQUEBOT'
and unloaded at Queenstown for
transportation by train to Dublin. On
board the Dublin train the postcard
received the cancellation of the Dublin
and Queenstown Travelling Post Office
(TPO). It was not unloaded at
Kingsbridge Station, Dublin, but made
the return journey to Queenstown. The
postcard arrived in Philadelphia on 5
January 1905. The message reads,
'3 pm. Dec 27-04. Dear Will, nearing
the Irish coast – had a calm voyage all
the way. Took 2nd cabin after leaving
N.Y. food fine etc. Am well this sea
voyage doing me good. Writing Frank
and Nellie, Your brother Arthur.'

[62]

The reciprocal love between a mother and her child was a common sentiment pictured on Edwardian postcards. This theme resonates throughout *Ulysses*.

One more for your album, with beauty and flowers;
Good fortune come with it, and bright, happy hours.

E. E. G.

[63]

The gold miners attempting to cross the White Pass, Yukon, in winter is a highly unusual postcard to turn up postally used in Dublin.

Colonial and Continental Church Society,
9, Serjeants' Inn, Fleet Street, London, E.C.   The White Pass, Yukon, in Winter

RUSSO-JAPANESE WAR. — No 2. — Port-Arthur : 8th. Feb. 1904.

Naval Combat. Immediate reply by the Russian Fleet.

64

RUSSIAN OUTRAGE ON HULL FISHING FLEET.
22.10.1904.

65

66

Hely's, Limited, Dublin.]　　　　MOTOR RACES, PORTMARNOCK.　　　　[Photo by Lafayette
AUTOMOBILE CLUB 200 GUINEA CHALLENGE CUP.　A. Lee Guinness and J. W. Stocks starting.

[64]

The Russo-Japanese War is mentioned several times in *Ulysses*. This postcard from London to Dublin received the scarce maritime cancellation at sea, 'H. & K. PACKET', i.e. Holyhead and Kingstown.

[65]

On 22 October 1904 the Russians opened fire on the Hull fishing fleet, creating a major international incident. This is another postcard from Ina to John MacGregor written partly in code, English and French.

[66]

This view of the Automobile Club 200 Guinea Challenge Cup motor race at Portmarnock, County Dublin, was published by Hely's Limited from a photograph by Lafayette of Westmoreland Street, Dublin.

[67]

Photographic postcards of famous Edwardian stage performers were sold in the millions each year. This writer tells her friend: 'I was hearing Marie Studholme made £2000 by her photos alone.'

67

226M
ROTARY PHOTO, E.C.　　MISS MARIE STUDHOLME.

[68]

Louis Wain was one of the most popular artists ever commissioned by postcard publishers and is famous for his cats. This postcard is from the 'Write Away' series of Raphael Tuck & Sons, England, and was chromographed in Saxony, Germany. The idea was to give the sender a start to his message: 'It's really too bad' at a time when the message and address were confined by regulations to separate sides of the postcard.

[69]

Hely's 'Write Away' postcards by Irish artist Frank Rigney were pale imitations of Louis Wain and relatively unsuccessful.

[70]

This is a 'Hold-to-Light' official souvenir postcard of the World's Fair held in 1904 in St Louis, Missouri, USA. The fair was immortalized in Judy Garland's legendary film, *Meet Me in St Louis*.

[71]

A gentleman has carefully selected this postcard with a view to influencing Miss Lodge, 8 Moyne Road, Rathmines. Amusingly, he writes: 'Will you and Mrs Lodge come over on Friday afternoon for tea and fun? H.'

70

71

72

Roadside Butter Market.

73

Irish Fair.

[72]

Irish peasant life is fairly
represented in this scene of
a roadside butter market. It
is a good example of social history
accurately portrayed on postcards.

[73]

Fairs, for the purpose of selling
animals and other farm produce,
were a common feature of Irish life.
These weekly and monthly events
were usually held on the main streets
of Irish country towns and villages.

74

2767. 8.   *Peasant & Curf Stack.*

Irish Piper.

John Carey

4/29/04

75

[74]

A plentiful number of bogs, scattered
throughout Ireland, provided ample
fuel for warmth and cooking. This old
character is obviously pleased with a
job well done.

[75]

The message on the back of this postcard by Irish artist John Carey reads:
'Saw King & Queen yesterday passing
through Westmoreland St going to lay
stone at College of Science.' The first
postcard illustration of this chapter
records this event.

Barney O'Hea.

[76]

This roguish scene by John Carey was one of the most popular postcards sold in Dublin during 1904. Despatched by a lovesick Clongowes student to his estranged girlfriend, Miss Ennis, his heartfelt plea is: 'Why don't you answer my letters. Bernard.'

[77]

Turn-of-the-century chromo-lithographic printing from Germany is suitably demonstrated by this attractive postcard. It is an undivided back with room in front to the right of the cartouche for this message: 'Please send a message by Jack if you can come Portmarnock on Tuesday instead of Wednesday. I can call about 3.30. W. Anderson.'

I know a bank.

Louqsor.   Luqsor.   Luxor.

Not quite sure whether I can get to Bray to night, if I do I will catch the 6.45

[78]

Luxor is one of many postcards sent by Jack Millar to his sweetheart, Maude Tighe. Jack shows his confidence in the postal system with his pencil-written message on the front: 'Not quite sure whether I can get to Bray tonight, if I do I will catch the 6.45.'

[79]

Words like 'Coon' and 'Nigger', originating in American slang, were not considered offensive by Edwardians. However, they were used in contempt, as in *Ulysses* when John Henry Menton refers to Mr Bloom as a 'Coon'. This postcard is from Valentine's 'Coon' series.

Valentine's "Coon" Series

IN THE SPRING A YOUNG MAN'S FANCY

With Best Wishes

Published by Sallo Epstein & Co., Durban

Riksha boys

6 a mile and very comfortable ═══

I'm sure you heard of this match of this fine your esthetic? I no longer only a trapeze thought you ought have written in 9 Still you be over this side now. or when away for & far Remembrance to Nora. Yours &c M.

Thursday

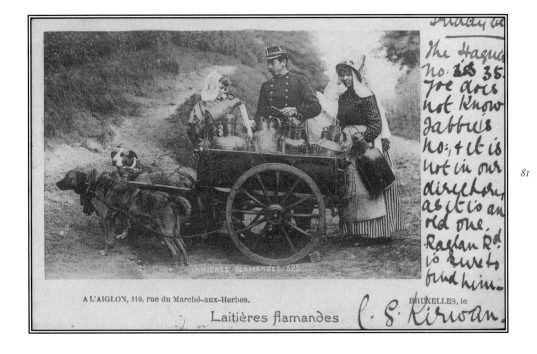

LAITIÈRES FLAMANDES, 625

A L'AIGLON, 110, rue du Marché-aux-Herbes.

Laitières flamandes

BRUXELLES, le

C. P. Kirwan

Sunday 6.
The Hague
No: is 35.
Joe does
not know
Jabbus
No:, & it is
not in our
direction,
as it is an
old one.
Raglan Rd.
is sure to
find him—

[80]

Miss Mary Bowler, 15 Upper Pembroke Street, City, was probably flabbergasted to receive this fine study of native transport in Durban, South Africa.

[81]

Flemish milk sellers are appealingly portrayed on this Belgian postcard.

[82]

This attractive advertising postcard was issued by Woods, Webb and Co. Ltd, Temple Lane, Dublin, to promote their 'New Idea' of liquid coffee.

[83]

'Quaker Oats Smiles' were issued in ten different designs, which could be obtained from their London office for three pence, post-paid, and three white squares cut from the fronts of Quaker Oats packets.

Irish spinning Wheel.

Shelbourne Hotel.
Dublin.

[84]

The message on this postcard tells us that the sender is enjoying himself in Dublin: 'I came over here on Sunday for a fortnight with my Auntie. I am having a very good time. Dublin is a grand town & this Hotel is full of awfully nice people. M.E. West. 11-10-04.'

[85]

In 1904 Frank O'Connor published a series of postcards after Bartlett depicting peasant life in Connemara. The life and privations of the Connemara peasantry also found expression in the plays of John Millington Synge. His *Riders to the Sea* was first performed in 1904 by the Abbey Group.

For Galway Fair. *Connemara.*

This attractive Christmas postcard by highly respected artist
Frank Haviland was published
by Raphael Tuck & Sons and
chromographed in Berlin.

Although self-evidently written
on 16 June 1904, this leap
year postcard by artist Lance
Thackery bears a Dublin
postmark of 17 June 1904.
The writer indicated 'awfully
showery' weather, mirroring
a remark in *Ulysses* by Simon
Dedalus that the weather of
the day was as uncertain as a
baby's bottom.

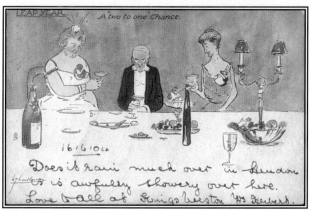

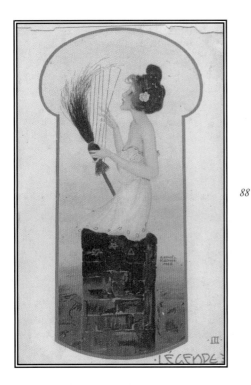

88

89

[88]

Raphael Kirchner produced this attractive art nouveau design for a series called 'Légendes', published in Paris at the turn of the century. Peeping at a young woman in déshabillé would have delighted Leopold Bloom, the aficionado of ladies' underwear.

[89]

The 'Gibson Girl' look became fashionable after the many published drawings by C. Dana Gibson. Obviously Tim, the sender of this postcard, is impressed: 'Am looking for a girl similar to this lady. The first one I meet, I intend to marry, whether she likes it or not.'

[90]

The *S.S. Scotia* was owned by the London and North Western Railway and plied between England and Ireland via Holyhead and Dublin. This passenger encountered some difficulties as the pencil-written message explains: 'Missed connection with Mail had to come by North Wall, stop night and go on by Mail leaving at 6.5. This is boat we came over on, rough crossing and was seasick. Had a good time and saw Llandudno, Bangor and Menai Bridge. Dont forget Wednesday and dont confine yourself to two sheets. Have you started collecting Picture Post Cards.'

[91]

This series of 'Dublin Sketches' was designed and printed in Ireland by B. & N. Limited, Dublin. This example, 'Evening, Kingstown Harbour', depicts the arrival of the mail boat.

92

93

The postmark on this postcard reads, 'Dublin, 5.30 am, De 25, 04'. We may be fairly certain that this Christmas greeting from Lillie was delivered before his Christmas dinner to W. Lanigan Esq., c/o Mrs Byrne, 17 Bath Avenue, Sandymount.

[93]

Raphael Tuck & Sons, the maestros of superb colour, had this beautiful Christmas postcard chromographed in Prussia.

[94]

This is a fine advertisement for 'Milkmaid Brand Milk' and is from a much sought-after series by Raphael Tuck & Sons called 'Celebrated Posters'.

[95]

Another Christmas postcard, from a Dublin girl called Nelly, was posted at the James's Street post office on 21 December 1904. It was received at Vlissingen, Holland on 23 December 1904 for delivery to her boyfriend, Mr T.J. Flood.

94

MILK ARRIVING AT ONE OF OUR FACTORIES.
The Milk of 60,000 Cows is Condensed daily at our Eleven Factories.

95

WITH BEST CHRISTMAS
WISHES
From Nelly

FOOTBALL INCIDENTS. *After the black & white drawing by S.T. DADD*
CHARGED THROUGH (*Association*).

96

Linden, Convalescent Home-Blackrock, Co. Dublin

97

[96]

The famous 'Oilette' series was designed and printed in England by Raphael Tuck & Sons. This example, after a black-and-white drawing by S.T. Dadd, depicts an all-action soccer incident. Tuck are at pains to point out that this is association football as opposed to rugby football.

[97]

Gerrard Brothers, Dublin, published this extremely fine photographic view of the Linden Convalescent Home, Blackrock, County Dublin. The printed photo has been tastefully hand-coloured to give a pleasing overall imitation of the chromo-lithographic printing process.

[98]

Postmarked on Bloomsday, this postcard reflects a reliable postal service for written communication. The 16 June 1904 being a Thursday, Mr French was confidently relying on the system for a reply by Friday. It is interesting to speculate about Mr French's choice of John Knox's House, Edinburgh, by A.Y. Wishaw. Perhaps there is a religious significance or it may have been merely a postcard lying about the house from a past trip to Scotland. The addressee is Miss Lister, 29 Upper Temple Street, Dublin, and the message reads: 'Dear Mary I will not be able to call to see you till Friday afternoon about 4.30. If that day does not suit you kindly drop me a line. L.E. French, 8 Palmerston Villas, Palmerston, P.R.'

98

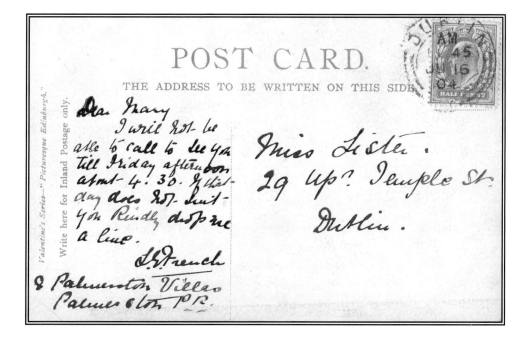

Homeric Background
and Schema of 'Ulysses'

Homer's 'Odyssey' relates the epic story of Odysseus, King of Ithaca, and of his wanderings throughout the Mediterranean after the siege of Troy. The homeward journey lasts ten years, during which time he has an extraordinary series of adventures. Many obstacles are placed in his path by the gods and he is forced to endure severe privations. His patience and presence of mind eventually triumph over adversity and he returns to his kingdom and to his faithful wife, Penelope, where he rights all the wrongs perpetrated against him.

Odysseus, known in Latin and English as Ulysses, was a hero of Joyce's in his schoolboy days and it is not surprising that he used the framework of the *Odyssey* on which to base the story of his own epic novel, *Ulysses*. To some extent he followed the Homeric parallel but where the original did not suit his purpose he made alterations or discarded unwanted details, sometimes entire episodes. In addition to naming his book *Ulysses* he gave each chapter a Homeric title, but a decision was taken to leave these titles out prior to publication.

The eighteen chapters of *Ulysses* are themselves divided into three books. 'Book One' consists of three chapters and relates mainly to the activities of Stephen Dedalus. 'Book Two' comprises twelve chapters, which are principally concerned with the wanderings and adventures of Leopold Bloom in the city of Dublin. 'Book Three' contains the final three chapters, recounting the homeward journey of Stephen and Mr Bloom, their arrival at Eccles Street, and the closing monologue of Molly Bloom.

Mr Bloom undergoes a series of extraordinary adventures in the course of a single day. Like his Homeric counterpart, he also triumphs over adversity through his patience and endurance. The story begins at 8 am and ends eighteen hours later. There is an elaborate hidden structure in the narrative of considerable complexity. Each chapter has been allocated a particular science or art form, colour, organ of the body, technique, symbol, style of writing and Homeric correspondences, and is equivalent in time to one hour of the day. The narrative is sometimes expressed in words of ancient derivation or uncommon usage. There are passages of text in which it is open to conjecture as to whether they represent reality or fantasy.

Joyce relished the idea that readers and scholars would struggle interminably with the mysteries of his comic masterpiece. Yet he was concerned that the special techniques and Odyssean parallels would prove too complex for scholarly interpretation. Accordingly he discreetly circulated his plan, or schema, for the book before publication. This schema was sent first to Carlo Linati and, later, a new schema was sent to Valery Larbaud and others. These schemas were eventually authorized for publication by Joyce and formed the basis for all later scholarly interpretation of *Ulysses*.

Today it is common practice to refer to each chapter of *Ulysses* by the Homeric titles originally assigned by Joyce. This is the case in the following eighteen chapters, which relate a selective and interpretive account of the bare thread of the narrative. Like any retelling of the plot of *Ulysses* it will completely lack the power and interest of the original but, hopefully, will encourage fresh odysseys through the pages of Joyce's sometimes difficult and intricate masterpiece. A brief explanation of each of the Homeric titles follows:

Homeric Titles of 'Ulysses'

TELEMACHUS	Son of Ulysses and Penelope. He searched fruitlessly for his long-lost father. When Ulysses eventually returned from the Trojan War, Telemachus helped him to slay all of his mother's suitors.
NESTOR	King of Pylos. He was the eldest and wisest of the Greek leaders at the siege of Troy.
PROTEUS	A sea-god with the power of metamorphosis and the gift of prophecy.
CALYPSO	A sea-nymph and ruler of the island of Ogygia who detained Ulysses for seven years. Ulysses refused her offer of immortality.
LOTUS-EATERS	A people who ate a narcotic fruit that induced forgetfulness and listless dreaming. Ulysses had to use force to bring his followers back to the ship after they had eaten the fruit of the Lotus plant.
HADES	The abode of the dead, where Ulysses encountered many ghosts, including Elpenor, one of his own men who pleaded for a proper burial. Ulysses also met the ghost of his mother, Anticlea, of whose death he was unaware. She told him that the cause of her death was grief over his long absence.
AEOLUS	King of Aeolia and god of the winds, which he kept confined in a cavern. Aeolus gave Ulysses a bag of winds to help with his journey. Within sight of Ithaca, the sailors opened the bag and, in the storm that followed, their ship was blown back to the island of Aeolia.

LESTRYGONIANS	A savage race of cannibals ruled by King Lamos who destroyed all the ships of Ulysses except one. They killed and ate most of his men.
SCYLLA AND CHARYBDIS	Scylla was a six-headed sea-monster who dwelt in the rocks on the Italian side of the Straits of Messina. Charybdis was a dangerous whirlpool and alternating waterspout directly opposite Scylla on the Sicilian side. Following the advice of Circe, Ulysses passed just outside Charybdis and, in so doing, six of his followers were eaten by Scylla.
WANDERING ROCKS	Two rocks that were supposed to suddenly close in on ships attempting to sail between them. Circe advised Ulysses to avoid the Wandering Rocks and to sail instead between Scylla and Charybdis.
SIRENS	Beautiful sea-nymphs who lured sailors to their destruction with their enchanting singing. Before passing their island Ulysses stuffed the ears of his followers with wax and lashed himself to the mast so that he could hear their beautiful song.
CYCLOPS	A race of giants with only one eye in the middle of their foreheads, one of whom, Polyphemus, captured Ulysses and his followers. They engineered an escape by getting Polyphemus drunk on wine and then blinding him with a stake.
NAUSICAA	A beautiful young princess and the daughter of Alcinous, King of Phaeacia. She fell in love with Ulysses after she found him on the shore following his shipwreck.
OXEN OF THE SUN	The sacred cattle of the sun god Helios on the island of Trinacria. Despite warnings, the followers of Ulysses, driven by starvation, killed the cattle. They were subsequently punished when all of them except Ulysses were drowned after their ship was wrecked.

CIRCE	A sorceress, temptress and daughter of Helios. She changed the followers of Ulysses into swine.
EUMAEUS	A faithful old swineherd whose hut is visited by Ulysses on his return to Ithaca. Disguised as a beggar, Ulysses tells Eumaeus a lengthy lie about his adventures and wanderings.
ITHACA	An island off the west coast of Greece and homeland of Ulysses, King of Ithaca.
PENELOPE	The faithful wife of Ulysses, who awaited his return from the Trojan War. Her suitors assumed that Ulysses was dead and pestered her to marry one of them. She promised to consider marriage when a shroud, being woven for her father-in-law, Laertes, was completed. By undoing at night what was woven during the day, she managed to keep her suitors at bay until the return of Ulysses.

— 4 —

Telemachus

O N THE TOP OF SANDYCOVE TOWER Stephen Dedalus watches, in a cold and displeased manner, as Buck Mulligan performs a mock Latin Mass, using a shaving bowl and razor. Mulligan's plump face breaks into a smile as he ridicules the absurdity of Stephen's Greek surname, adding that his nickname, Kinch, is ideally suited to Stephen. Stephen enquires if Haines will be remaining in the tower, as Haines had been raving overnight about shooting a black panther. He informs Mulligan that he will have to leave if Haines remains.

From the parapet Stephen and Mulligan watch as the mail boat leaves Kingstown Harbour. In an abrupt manner, Mulligan rounds on Stephen with an accusation that his aunt thinks Stephen killed his own mother. As a result his aunt wants Mulligan to disassociate himself from Stephen. Mulligan chides Stephen for refusing the last request of his dying mother to kneel down and pray for her. Stephen refuses an offer from Mulligan of a pair of grey trousers because he feels obliged to wear black in mourning for his mother.

Arm in arm, they walk around the tower, stop, and glance towards Bray Head. Mulligan asks Stephen why he does not trust him any more and wonders if Haines is the cause. The difficulty between them, according to Stephen, is the insulting remark about his mother made by Mulligan on their first meeting after her death.

A voice from below calls out for Mulligan and he descends the stairs chanting a verse from 'Who Goes with Fergus' about abandoning brooding.

Pier.   *Kingstown.*

Copyright Chas. Cook, Kingstown.   *Tuesday August 5 1902*

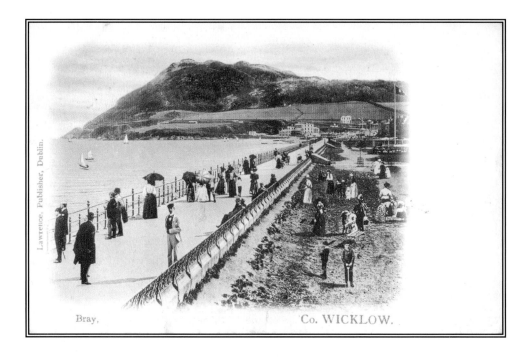

Bray,   Co. WICKLOW.

[99]

From the parapet Stephen
and Mulligan watch as the
mail boat leaves Kingstown
Harbour.

[100]

Arm in arm, they walk around
the tower, stop, and glance
towards Bray Head.

Stephen is reminded that he sang the same song at his mother's deathbed. He recalls a dream in which she had appeared to him wrapped in a shroud, her wasted body exuding the horror of death. Memories of the terrible deathbed scene with everyone on their knees cause Stephen to scream out to his mother to leave him alone.

A breakfast call from Mulligan ends his waking nightmare. Mulligan's head reappears, mouthing a request for the loan of a pound for a drinking session when Stephen receives his wages. As he is about to leave the parapet, Stephen notices Mulligan's shaving bowl and picks it up, wondering if he should bring it downstairs. Stephen is reminded of the incense bowl he carried as an altar boy at Clongowes.

In the dark and gloomy living-room of the tower Haines, Mulligan and Stephen settle down to breakfast. The meal is apportioned by Mulligan, who delivers a short Latin grace followed by a humorous story about 'Old Mother Grogan' and the making of tea. The old milk woman arrives and leaves after collecting two shillings for the milk bill. Haines announces his intention of visiting the National Library while Mulligan proposes a swim.

The three men make their way out of the tower. Stephen takes his ashplant and Latin Quarter hat, then locks the iron door behind him, placing the large key in his inside pocket.

As they walk along the path Stephen refuses to be drawn on his theory of *Hamlet*. Haines remarks that the surrounding cliffs and tower remind him of Elsinore. He propounds a theological interpretation of *Hamlet* that he has read, which argues that the whole idea of the play was that of a son striving for atonement with his father.

Singing a blasphemous ballad, Mulligan skips joyfully down the path towards the bathing place at Sandycove. Stephen and Haines follow at a distance discussing religion and politics in a friendly manner. Stephen is

Lawrence, Publisher, Dublin.

Higher Line Library, Clongowes Wood College, Co. KILDARE.

distracted by the thought that, although he pays his share of the rent for the tower, Mulligan will want the key.

A businessman and a boatman stand at the edge of the cliff and watch as a boat sails towards Bullock Harbour. The boatman expresses an opinion that the body of a drowned man will be washed up on the one o'clock tide, as it is nine days since the drowning.

Stephen and Haines follow the winding path down to the bathing place. Standing on a stone, Mulligan converses with a young man already in the water about a mutual friend called Bannon from Mullingar, County Westmeath. The young man mentions a postcard received from Bannon, describing his new girlfriend who works for a photographer in Mullingar.

Stephen announces his departure and Mulligan asks for the key to the tower and two pence for a pint. The key and money are handed over and Stephen makes his way up the winding path. Plunging into the sea, Mulligan surfaces to shout arrangements for a meeting in The Ship public house at half-past twelve. Stephen acknowledges,

[101]

Stephen is reminded of the incense bowl he carried as an altar boy at Clongowes.

[102]

Singing a blasphemous ballad, Mulligan skips joyfully down the path towards the bathing place at Sandycove.

[103]

A businessman and a boatman stand at the edge of the cliff and watch as a boat sails towards Bullock Harbour.

102

Storm at Bathing Place.
Copyright, Chas. Cook, Kingstown.

27. 9. 04. I was here yesterday, but had not time to post this. Sandycove. The Sea was not like this, quite Calm. Affectionately Millicent

103

Dalkey Island, Dublin (Rave Flora)
J. V.   Published by Richardson, Leinster Restaurant, Dalkey

while inwardly resolving not to sleep in the tower that night or to stay at his own home. As he turns the curve of the path Stephen waves goodbye, yet he is acutely mindful of Mulligan's unjust conduct.

~5~

Nestor

AT Mr Garrett Deasy's school in Dalkey, Stephen Dedalus is teaching a class of local boys. Questions arise about Greek history and the so-called victory of Pyrrhus at the battle of Asculum. Stephen queries Armstrong, who is slyly consuming biscuits, about his knowledge of Pyrrhus. Armstrong, the son of well-to-do parents from Vico Road, Dalkey, is caught unawares. His answer that Pyrrhus is something out in the waves, like Kingstown Pier, causes the class to explode with exaggerated laughter. Conscious of his lack of control, Stephen restores order by affirming that Kingstown Pier was also a failed bridge.

Talbot is asked to recite from Lycidas and the verses remind Stephen of his student days in Paris, where he studied Aristotle in the silence of the library of Saint Genevieve. When Talbot finishes the poem the boys bundle their books away in preparation for a game of hockey.

After their departure only young Cyril Sargent remains behind to have his sums checked by Stephen. The boy's ugly and unattractive appearance reminds Stephen that, at least, Sargent's mother loved him. Stephen wonders if a mother's love is the only true aspect of life. Sitting side by side, Stephen guides Sargent to work out the second sum by himself. As the young boy nervously copies the sum, Stephen reflects on the gracelessness of his own boyhood.

They leave the classroom and in the corridor the headmaster's voice is heard calling for Sargent. In the porch of the school Stephen observes Mr

Sorrento Terrace and Dalkey Island.

The Wrench Series, No. 1703

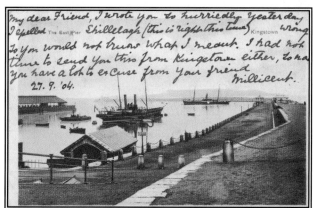

my dear Friend, I wrote you so hurriedly yesterday I spelled *The East Pier* Shillelagh (this is right this time) wrong so you would not know what I meant. I had not time to send you this from Kingstown either, to *Kingstown* you have a lot to excuse from your friend Millicent. 27. 9. '04.

[104]

Armstrong, the son of well-to-do parents from Vico Road, Dalkey, is caught unawares.

[105]

Conscious of his lack of control, Stephen restores order by affirming that Kingstown Pier was also a failed bridge.

Deasy sorting out the teams and settling altercations between the boys. Mr Deasy tells Stephen to wait in his study while he restores order among the squabbling schoolboys.

In the study, which smells of stale smoke and old furniture, Stephen waits. Mr Deasy arrives and settles the wages of three pounds and twelve shillings. He gives Stephen unsolicited advice on thrift and proclaims that his proudest boast is that he has paid his way and never borrowed in his life. Stephen mentally calculates his

Stephen wonders if a mother's love is the only true aspect of life.

overwhelming debts, against which his wages are worth-less. Mr Deasy puts away his savings box and laughs as Stephen admits that he is unable to pay his way, for the moment.

Although a self-confessed Tory and Orangeman, Mr Deasy is anxious to portray himself to Stephen as hav-ing some rebel Irish blood. He informs Stephen that Orangemen lobbied for the Repeal of the Union some twenty years before O'Connell began his campaign.

Mr Deasy asks Stephen to do him a favour with his literary friends by way of having a letter published. Stephen waits as Mr Deasy types in the finishing touches.

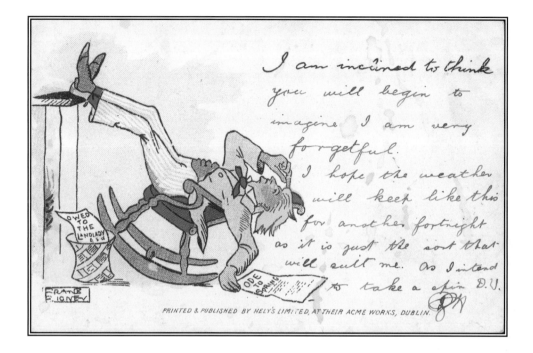

I am inclined to think you will begin to imagine I am very forgetful.
I hope the weather will keep like this for another fortnight as it is just the sort that will suit me. As I intend to take a spin D.V.

PRINTED & PUBLISHED BY HELY'S LIMITED, AT THEIR ACME WORKS, DUBLIN.

[107]

Stephen mentally calculates his overwhelming debts, against which his wages are worthless.

Stephen is reminded, by images of horses on the wall, of the times when Cranly led him to get rich by backing horses at race meetings.

Rising from the table, Mr Deasy asks Stephen to glance over his letter, which laboriously advocates the Austrian method of treating foot-and-mouth disease. With the possibility of an embargo on Irish cattle at the next outbreak of the disease, Mr Deasy is anxious to have his letter published and read. Believing himself to be surrounded by difficulties and suspicious influences, Mr Deasy informs Stephen that England is being destroyed by Jewish merchants. Although Stephen attempts a defence of the Jewish people, Mr Deasy condemns them out of hand for sins against God and cites their inevitable punishment to wander eternally on the face of the earth. The two men argue about religion and history. Mr Deasy declares that all human history moves towards a single goal that is the manifestation of God. Stephen believes history is a nightmare and his definition of God is the shout of children at play in the streets.

The conversation turns to women, whom Mr Deasy blames for bringing sin into the world. He cites Helen, the estranged wife of Menelaus who caused the ten years of war waged by the Greeks on the city of Troy. For good measure Mr Deasy adds that MacMurrough's faithless wife brought the foreigners to Ireland and Parnell was brought down by a woman.

Stephen ignores the diatribe and offers to try and have Mr Deasy's letter published in the *Evening Telegraph* and the *Irish Homestead*. Stephen bids good morning and walks out the door. He hears Mr Deasy calling his name and turns back towards the gate as Mr Deasy halts, hard of breathing, after a short run. He informs Stephen that Ireland was the only country that did not persecute Jews. With a smile, Stephen asks the required question. A delighted Mr Deasy, in the throes of laughter and a coughing fit, triumphantly proclaims that it was because Ireland never let the Jews into the country.

~ 6 ~

Proteus

O N SANDYMOUNT STRAND, Stephen Dedalus walks, eyes closed, listening to the sound of his boots as they crush and crackle the sea-wrack and shells. He resists the temptation to open his eyes and makes his way along with the help of his ashplant. As he opens his eyes, Stephen sees two women carefully descending the steps of Leahy's Terrace. One of the women, Mrs Florence MacCabe, carries a midwife's bag, bringing to mind his own birth and the link of all mankind back to Eve.

Mr Deasy's letter and the appointment with Mulligan at The Ship public house are on his mind as he ponders whether he should visit his Aunt Sara and Uncle Richie in Strasburg Terrace. He recalls childhood days with Uncle Richie and his father's low opinion of his in-laws, particularly Uncle Richie, the drunken cost-drawer. Stephen remembers boasting to his friends at Clongowes about his high-ranking relations whereas, in reality, his family is in decline. The beauty he seeks in life was not to be found within his family, neither was it in Marsh's Library where he had read books on prophesies.

As he pictures himself as a priest, he is reminded of the sexual temptations of his early youth. In those days he read two pages from seven different books every night and there were books he was going to write which, in the event of his death, would be sent to all the great libraries of the world.

The fishermen's houses at Ringsend come into view. Stephen halts and

Higher Line Playroom, Clongowes Wood College,   Co. KILDARE.

realizes that he has gone past the way to his Aunt Sara's house in Irishtown. Deciding against a visit, he changes direction and walks across the harder sand towards the Pigeon House. The name reminds him of his student days in Paris and Kevin Egan's joke about a pigeon and the conception of Christ.

Stephen ruefully reflects on how little he actually achieved during his sojourn in Paris. He remembers the miserable collection of possessions he brought back to Dublin after the receipt of his father's telegram advising that his mother was dying. Mulligan's jibe about his aunt thinking that Stephen killed his mother again comes to mind.

Striding over the sand furrows, along by the rocks of the South Wall, Stephen remembers the exiled Irish revolutionary Kevin Egan and his son Patrice. In the cafés and taverns of Paris, Egan had tried to influence Stephen in the cause of Irish Freedom by citing daring deeds. Egan had recounted the story of a Fenian leader who escaped captivity by taking the road to Malahide disguised

[108]

Stephen remembers boasting to his friends at Clongowes about his high-ranking relatives whereas, in reality, his family is in decline.

[109]

Egan had recounted the story
of a Fenian leader who
escaped captivity by taking
the road to Malahide
disguised as a young bride.

[110]

Stephen sings a few words
from 'The Boys of Kilkenny',
an old ballad associated with
Kevin Egan and his son,
Patrice.

as a young bride. Now, Kevin Egan hides in Paris, a man
without love, land or wife, doing his daily rounds of the
taverns. Stephen sings a few words from 'The Boys of
Kilkenny', an old ballad associated with Kevin Egan and
his son, Patrice.

The wet sand sinks beneath his feet as he walks at the
edge of the sea. Looking towards the south shore where
the Sandycove tower is located, Stephen again resolves
that he will not sleep there at nightfall. Moving before
the incoming tide, he finds a rock to sit on where he can
watch the water flow past. The swollen carcass of a dead
dog and the gunwale of a boat are visible in the sand. A
live dog runs towards him and Stephen is fearful of an
attack, but the dog turns and runs back to his owners.

Dalkey Island, Dalkey   10.9.'04. In Dublin again Co, Dublin
to-day — I have been hunting up a few post cards and hope you have not already had any of these. The heartiest of hearty hand shakes.
millicent.

Stephen reflects on his own cowardice at the barking dog, compared to Mulligan's bravery in saving a drowning man. The body of the man drowned nine days ago near Maiden's Rock, Dalkey Island, is shortly due to surface.

In the distance two cockle-pickers are wading in the water, stooping and lifting bags. Their dog jumps up on them, drops on all fours, then wanders off ahead only to discover and smell the carcass of the dead dog. A loud call brings him to heel and a kick from his master sends him flying across the sand.

Stephen feels the urge to write and, tearing a piece of blank paper from Deasy's letter, he scribbles a few words. He wonders if anyone is watching him or if anyone will ever read his written words.

The beautiful young virgin he had encountered last Monday at the window of Hodges Figgis' bookshop springs to mind. He longs for her touch because he is lonely and sad. He does not answer his own mind's question as to the word known to every man but asks again to be touched.

[111]

The body of the man drowned nine days ago near Maiden's Rock, Dalkey Island, is shortly due to surface.

Stephen puts the scribbled note in his pocket and lies back, fully stretched out on the rocks. He gazes with displeasure at Mulligan's cast-off boots and is reminded how delighted he was in Paris when Esther Osvalt's shoe fitted him.

The tide makes its way slowly inward from the Cock Lake. He urinates in the sea. The action of the incoming tide reminds him of the drowned man, and in his mind the white corpse rises from underneath the waves and slowly bobs and weaves landwards. It is seen, hooked and hauled in over the gunwale of the rescue boat. The corpse reeks with the leprous stench of its watery grave. Stephen is struck by the thought that death by drowning at sea is one of the easiest of all deaths known to mankind.

The sky clouds over. Stephen anxiously reassures himself that a thunderstorm is not imminent because there are no black clouds to be seen. He takes his ash-plant and gets ready to leave. Stephen looks over his shoulder and sees a three-masted sailing ship moving slowly up the mouth of the River Liffey.

[112]

Stephen looks over his shoulder and sees a three-masted sailing ship moving slowly up the mouth of the River Liffey.

~7~

Calypso

MR LEOPOLD BLOOM has kidneys on his mind as he saunters about the kitchen preparing breakfast for himself and his wife, Molly. The cat walks around the leg of the table and mews for milk, which he pours into a saucer and watches as the cat hungrily laps it up. He decides to buy a pork kidney for his own breakfast and wonders if Molly would like something tasty. From outside the bedroom door he enquires if she wants anything and concludes from the soft sleepy grunt that she does not.

Mr Bloom takes his hat from the peg and checks that a white slip of paper, concealed inside the leather headband, is safe. On the doorstep he realizes that he has left the door key in his other trousers. Not wishing to disturb Molly, he leaves the door closed but unlocked. He crosses to the sunny side of the street and observes that the sun is close to the steeple of George's Church.

As he approaches Larry O'Rourke's public house and grocery, Mr Bloom decides against canvassing the cute O'Rourke for an advertisement. Mr Bloom is reminded of how, hilariously, Simon Dedalus could caricature O'Rourke's opinion that the Russians would be easy meat for the Japanese. Mr Bloom turns into Dorset Street, bids O'Rourke the time of day and is greeted graciously in return. Mr Bloom wonders where publicans get their money. They come up from the country with nothing and later they seem able to afford their own businesses. Mr Bloom is struck by a good idea for

RUSSO-JAPANESE WAR. — N° 8. — Talien-Wan : 11th. Feb. 1904.

Landing of six hundred Japanese near Talien-Wan. — Charge of Cossacks.

[113]

Mr Bloom is reminded of how, hilariously, Simon Dedalus could caricature O'Rourke's opinion that the Russians would be easy meat for the Japanese.

[114]

Mr Bloom is struck by a good idea for a puzzle, which would be to cross the city of Dublin without passing a public house.

a puzzle, which would be to cross the city of Dublin without passing a public house.

Mr Bloom stops and stares at the black-and-white sausages in the window of Dlugacz's pork shop. He enters and waits as a neighbour's servant girl receives attention at the counter. Mr Bloom takes one of the cut pages from the pile at the counter and reads with interest an advertisement for a model farm at Kinnereth by the shore of the Sea of Tiberias. The servant girl's rear view reminds Mr Bloom of her swinging skirt and bottom as

"TAKING IN THE SHEET"

"Valentine's Series"

[115]

The servant girl's rear view reminds Mr Bloom of her swinging skirt and bottom as she whacks the carpet on his neighbour's clothesline.

she whacks the carpet on his neighbour's clothesline. Mr Bloom decides it would be a pleasant idea to walk behind her and watch the moving cheeks of her bottom. The butcher takes two sheets and wraps her sausages. She pays and leaves, pausing momentarily outside the shop before turning slowly to the right. Impatiently, Mr Bloom points to the pork kidney, pays his three pence and leaves.

Outside the shop Mr Bloom is disappointed to find the girl has disappeared. He walks slowly along Dorset Street, reading the advertisement of the Planters Company, offering to sell plots of land north of Jaffa for fruit-growing.

The olives and oranges remind him of happier days with old friends, Citron and Mastiansky, and the pleasant evenings as Molly relaxed, sitting on Citron's basket chair. A cloud begins to cover the sun as he turns into Eccles Street.

On the hall floor there are two letters and a postcard. His heart flutters as he notices the bold handwriting of Blazes Boylan on a letter addressed to Mrs Marion Bloom. The other letter is for himself from his daughter Milly in Mullingar and the postcard is from Milly to her mother. Mr Bloom enters the bedroom and hands over the letter and postcard. Molly tucks Boylan's letter under the pillow and reads Milly's postcard.

Mr Bloom returns down the stairs to the kitchen where he draws the tea and drops the kidney on the pan. He opens Milly's letter, glancing briefly at references to the picnic at Lough Owel and the young student she had met in Mullingar. When the tea is drawn he fills his own cup, remembering that it was a birthday gift from Milly when she was only four years old. He smiles as he recalls the night Milly found Professor Goodwin's little mirror hidden in his silk hat and brought the mirror into the parlour amid hilarious laughter. Professor Goodwin, Molly's piano accompanist, was an incorrigible character when the worse for drink. However, Mr Bloom remembers him fondly for his old-fashioned and courteous manners, even to the extent of bowing Molly off the stage.

Mr Bloom sticks a fork into the kidney and turns it over on the pan. Carefully, checking that everything is on the tray, he moves up the stairs, pushing the bedroom door open with his knee. Molly criticizes the delay and raises herself on the bed to pour the tea. A torn envelope under the pillow causes him to ask the name of the sender. Casually, she replies that the letter is from Boylan, who will be calling later that day to discuss the forthcoming concert and bring the programme. Molly drinks her tea, enquiring about the time of Dignam's

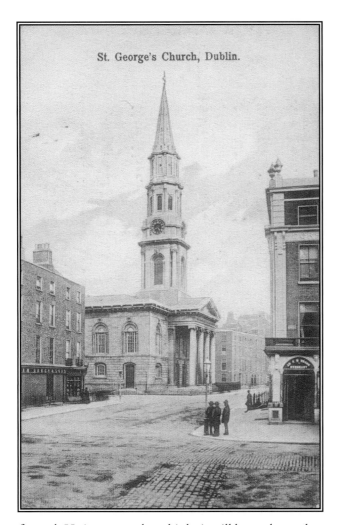

St. George's Church, Dublin.

[116]

As he comes out into the light the ringing bells of George's Church remind him of Patrick Dignam's funeral.

funeral. He is not sure but thinks it will be at eleven that morning.

Molly wants him to explain the word 'metempsy-chosis', which she has encountered in a book. He finds the book and explains that the word is from the Greek language meaning the transmigration of souls to another body after death. Molly does not understand and asks him to explain in plain language. Mr Bloom turns the pages of her cheap novelette, noting the lurid cover of a naked girl at the feet of a fierce-looking Italian wielding a whip. Molly has finished reading the book and asks him to get her another by the same author.

Mr Bloom continues to explain that some people believe that after death we all continue living in another body, which is called reincarnation. The Greeks believed that a person could be changed into an animal or even a nymph, like the nymph taking a bath on the print over their bed.

Molly smells the burning kidney and he rushes down the stairs, just in time to save his breakfast. He reads Milly's letter as he eats his kidney and bread, steeped in gravy. Milly thanks him for a lovely birthday gift and describes a young student called Bannon she has met in Mullingar who sings Boylan's song about lovely seaside girls. He reflects sadly on the thought that Milly was fifteen yesterday and his son, Rudy, would be eleven if he had lived.

After finishing breakfast Mr Bloom visits the outside lavatory, taking a copy of *Titbits* with him to read. He notes with interest that a Mr Philip Beaufoy has won a monetary prize for an article in the magazine. He recalls his own failed efforts to make money from writing by jotting down what Molly said. His thoughts turn to the bazaar dance at which the band played 'The Dance of the Hours' by Ponchielli. That was the first night that Molly had met and danced with Boylan.

Finishing his toilet, he tears half of Beaufoy's prize-winning article to wipe himself. As he comes out into the light the ringing bells of George's Church remind him of Patrick Dignam's funeral.

~ 8 ~

Lotus-Eaters

Mʀ Bʟᴏᴏᴍ ᴡᴀʟᴋs ǫᴜɪᴇᴛʟʏ along Sir John Rogerson's Quay, turns and walks through Lime Street. As he passes an undertaker's establishment, he is reminded of how Corny Kelleher had landed the job of burying Dignam for his employer. Mr Bloom surmises that Corny Kelleher is a police informer.

In Westland Row he stops outside the window of the Belfast and Oriental Tea Company to read the advertising on the tea packets. Furtively he fingers the headband of his hat, finds a card and quickly transfers it to his waistcoat pocket. The Ceylon tea brands remind Mr Bloom of how pleasant it would be to be lazing around doing nothing in the warmth of the Far East. He thinks the natives of Ceylon spend their time idling and sleeping in the sun, in a warm lethargic climate similar to the hothouse in the Botanic Gardens.

Mr Bloom turns away from the window, crosses the road and enters the Westland Row post office. He hands his card to the postmistress and receives a typed letter addressed to Henry Flower. He slides the letter and his card into a pocket.

Outside the post office he meets M'Coy who notices the black tie and clothes. Mr Bloom explains that the clothes are for Dignam's funeral and M'Coy indicates that he will try to attend. Mr Bloom is distracted by a well-dressed, stylish woman about to board a jaunting car outside the Grosvenor Hotel. Almost ignored, M'Coy chatters on about having just

THE PALM HOUSE, BOTANIC GARDENS, DUBLIN.
Signal Series. 10031=5. 28/12/04 E. & S., Ltd., Dublin.

[117]

He thinks the natives of Ceylon spend their time idling and sleeping in the sun, in a warm lethargic climate similar to the hothouse in the Botanic Gardens.

[118]

Mr Bloom is distracted by a well-dressed, stylish woman about to board a jaunting car outside the Grosvenor Hotel.

The Grosvenor Hotel
DUBLIN
opposite Westland Row Railway Station.

left Bob Doran and Bantam Lyons in Conway's public house. Mr Bloom continues to ogle the high brown boots of the attractive woman and hopes to catch a glimpse of her stockings as she boards the car. To his annoyance, a passing tram spoils the view.

M'Coy enquires after Molly. Mr Bloom acknowledges, opening his newspaper to read an advertisement for Plumtree's Potted Meat. M'Coy announces that his own wife has just obtained a singing engagement and Bloom responds with news of Molly's concert in Belfast. M'Coy asks pointedly for the name of the person getting it up and Mr Bloom explains that it is a tour, with a committee, including a distribution of shares and profits. Before parting, M'Coy asks Mr Bloom to put his name down on the list of mourners, as a drowning at Sandycove may require his presence there with the coroner.

Mr Bloom walks slowly into Brunswick Street, turns into Cumberland Street and halts beside the wall of the railway station. He opens and reads the typed letter from Martha Clifford, which contains a yellow, flattened flower. Martha thanks him for his last letter and indicates that she will punish him for sending her stamps. She asks to be told why he is unhappy at home and thinks that he has a beautiful name. Martha declares herself drawn strongly to him and threatens to punish him like a naughty boy if he does not write to her. She longs to meet him and begs her dear Henry not to deny her request. In the postscript she wants to know what kind of perfume his wife uses.

Mr Bloom puts the flower in his pocket and walks along rereading the letter. Martha seems to have changed since her first letter and he wonders if she wrote this one herself. He decides that he will not meet her because of the difficulties in carrying on a love affair. However, he will be more daring the next time he writes, placing more emphasis on the theme of punishment.

At the back door of All Hallows Church he doffs his hat and replaces the card in the hatband. A sign on the

[119]

At the back door of All Hallows Church he doffs his hat and replaces the card in the hatband.

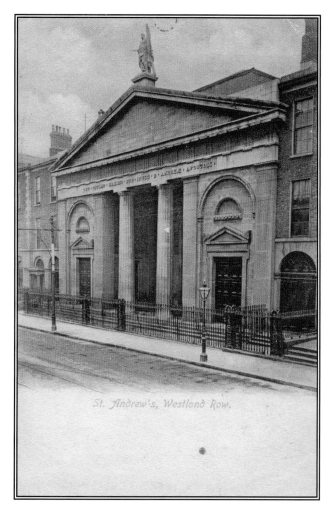

St. Andrew's, Westland Row.

door advertises a sermon by the Very Reverend John Conmee SJ. As he enters the church he notices that a priest is giving out communion to the congregation. The priest puts away the communion cup, genuflects, drinks the remaining wine and rinses the chalice. Mr Bloom considers that wine makes the ceremony more dignified than Guinness's porter. In any event it is more prudent that the priest does not give wine to everybody, otherwise every old alcoholic would be coming along for a slug. The priest bends down, kisses the altar then turns around to bless the congregation. Mr Bloom is impressed with the organization of the Catholic Church,

Westland Row   Dublin

particularly confession, with penance and punishment. There is a final prayer and the priest and altar boy walk off. Mr Bloom walks down the aisle, out through the main door of All Hallows Church.

As he walks along Westland Row Mr Bloom remembers to collect a lotion for Molly at Sweny's, Lincoln Place. The recipe for the lotion and his latchkey are in his ordinary trousers but the chemist in Sweny's locates the recipe from a previous order. The smell of soap puts Mr Bloom in mind of a bath, so he orders a bar of lemon soap.

Newspaper under his arm, he strolls out of Sweny's and bumps into Bantam Lyons. Noticing the newspaper, Bantam Lyons asks for a look to check the prospects of a French horse running in the Gold Cup. Mr Bloom tells Lyons he can keep the newspaper as he was about to throw it away. A startled Lyons asks Mr Bloom to repeat what he had just said, and leers when Mr Bloom repeats the throwaway remark. Bantam Lyons returns the newspaper and announces that he will risk it. Mr

[120]

As he walks along Westland Row Mr Bloom remembers to collect a lotion for Molly at Sweny's, Lincoln Place.

King's Hospital and Cricket Ground.　　　　　　　　　　　Dublin.

[121]

Mr Bloom reflects on the balmy pleasantness of the weather and of how ideally suited it is for watching a leisurely game of cricket.

Bloom watches as Bantam Lyons speeds away, wryly observing that betting on horses has become a problem recently, giving rise to stealing and embezzlement.

Mr Bloom walks in the direction of the baths. He sees a poster advertising the sports to be held later that day in College Park. He greets Hornblower, who is standing at the porter's lodge, and is greeted in return. Mr Bloom reflects on the balmy pleasantness of the weather and of how ideally suited it is for watching a leisurely game of cricket. He foresees a warm soapy bath with pleasurable anticipation.

9

Hades

HE FUNERAL CORTÈGE of three horse-drawn vehicles is assembled before the home of Patrick Dignam. In the first mourning carriage behind the hearse Martin Cunningham, Mr Power, Simon Dedalus and Mr Bloom take their seats. The cortège moves slowly away from the Dignam home, gaining speed as it proceeds down Tritonville Road. The four men watch while the passers-by lift their hats as a mark of respect.

Mr Bloom notices a young man in mourning dress and a wide hat. He informs Simon Dedalus that he has just seen Stephen walking alone. Simon Dedalus launches a verbal attack on Buck Mulligan and the Goulding family. He denounces Mulligan as a dishonourable bastard and declares his intention of writing to Mulligan's aunt to inform her that her nephew is ruining his son.

The cortège proceeds along the Ringsend Road and crosses over the Dodder Bridge. The outburst of Simon Dedalus turns Mr Bloom's thoughts to his dead son, Rudy. He wonders what it would have been like to see him grow up and remembers the moment of Rudy's conception in Raymond Terrace. Molly was so big during her pregnancy with Rudy, she had to refuse a concert in Greystones.

The cortège halts before crossing the Grand Canal. Mr Bloom sees the Dogs' Home and remembers his father's dying wish that he should be good to his dog, Athos. They move again, on past the Antient Concert Rooms,

Grand Hotel, Greystones   Published by E. Greer, Greystones,

[122]

Molly was so big during
her pregnancy with Rudy,
she had to refuse a concert
in Greystones.

under the railway bridge and on past the Queen's Theatre.

On D'Olier Street Blazes Boylan exchanges salutes with the carriage from the door of the Red Bank restaurant. Mr Bloom looks at his fingernails and wonders why his wife is fascinated with one of the worst men in Dublin. Mr Power enquires about Molly's forthcoming tour. Mr Bloom explains that it will be a big event featuring the very best performers, including J.C. Doyle and John McCormack. Mr Power makes a flattering reference that Molly is last but not least of the performing artists. Mr Bloom likes Mr Power and wonders whether it is true that he keeps another woman. Crofton had told him that Power's affair with a barmaid from Jurys or the Moira was not a carnal relationship. Mr Bloom can see no benefit in such a situation.

They cross the Liffey and proceed past the large cloaked statue of Daniel O'Connell. In O'Connell Street they observe Reuben J. Dodd striding around the corner of Elvery's Elephant House. Mr Bloom and Martin Cunningham combine to relate the story of Dodd's son and his involvement with a girl. Reuben J. Dodd, anxious

O'Connell's Statue, Dublin   J.V.

[123]

They cross the Liffey and proceed past the large cloaked statue of Daniel O'Connell.

to get him out of harm's way, decided to send the boy to the Isle of Man. On the way to the boat the boy jumped into the Liffey and had to be rescued by a boatman. Mr Bloom explains that the funny part of the story was that Dodd only gave the boatman a silver florin for saving his son's life.

The conversation returns to the sudden death of Patrick Dignam, which Martin Cunningham suggests was due to heart trouble. Mr Bloom attributes the cause to alcohol but keeps his thoughts to himself. At the

just like it.

Mater Misericordiae Hospital — Dublin

Rotunda the funeral of an illegitimate child gallops by their carriage, at speed. Simon Dedalus stoically remarks that the dead child is fortunate to be finished with life.

As their carriage moves through Rutland Square, Mr Power expresses the view that suicide is the greatest disgrace to have in a family. Martin Cunningham rushes to excuse suicide as temporary insanity, adding that in any event it was not a matter for them to judge. Mr Bloom decides not to add to Cunningham's charitable remarks about suicide. He respects Cunningham as a sympathetic human being who always has a good word to say. Mr Bloom is sorry that Cunningham's wife is an inveterate drunkard who pawns his furniture and gives him a life of hell. Mr Bloom reflects on the afternoon of his father's inquest and the coroner's verdict of an overdose and death by misadventure.

They move quickly along Blessington Street and turn into Berkeley Street. Mr Bloom sees the Mater Misericordiae Hospital and is reminded of their ward for incurables and his home in Eccles Street. The carriage stops to let cattle and sheep bound for Liverpool pass noisily by. Mr Bloom recalls that when he worked for Cuffe's they exported young cattle to England for twenty-seven pounds each. They move through the herd, turn right at Dunphy's corner and proceed along the Phibsborough Road.

A man and his barge, loaded with turf, are between the sluices as they cross the Royal Canal. At the Brian Boroimhe public house the carriage bears left, out the Finglas Road. Mr Power points to the house where a man called Childs was murdered. Simon Dedalus confirms that it was a brutal case of a man who murdered his brother but escaped with the aid of a good barrister, Seymour Bushe.

At Prospect Cemetery, Glasnevin, the occupants step out of the first carriage. Corny Kelleher from O'Neill's is there, standing by an open hearse. Dignam's coffin is carried into the graveyard, followed by his friends. Corny Kelleher and Dignam's eldest son, Patsy, carry two wreaths. They are accompanied by Dignam's brother-in-law, Bernard Corrigan.

As the funeral party proceeds towards the mortuary chapel, Martin Cunningham whispers to Mr Power about the indiscretion of mentioning suicide in front of Bloom. Mr Power is shocked to hear the news, as he had not been aware that Bloom's father had poisoned himself. Mr Bloom and Tom Kernan discuss Dignam's insurance policy and the sorry plight of his wife and five children. Simon Dedalus and Ned Lambert greet one another cordially and exchange news about Cork city. Ned Lambert tells him that Martin Cunningham is taking up a collection to keep the Dignam family going until the question of the insurance is cleared up. The sight of John Henry Menton reminds Ned Lambert that Menton, Dignam's former employer, had contributed a pound to the collection. Simon Dedalus explains that he had often warned Dignam to take care of his job with Menton.

Simon Dedalus points to the
O'Connell Circle.

O'Connell Monument, Glasnevin.   Dublin.

From Dick

The Wrench Series, No. 1699

The procession halts before the door of the mortuary
chapel and the coffin is carried inside. Father Coffey
performs the burial service and leaves, followed by the
server. The grave-diggers carry out the coffin and load it
on their cart. The mourners follow the coffin as it is
wheeled slowly along the lane of sepulchres. Simon
Dedalus points to the O'Connell Circle. Mr Power
opines that, although O'Connell is at rest in the middle
of his people, his heart is buried in Rome. Simon Dedalus
breaks down and weeps at the thought of his wife, buried
nearby. In sympathy, Mr Power takes his arm.

John Henry Menton asks Ned Lambert about the man walking with Tom Kernan. Ned Lambert explains that he is Bloom, married to the soprano, Madam Marion Tweedy. John Henry Menton remembers dancing with her at Mat Dillon's party in Roundtown, where he had a row with Bloom over a game of bowls. Ned Lambert smiles and comments that Bloom once worked for Wisdom Hely as a traveller for blotting-paper. John Henry Menton expresses astonishment that a good-looking, flirtatious woman could marry a coon like Bloom. Ned Lambert acknowledges that Mrs Bloom is still gamey and that Bloom himself now works as a canvasser for advertisements.

The funeral party is greeted by the caretaker of the cemetery, John O'Connell. He shakes hands with all the mourners and recounts a funny story. Corny Kelleher and John O'Connell exchange the burial papers. The mourners gather around the grave. Mr Bloom notices a man in a macintosh and wonders who he could be. Including the man in the macintosh, Mr Bloom counts death's number of thirteen mourners at the final moment of the burial.

The coffin is lowered into the grave. Mr Bloom reflects on the unpleasantness of approaching death. The dying man is unable to believe that death is near and at first thinks it is a mistake. Then he becomes aware of the darkened room of death, the whispers of those around him and the offers of a priest. A death struggle ensues and the moment of expiry inevitably arrives. The dead man is forgotten in a short time, like Parnell whose Ivy Day remembrance is dying out. Mr Bloom is reminded that his own burial plot is in this cemetery towards the Finglas side, where his mother and son Rudy lie buried.

The grave-diggers begin to fling heavy lumps of clay into the grave. John O'Connell puts on his hat and the mourners follow suit. Hynes the reporter is taking the names of mourners. He approaches Mr Bloom to ask for his Christian name. Mr Bloom asks Hynes to add

Parnell's Grave.   Dublin.

2492. 20.

[126]

Mr Power remarks that there
are people who say that
Parnell is not in that grave and
that he will return one day.

M'Coy's name to the list of mourners. Hynes remembers that Charley M'Coy had at one time worked for the
Freeman's Journal. However, Mr Bloom inwardly recalls
that M'Coy was sacked from the newspaper for stealing
and afterwards got a job at the city morgue. A misunderstanding develops between Hynes and Mr Bloom
about the name of the man in the macintosh, which
causes Hynes to scribble the name 'M'Intosh' down as a
mourner.

The mourners move slowly away from the graveside
by various paths. Hynes suggests a visit to Parnell's grave
and Mr Power agrees. Mr Power remarks that there are
people who say Parnell is not in that grave and that he
will return one day. Hynes shakes his head in disagree-
ment, declaring that Parnell will never return because he
is truly dead and buried in that grave.

Mr Bloom walks alone among the crosses, tombs and
headstones, reflecting on the futility of death. He thinks of
all those buried in this cemetery who once walked the
streets of Dublin. He hears the rattle of pebbles and sees an
old grey rat moving beside a crypt. Mr Bloom remembers

that Robert Emmet was secretly buried by torchlight in this graveyard.

The gates of the cemetery appear before him and Mr Bloom is glad to be back in the real world. He recalls that his last visit to Prospect Cemetery was for the burial of Mrs Emily Sinico.

Martin Cunningham and John Henry Menton walk towards him. Mr Bloom remembers the solicitor Menton and the row over a bowling match at Mat Dillon's party. Politely, he points to a dent in Menton's hat and is snubbed for his trouble. Mr Bloom is confident that Menton, with his peculiar oyster eyes, will be sorry for his insulting behaviour.

10

Aeolus

IN FRONT OF NELSON'S PILLAR, southbound trams shunt and clang noisily. The tram company timekeeper shouts the starting command to the driver of the Palmerston Park tram. A cacophony of sound issues from the boot-blacks at the General Post Office, the mailmen in North Prince's Street and the draymen rolling and loading barrels.

In the offices of the *Freeman's Journal*, Mr Bloom is looking for an advertisement of Alexander Keyes. Red Murray finds and slices the advertisement from the newspaper. He offers to give Keyes a free paragraph. Mr Bloom accepts the offer and leaves through the printing works.

Mr Bloom makes his way along the noisy passage and enters the foreman's office. Hynes is with Councillor Nannetti, the foreman of the *Freeman's Journal* and member of parliament for College Green. Hynes suggests that his article on the Dignam funeral should appear in the evening edition. The foreman scribbles an instruction to print and hands it to a typesetter. As Hynes is leaving, Mr Bloom helpfully urges him to hurry if he wishes to draw from the cashier. Mr Bloom is acutely aware that this is the third time he has hinted to Hynes about a debt of three shillings.

Mr Bloom lays the cutting on the foreman's desk and explains the design of two crossed keys. The foreman agrees to publish a paragraph drawing attention to the firm of Keyes, on condition that a three-month renewal of the advertisement is given. Mr Bloom leaves to discuss the matter with Mr Keyes and to obtain a copy of the new design, which had been published in

Palmerston Park   Rathmines

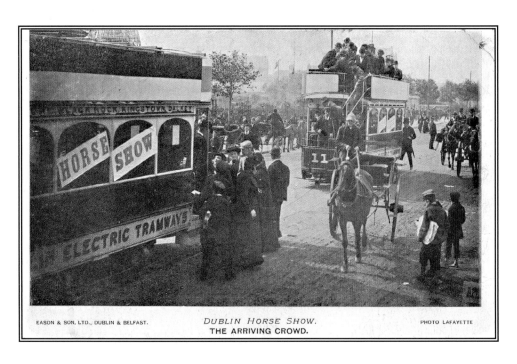

EASON & SON, LTD., DUBLIN & BELFAST.   *DUBLIN HORSE SHOW.*   PHOTO LAFAYETTE
THE ARRIVING CROWD.

[127]

The tram company timekeeper shouts the starting command to the driver of the Palmerston Park tram.

a Kilkenny newspaper. Mr Bloom considers that August is an excellent month for advertisements with the tourists over for the Dublin Horse Show.

As Mr Bloom makes his way down the staircase he hears a loud shout of laughter echoing from the office of the *Evening Telegraph*. He enters the room where Ned Lambert is reading a newspaper report of Dan Dawson's speech, to the jeers and laughter of Simon Dedalus and Professor McHugh. J.J. O'Molloy comes in and asks for the editor, Myles Crawford. Mr Bloom is inwardly reminded that J.J. O'Molloy was once a brilliant junior barrister but now is in serious decline, with money worries, a dwindling practice and gambling debts. Ned Lambert continues to read the pretentious, patriotic rhetoric of Dan Dawson against the din of further ridicule and criticisms.

[128]

Mr Bloom considers that August is an excellent month for advertisements with the tourists over for the Dublin Horse Show.

Myles Crawford bursts into the room screaming about the uproar. He engages in banter with Professor McHugh. Simon Dedalus and Ned Lambert prepare to leave and invite Crawford to join them for a drink at the Oval. Mr Bloom makes for the inner room, telling Crawford he needs to make a telephone call. He carefully dials the office number of Alexander Keyes.

Lenehan appears with racing forms by *Sport* in his hands. He proclaims that Sceptre is a certainty to win the Gold Cup at Ascot. An altercation between newsboys in the hall results in the door being blown open and papers scattering around the room. Professor McHugh grabs the cringing boy and Crawford urges McHugh to fling him out because a hurricane wind is blowing. The boy is ejected and the door banged closed.

Meanwhile Mr Bloom has learned by telephone that Keyes is at Dillon's auction rooms. He leaves, telling Crawford he will return after he has checked details of the advertisement with Keyes. Crawford is anxious to join Simon Dedalus and Ned Lambert for a drink at the Oval.

Mr O'Madden Burke and Stephen Dedalus enter the room. Stephen is introduced to Crawford and mentions

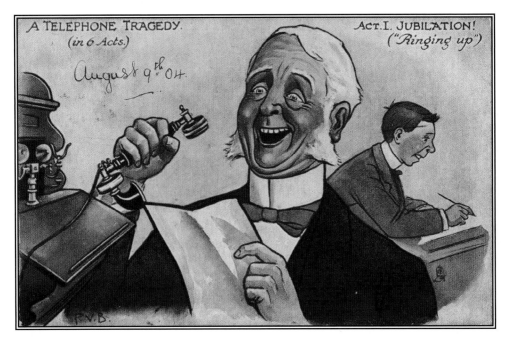

A TELEPHONE TRAGEDY.
(in 6 Acts.)

August 9th 04.

ACT.I. JUBILATION!
("Ringing up")

F.V.B.

a letter from Mr Garrett Deasy. Crawford knows Deasy and his wife, an awful woman, infamous for throwing soup in a waiter's face at the Star and Garter Hotel. Stephen asks if Deasy is a widower. Crawford, glancing at the letter, replies that Deasy is separated from his wife.

The conversation turns to the misplaced loyalty of the Irish to various emperors and princes of Europe. Professor McHugh blames the Irish for always being loyal to lost causes and not successful ones. He extols the virtues of the Greeks and their language, but adds that they too followed lost causes. Professor McHugh explains that Pyrrhus took the advice of an oracle and failed in a final attempt to regain the former glory of Greece.

Myles Crawford puts Deasy's letter in his pocket, telling Stephen he will publish it. He asks Stephen to write something with a strong theme to include himself and everyone else. To emphasize his point Crawford cites Ignatius Gallaher, the journalist who brought off a coup reporting the murders perpetrated by the Invincibles in the Phoenix Park. Gallaher, responding to a cabled request from the *New York World*, developed an

[129]

He carefully dials the office number of Alexander Keyes.

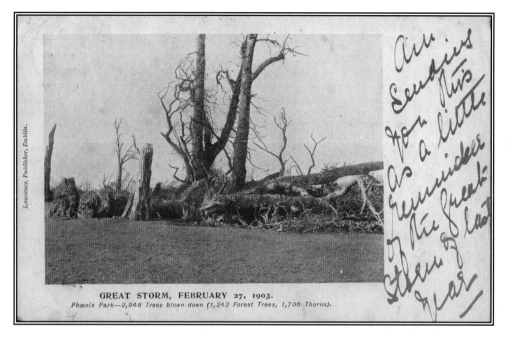

Lawrence, Publisher, Dublin.

GREAT STORM, FEBRUARY 27, 1903.
Phœnix Park—2,948 Trees blown down (1,242 Forest Trees, 1,706 Thorns).

All sending for this as a little reminder of the great storm of last year!

[130]

Lady Dudley was walking through the Phoenix Park to see the trees blown down by last year's great storm.

ingenious code based on an advertisement in the *Weekly Freeman*. This code enabled him to transmit secret messages about the movements of the Invincibles. Mr O'Madden Burke mentions that Skin-the-Goat, the man who drove the car for the Invincibles, was now in charge of the cabman's shelter at Butt Bridge, while another Invincible, Gumley, works nearby as a night-watchman for the Corporation.

Professor McHugh comments on the recent appearance of hawkers to answer charges before the recorder of Dublin. J.J. O'Molloy intervenes to tell his side of this story. Lady Dudley was walking through the Phoenix Park to see the trees blown down by last year's great storm. She decided to buy a postcard of Dublin from the hawkers who were trading outside the Viceregal Lodge. She discovered that it was a commemorative postcard of one of the Invincibles. J.J. O'Molloy invites the company to consider this astonishing story and the implications of Lady Dudley's involvement.

Myles Crawford expresses an opinion that the standards in journalism and law have deteriorated. An argument

develops on the merits of oratory, past and present. J.J.
O'Molloy remembers the polished performance of
Seymour Bushe, acting for the defence in the Childs'
murder case. Professor McHugh informs the company
that the finest display of oratory that he has heard was
by John F. Taylor at the College Historical Society.
Although sick, Taylor had come to the debate to speak
in favour of the revival of the Irish language. Professor
McHugh quotes Taylor's speech, which argued that if
Moses and the Jews had accepted the admonitions of
their captors to abandon their culture, religion and language and to adopt those of Egypt, the Jews would never
have escaped bondage. If Moses had received the gods of
Isis, Osiris, Horus and Ammon Ra, he would never have
spoken to the true God on Mount Sinai or received the Ten
Commandments written on stone. Professor McHugh's
words are received in silence.

Stephen proposes that the house be adjourned.
Lenehan declares the motion carried and suggests a visit
to Mooney's public house. The company emerges from

[131]

A short circuit in the electricity
stops all the southbound trams
dead in their tracks, including
those to or from Rathmines
and Upper Rathmines.

the offices of the *Evening Telegraph* and proceeds along Abbey Street. Stephen recounts a story to Professor McHugh about two old Dublin women and their visit to the top of Nelson's Pillar. Mr Bloom catches up with Myles Crawford. He explains that Keyes will be willing to give a two-month renewal in return for a paragraph and asks Crawford what he should tell Keyes. Myles Crawford proclaims loudly that Keyes can kiss his arse and walks away.

J.J. O'Molloy and Myles Crawford are walking together, talking about money. Myles Crawford explains that he is heavily in debt himself and had been looking for someone to guarantee a loan as recently as last week. He is sorry but is quite unable to raise a loan for O'Molloy. They catch up with the others who are preparing to cross O'Connell Street in the direction of Mooney's.

A short circuit in the electricity stops all the southbound trams dead in their tracks, including those bound to or from Rathmines and Upper Rathmines.

—11—

Lestrygonians

IN O'CONNELL STREET, outside Graham Lemon's, a young man hands Mr Bloom a throwaway leaflet. Mr Bloom walks towards the Liffey reading the throwaway, which proclaims the coming of Elijah in the person of Dr John Alexander Dowie. At Butler's Monument House corner he glances down Bachelor's Walk and sees one of the Dedalus girls waiting outside Dillon's auction rooms. He reflects on the plight of the Dedalus family with fifteen children and how the home tends to break up when the mother dies. Mr Bloom is critical of the Catholic priests who force women to have children by refusing absolution for the sin of contraception.

As he arrives on O'Connell Bridge a puff of smoke rises from a Guinness Brewery barge. Mr Bloom flings his throwaway into the Liffey, among the gulls flying between the walls of the quayside. He buys two small cakes for a penny and feeds the gulls. From the bridge he notices that the timeball on the Ballast Office has fallen. The fact that the timeball is linked to Dunsink Observatory reminds him of a book that he has read on astronomy by Sir Robert Ball. Like Molly, there were words in that book that he never quite understood.

A procession of five sandwich-board men walk along the gutter of the pavement towards Mr Bloom. He reads the five letters on each of their tall hats that spell Hely's, the name of his former employer. Mr Bloom remembers suggesting a good advertisement to Wisdom Hely. It would consist of two smart girls sitting inside a transparent show-cart, writing letters, surrounded

Dublin. 20th Sept, '04 — Guinness' Dublin Stout creates strength and energy. It is bottled in Dublin by E.& J. Burke, (see label) Beware of imitations. Boston office — 7. Water Street.

[132]

As he arrives on O'Connell Bridge a puff of smoke rises from a Guinness Brewery barge.

by Hely's stationery. Mr Bloom ruefully recalls that Wisdom Hely rejected the idea because he did not think of it himself. In retrospect he is happy to be out of Hely's, because of the difficulties in collecting accounts from the convents, particularly the Carmelite nuns.

As he crosses Westmoreland Street Mr Bloom recalls that he landed the job in Wisdom Hely's the year he married Molly. That was 1894, when Val Dillon was lord mayor and also the year of the Glencree Dinner. He remembers how Alderman Robert O'Reilly emptied his port into the soup before the dinner started. Mr Bloom was happier then, remembering their cosy room and the pleasant smell of Milly's bathing water. He tries but fails to recall the name of the young man who habitually stared in their window as he passed. Mr Bloom recalls with displeasure Bartell d'Arcy, the tenor, who brought Molly home after singing practice. D'Arcy was a conceited man with a pretentious waxed moustache. Mr Bloom reflects on the night of the meeting of his Freeman's Lodge on the issue of lottery tickets. After the meeting he had collected Molly and Professor Goodwin, both of whom had been performing at the Mansion House. He recalls the pleasant night with Molly when they got home, with good food and mulled rum.

Outside Harrison's Mr Bloom meets Mrs Breen and they exchange pleasantries. Mrs Breen notices his black attire, which he explains. Mrs Breen discloses that her husband is acting irrationally and is now consulting legal books on the law of libel. She takes a postcard out of her handbag and asks Mr Bloom to read the coded message of just four letters. Mrs Breen believes that someone is playing a hoax on her husband. She sighs as she tells Mr Bloom that her husband is going to see John Henry Menton with a view to a suit for libel for £10,000. Mr Bloom notices her dowdy attire and the lines on her face although she is only a year older than Molly. He recalls, with unease, that she was once the lovely Josie Powell with whom he played charades a long time ago at Luke Doyle's party in Dolphin's Barn.

The subject turns to Mina Purefoy and her confinement at the lying-in hospital, Holles Street, under the care of Dr Horne. Mrs Breen informs Mr Bloom that Mina Purefoy has been in a very poor condition for three days and a difficult birth is expected. Mrs Breen sees her husband and departs, sending her good wishes to Molly. Mr Bloom watches Denis Breen walk out of Harrison's carrying two heavy books and concludes he is mad. He suspects that the postcard hoax is the concoction of Alf Bergan or Richie Goulding.

As he passes the offices of the *Irish Times* he remembers his advertisement seeking a lady typist to assist a literary gentleman. Martha Clifford and Lizzie Twigg replied. Mr Bloom concludes that the *Irish Times* is the best newspaper for small advertisements as it is read by a better class of person, like the attractive woman at the Grosvenor Hotel. Mr Bloom recalls another horsy-type, Mrs Miriam Dandrade, who sold him her old clothes and black underwear in the Shelbourne Hotel.

[133]

Mr Bloom recalls another horsy-type, Mrs Miriam Dandrade, who sold him her old clothes and black underwear in the Shelbourne Hotel.

[134]

The pigeons flying in front of the high door of the Bank of Ireland distract his attention as he passes under the statue of Tom Moore.

Dublin. Stephen's Green from Shelbourne Hotel. *Where will you find its like?*

Lawrence]   THE ROYAL VISIT, DUBLIN, JULY, 1903.   [Dublin
WESTMORELAND STREET DECORATED

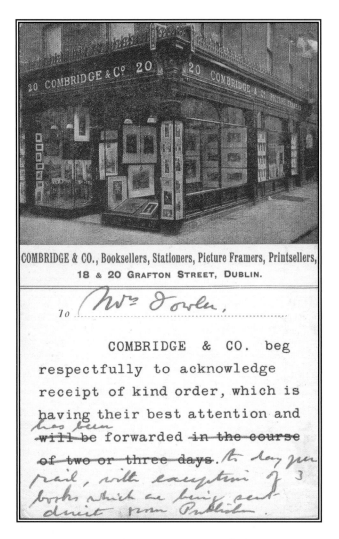

COMBRIDGE & CO., Booksellers, Stationers, Picture Framers, Printsellers,
18 & 20 GRAFTON STREET, DUBLIN.

To *Mrs Fowler,*

COMBRIDGE & CO. beg
respectfully to acknowledge
receipt of kind order, which is
having their best attention and
~~will~~ *has been* be forwarded ~~in the course~~
~~of two or three days.~~ *the day per
mail, with exception of 3
books which are being sent
direct from Publisher.*

[135]

He turns around Combridge's
corner into Duke Street and
enters the Burton restaurant.

He walks through the intersection of Fleet Street and Westmoreland Street, heading for College Street. The pigeons flying in front of the high door of the Bank of Ireland distract his attention as he passes under the statue of Tom Moore. He is amused by the thought that Moore's statue is over a urinal, in view of his legendary song about the meeting of the waters in the Vale of Avoca.

A dark cloud covers the sun when he walks past the front of Trinity College. As he passes the Provost's House he sees John Howard Parnell, the city marshall, walking on the other side of the street. The haunted face and sorrowful walk of Parnell's brother reminds Mr Bloom that all the Parnell family were slightly peculiar. He is overtaken by George Russell in the company of a young woman. Mr Bloom wonders if she might be Lizzie Twigg, the young lady who claimed to know the eminent poet when replying to his advertisement in the *Irish Times*.

In Grafton Street he looks in windows of shops bedecked with awnings. He turns around Combridge's corner into Duke Street and enters the Burton restaurant. He is revolted by the sight, smell and sound of men feeding like pigs at a trough. He decides instead on a light snack at Davy Byrne's. As he enters, Mr Bloom recalls that Davy Byrne is not over-generous to his customers by way of free drink, although he did cash a cheque on one occasion. Nosey Flynn, sitting in a corner, greets his arrival. Mr Bloom orders a glass of burgundy and a Gorgonzola cheese sandwich.

Nosey Flynn enquires about Molly and the forthcoming concert tour. Mr Bloom answers in general terms, evading the direct question about the name of the organizer. Nosey Flynn remembers that someone told him that it was Blazes Boylan who was getting up the concert. Mr Bloom is momentarily shocked and looks at the clock. It is two o'clock and not yet time for Boylan's visit to Molly. Mr Bloom confirms that Boylan is, in fact, the organizer but he is not suspicious of the motives of his companion. Davy Byrne joins the company and the conversation turns to gambling and the Gold Cup race at Ascot.

Mr Bloom quietly savours his wine and cheese, musing over the various foods that people eat. He considers the aphrodisiac effect of oysters and wonders if Boylan had eaten oysters at the Red Bank restaurant that morning. Memories of Howth come to mind, where he and Molly lay hidden among the wild ferns and heather. He remembers the kisses, her soft lips and her eyes willing him on. Then there was the final moment when she yielded, tossing his hair and exchanging wild kisses.

Mr Bloom drains his glass and walks outside to the toilet. Nosey Flynn and Davy Byrne discuss Mr Bloom's job as a canvasser for the *Freeman's Journal.* Nosey Flynn is of the opinion that Bloom derives additional income and help from the Freemasons. Davy Byrne describes Bloom as a decent man who often calls in for a drink but never gets drunk or misbehaves himself. Nosey Flynn agrees, adding that Bloom is always generous to people down on their luck.

Paddy Leonard, Bantam Lyons and Tom Rochford come in for a drink. Paddy Leonard orders drinks and informs the company that Bantam Lyons has a dead cert for the Gold Cup. Paddy Leonard demands to know the source of Lyons' information. At this point Mr Bloom raises his hand in greeting as he leaves the premises. Bantam Lyons furtively whispers that Bloom is the man that gave him the tip.

Mr Bloom walks toward Dawson Street. He calculates that his good financial position would allow him to buy Molly a silk petticoat to match her new garters. He forces

[136]

Mr Bloom surmises that Falkiner was just after a good lunch with old friends from King's Hospital school.

King's Hospital.   Dublin.

himself not to think of Boylan and the impending meeting with Molly. In Dawson Street Mr Bloom helps a blind boy across the road and watches with compassion as he taps his way along. He remembers to answer Martha Clifford's letter and decides to send her a postal order for a half-crown.

As he walks through Molesworth Street he sees Sir Frederick Falkiner, the recorder, entering the Freemasons' Hall. Mr Bloom surmises that Falkiner was just after a good lunch with old friends from King's Hospital school. He recalls that Falkiner is particularly tough on money-lenders and dealt harshly with Reuben J. Dodd. An advertisement for the Mirus Bazaar in Ballsbridge catches his eye. He decides against visiting Keyes in Ballsbridge because it would be more prudent not to wear out his welcome with Keyes.

As Mr Bloom arrives in Kildare Street he thinks that he sees Boylan's straw hat. His heart pounding, he turns right and escapes through the gate of the National Museum.

~12~

Scylla and Charybdis

IN THE OFFICE OF THE DIRECTOR of the National Library a discussion is in progress on the nuances of *Hamlet*. Lyster, the librarian and Quaker, cites Goethe's opinion of Hamlet as being a hesitating and incompetent dreamer who fails disastrously when faced with the harsh realities of life. Lyster is called away by an attendant. Stephen makes a contemptuous remark about Lyster's statements. John Eglinton counters by mocking the literary ability of Stephen and his student friends, adding that they have produced nothing to equal Shakespeare.

Russell enters the argument to disagree with theories that treat Hamlet as an actual person. He opines that the function of art, like that of Plato's theories, is to reveal hidden spirituality, and that other descriptions are merely schoolboy speculation. Politely, Stephen informs Russell that the followers of Aristotle were schoolboys to begin with and that Aristotle himself was once a schoolboy of Plato. John Eglinton makes a sneering reference to Aristotle as a model schoolboy. Mr Best, a tall young man, enters the room. Stephen argues that even the schoolboy Aristotle would find Hamlet's thoughts on the afterlife of his soul as improbable and insignificant as those of Plato. John Eglinton vents his anger with Stephen comparing Aristotle to Plato. Inwardly, Stephen prepares himself for a battle of definitions and girds himself to hold on to the present moment.

Mr Best recounts a description of a performance of *Hamlet* in a small French town that advertised the hero as a distracted or absentminded individual.

The National Library.. *My Dearest Mother* Dublin. *I will write a long letter to you on Wednesday I got Ma's letter today. Your loving son Anthony*

[137]

In the office of the director of the National Library a discussion is in progress on the nuances of *Hamlet*.

Stephen criticizes the exaggeration of murder in *Hamlet* where nine people are killed in revenge for the murder of Hamlet's father. John Eglinton expresses the view that Stephen would like the company to believe that *Hamlet* is a ghost story.

Stephen suggests that Shakespeare had identified with the ghost, Hamlet's murdered father, and played the role on stage. He argues that it is possible to conclude that Shakespeare, when playing the role of the murdered father, is in effect speaking to his real life son, Hamnet. Shakespeare is telling Hamnet that he is the disinherited son and his mother, Anne Hathaway, the guilty queen. Russell intervenes to complain that it is wrong to examine the private life of Shakespeare. Stephen inwardly reflects that he owes Russell a pound, which he borrowed to spend on a prostitute called Georgina Johnson.

John Eglinton expresses the long-held opinion that Anne Hathaway was of little importance in the life of Shakespeare. Stephen takes the view that Shakespeare, as evidenced in his writings, retained a vivid memory of his

COPYRIGHT S. HILDESHEIMER & C? L?? LONDON & MANCHESTER

M? WILSON BARRETT AS HAMLET.　PHOTO BY BARRAUD

Dear may. why have you not written to me I have not had a letter for over a week. & send me my collars. with love, from Clare.

John Eglinton expresses the view that Stephen would like the company to believe that *Hamlet* is a ghost story.

seduction in a cornfield by a determined woman of twenty-six. Richard Best remarks that it was a ryefield.

Russell rises and says that he is due at the offices of the *Irish Homestead*. John Eglinton enquires if Russell will be at Moore's party later that night. Russell explains that he has a meeting but will try to attend. Stephen reflects on the activities of Russell and the Hermetists at their meetings in Dawson Chambers. The company discusses Russell's forthcoming anthology of Ireland's younger poets and other literary gossip. Stephen silently ponders his exclusion from all these events, noting bitterly that Mulligan and Haines have been invited to Moore's party. Before leaving, Russell agrees to hand a copy of Deasy's letter in to the offices of the *Irish Homestead*.

After seeing Russell out, Lyster returns and introduces the question of whether Anne Hathaway was faithful to Shakespeare. Stephen believes that there was a reconciliation between Shakespeare and Anne Hathaway, so there must have been a break up. John Eglinton expresses the opinion that very little is known about Shakespeare's mode of living and suffering. Mr Best remarks that *Hamlet* is more or less a private account of Shakespeare's personal life. John Eglinton believes that Shakespeare is Hamlet, the prince, rather than the ghost and warns Stephen that he will have a hard task ahead to dissuade him of that belief.

The company discusses the issue of reconciliation in the later plays of Shakespeare. Stephen points out that the softening of Shakespeare's heart begins to show in *Pericles, Prince of Tyre*, with the story of the recovery of a long-lost daughter. According to Stephen, Shakespeare is celebrating the birth of a beloved granddaughter. Lyster points out that the dark lady of Shakespeare's sonnets or the Earl of Pembroke would be more obvious candidates for his feelings of rejection than Anne Hathaway. Stephen speculates that Shakespeare lost belief in himself after his seduction by Anne Hathaway in a ryefield and was wounded irrevocably by the experience. Because Shakespeare is unaware of the poison in his soul, he only reveals himself in his plays. Shakespeare, Stephen tells the company, is a ghost, as it were, who can only be revealed by a son.

Buck Mulligan appears in the doorway and greets the company cheerfully. When asked about his theory of Shakespeare, Mulligan jokingly refers to Shakespeare as the fellow that writes like Synge. Mulligan reads Stephen's telegram and wails in a mock peasant accent about the plight of himself and Haines, left waiting by Stephen at The Ship public house.

From the open door an attendant calls for Lyster to look after a gentleman from the *Freeman's Journal* who wishes to see the files of *The Kilkenny People*. Lyster leaves to attend to the visitor. Mulligan identifies the caller as Mr Bloom by inspecting the business card. He informs the company that he had earlier encountered the Jew, Bloom, at the Museum, staring at the nude statue of Aphrodite.

John Eglinton and Mr Best wish to hear more of Stephen's opinion of Anne Hathaway. Stephen explains that Shakespeare had spent twenty years of pleasurable debauchery in London but is nonetheless obsessed by thoughts of her adultery. Evidence of her guilt is shown in the fifth scene of *Hamlet* where her misconduct is exposed. Stephen continues to argue that nothing is heard about Anne Hathaway for thirty-four years, other than a small debt and, to cap it all, Shakespeare deliberately left her the second-best bed in his will. Stephen compares this conduct with the final wishes of Aristotle, who asked to be buried near his dead wife and requested his friends to be kind to his former mistress.

The discussion turns to the question of whether Shakespeare was a Jew. Stephen attempts to prove it by citing Saint Thomas Aquinas, while Mulligan derides this effort with wails of mock anguish in Irish. Stephen returns to the subject of Shakespeare's contempt for Anne Hathaway, as evidenced in his will. John Eglinton echoes Russell's point that Shakespeare's family is of little importance. Inwardly, Stephen is conscious of the fact that William K. Magee, alias John Eglinton, has an uncouth peasant father who visits him periodically, much to Magee's embarrassment. Stephen recalls a poignant meeting with his own father at the quayside, after Stephen had returned from Paris to pay his respects to his dying mother on her squalid death bed. He remembers that his father's voice and eyes were warm and welcoming on that occasion, but his father does not really know him.

Stephen makes the point that it would be wrong to identify the thirty-five-year-old Shakespeare with Hamlet, a youthful student, because if you do you must hold that Shakespeare's mother is the adulterous queen. He concludes that fathering a child is not a conscious act, unlike a mother's love, which could be the only true aspect of life. Inwardly, Stephen queries the basis of his argument but nonetheless continues to expand on the relationship between father and son. Mulligan is fascinated by Stephen's theory and asks for time to produce a play on the subject.

The question of the various roles played by Shakespeare's family in his plays is outlined by Stephen. The death of Shakespeare's mother is recorded in *Coriolanus*. The death of his infant son is mirrored in *King John*. His son, Hamnet, is Hamlet. The girls appear in *The Tempest, Pericles, Prince of Tyre* and in *The Winter's Tale*. His three brothers, Gilbert, Edmund and Richard, are featured as villains. Gilbert is of little importance but the other two appear as Shakespeare's most villainous characters.

Lyster and John Eglinton press Stephen on the question of guilt by Shakespeare's brothers. Stephen admits that the names of Edmund and Richard were contained in the history books from which Shakespeare obtained the plots of his plays. However, in *Richard III*, Shakespeare deliberately selected Richard as an appalling hunchbacked villain to make love to and marry a widowed Anne. Furthermore Richard is the only king to be treated badly by Shakespeare. Stephen poses the question as to why Edmund is spuriously introduced to *King Lear* and argues that the theme of an adulterous brother preyed on Shakespeare's mind. John Eglinton sums up the debate by announcing that Shakespeare is both a ghost and a prince.

Stephen invites the company to consider the epilogue to Shakespeare's life. Shakespeare returns, a rich and prosperous man, to the place where he was born. The good Shakespeare is rewarded by the company of his beloved grandchild, Elizabeth, while the bad brother, Richard, is punished.

Dear D Thanks for card. am glad to hear you are looking so well M. is grand my cold still sticks but Y. is all right again. Love from all B G

Camden Street. Dublin

NATIONAL LIBRARY of IRELAND. KILDARE St DUBLIN.

John Eglinton asks Stephen if he believes his theory. Stephen answers negatively and Mr Best suggests that Stephen writes it like a dialogue by Wilde. John Eglinton smiles and proposes that Stephen should not be paid for writing something that he does not believe in. He adds that Stephen is the only writer who demands money for articles in *Dana.*

As Stephen and Mulligan prepare to leave, John Eglinton reminds Mulligan of the forthcoming party at Moore's. As they make their way out, Mulligan chides Stephen for his hostile criticism of Lady Gregory's book. He urges Stephen to be more like Yeats who praised the book as a work of art, reminiscent of Homer. Buck Mulligan stops at the foot of the stairs and reads for Stephen an extract from his obscene play, composed during the debate in the National Library. Buck Mulligan reminds Stephen of the night in the Camden Hall, when the young girls lifted their skirts to avoid Stephen as he lay in his own vomit. Stephen inwardly wonders if the time has come to part with Mulligan.

At the doorway Mr Bloom passes between Stephen and Mulligan, greeting both men. Buck Mulligan whispers, facetiously, that Bloom the Jew had looked at Stephen with lust in his eye. They follow Mr Bloom out through the gates into the pleasant air of Kildare Street.

—13—

Wandering Rocks

FATHER JOHN CONMEE SJ walks down the steps of the presbytery. He is on his way to Artane Industrial School at the request of Martin Cunningham to have a word with Brother Swan about the Dignam boy. At the corner of Mountjoy Square he stops and talks with three little boys from Belvedere College. He proceeds down Great Charles Street, turns the corner and walks along the North Circular Road.

Father Conmee raises his hat as he passes Saint Joseph's Church, Portland Row. William Gallaher salutes Father Conmee as he makes his way along the North Strand Road. At Grogan's shop he sees the news-boards recounting the appalling disaster in New York. He reflects on the misfortune of people who die suddenly, but reasons that they could still have time to say an act of perfect contrition. Father Conmee passes the funeral establishment of H.J. O'Neill, where inside Corny Kelleher is writing up the day-book.

At Newcomen Bridge Father Conmee sees a turf barge, horse and barge-man. He is delighted at the beautiful scene and reflects on the providence of the Creator who made it all possible. Father Conmee decides to board an outgoing tram because he dislikes the prospect of walking past Mud Island. The smiling face of Mr Eugene Stratton, with his large Negroid lips, greets Father Conmee from the hoardings. He is reminded of the millions of coloured people who die and are lost to God without the benefit of baptism. He takes consolation from a book by a Belgian priest that argues that these people could be saved without the sacrament of baptism.

Co. Dublin. *Malahiae Castle.*

Published by M. Hall, Malahide.

[141]

The name Malahide pleases
Father Conmee because it
reminds him of the legend of
Lord Talbot of Malahide Castle.

Father Conmee alights from the tram at the Howth Road stop and walks up the Malahide Road. The name Malahide pleases Father Conmee because it reminds him of the legend of Lord Talbot of Malahide Castle. Lord Talbot had been summoned to war on his wedding day and killed, giving rise to the well-known legend of a young girl being maid, wife and widow on the one day.

As he walks along the road he reflects on his own book about historical events and considers that another book might be written about Jesuit houses or perhaps Mary Rochfort, the Countess of Belvedere. He reflects on the adultery of Mary Rochfort with her husband's brother and concludes that only God, Lady Rochfort and Lord Belvedere's brother could know if full and complete adultery had taken place. Father Conmee imagines himself in olden days, mixing with the nobility and learning their secrets in confession.

The pleasant day reminds Father Conmee of his evening walks in Clongowes when he was rector of the college. He takes out his breviary and begins to read his office in Latin. A red-faced young man and a girl emerge through a gap in the hedge. The young man doffs his cap and Father Conmee blesses them both.

Corny Kelleher closes the day-book and walks to the door. Constable 57C stops and bids him the time of day. Corny Kelleher asks if there is any news and the constable replies that he had seen the person in question on the previous evening.

In Eccles Street a one-legged sailor on crutches proceeds with difficulty. He passes Katey and Boody Dedalus. From a house a blind is drawn aside, allowing a card advertising unfurnished rooms to fall. A woman flings a coin from the window onto the path. An urchin picks it up and hands it to the sailor.

Katey and Boody Dedalus arrive home and enter the steaming kitchen, where their sister Maggy is boiling clothes. Boody ascertains that Maggy has been unable to raise any money from the pawnbroker on Stephen's books. The three girls sit down to a meal of bread and pea soup obtained from Sister Mary Patrick. Maggy informs them that Dilly is gone to see their father. Boody passes a disparaging remark about her father and is rebuked by Maggy.

A throwaway proclaiming the coming of Elijah floats down the Liffey between the Custom House and George's Quay.

Custom House, Dublin.

[142]

A throwaway proclaiming the coming of Elijah floats down the Liffey between the Custom House and George's Quay.

In Thornton's a blonde girl is preparing a basket of fruit for Blazes Boylan. He hands her a bottle and a jar, asking that they be put in the basket for immediate delivery by tram. Blazes Boylan looks down her blouse as she calculates the bill. He asks permission to take a free carnation and the blushing girl concedes his request. Blazes Boylan, carnation between his teeth, asks flirtatiously if he may use the telephone.

Music teacher Almidano Artifoni and Stephen Dedalus are conversing in Italian outside the gates of Trinity College. The teacher pleads with Stephen to continue his singing career and Stephen promises to consider the advice. Almidano Artifoni catches sight of a Dalkey tram and bids a hasty goodbye. He signals in vain to the tram driver from among a large group of Highland bandsmen carrying their musical instruments through the gates of Trinity College.

I typed this all by my little self.

[143]

Miss Dunne types the date,
16 June 1904, then stares at a
poster of the beautiful actress,
Marie Kendall.

Miss Dunne hides a copy of a cheap mystery novel inside
her drawer. She muses to herself as to whether the hero of
the book is in love with a girl called Marion. Miss Dunne
types the date, 16 June 1904, then stares at a poster of the
beautiful actress, Marie Kendall. She daydreams about her
social night ahead and hopes that she will not be detained
late at the office. The telephone rings and she takes various business instructions from her employer, Blazes
Boylan. She gives Boylan the message that a Mr Lenehan
will meet him at four o'clock in the Ormond Hotel.

By the flickering light of a match Ned Lambert conducts Reverend Hugh C. Love around Saint Mary's Abbey. J.J. O'Molloy shouts from the top of the steps and comes down to join the two men. Ned Lambert outlines the historical associations of the buildings and gives permission to the Reverend Love to bring a camera on his next visit. Reverend Love thanks Ned Lambert and leaves the building. The two men follow the clergyman into the main part of the building where sacks of seeds are being loaded on floats by draymen. Ned Lambert informs J.J. O'Molloy that the nice young clergyman is writing a history of the Fitzgeralds. J.J. O'Molloy sneezes explosively from the dust of the seed bags.

Tom Rochford is demonstrating a machine to Lenehan, M'Coy and Nosey Flynn that indicates, by number, the music hall act in progress at any given time. Nosey Flynn comments favourably on the clever machine, while Lenehan offers to mention the idea to Blazes Boylan at the Ormond Hotel.

Lenehan and M'Coy leave, crossing Crampton Court and on past Dan Lowry's music hall. Lenehan mentions the heroism of Tom Rochford who climbed down a manhole to rescue a man choking from sewer gas. In Temple Bar Lenehan decides to check the starting price of Sceptre at Lynam's, the bookmakers. He returns to the waiting M'Coy with news that Sceptre is even money and Bantam Lyons is inside backing a horse with no chance of winning.

As they walk up the steps of Merchant's Arch they see Mr Bloom looking at the books on a hawker's cart. Lenehan is eager to relate a story about Bloom that happened on the night of the annual dinner at Glencree Reformatory. As they walk along the river wall of Wellington Quay

The Scalp, Co. Wicklow.

HELY'S, LIMITED, DUBLIN.

Lenehan outlines the details of the formal dinner. Val Dillon, the lord mayor, and Sir Charles Cameron were the chief guests. Dan Dawson gave a speech. There was plenty of music and songs from Bartell d'Arcy and Ben Dollard. Lenehan himself was in charge of the catering by Delahunt's of Camden Street and accordingly there was no shortage of food or drink.

Lenehan links M'Coy's arm and eagerly describes the return journey by horse-driven car through the Wicklow Mountains. Chris Callinan and Bloom sat on one side of the jaunting car while Lenehan and Molly were on the other side. They were all singing and looking at the stars on the lovely clear winter's night. Molly was tipsy and, to the delight of Lenehan, was bumping against him at each jolt of the car. Lenehan describes his sexual arousal, culminating in ultimate gratification of a kind. He stops and leans against the wall of the Liffey, gasping with laughter. M'Coy is not amused by the story. Glancing at M'Coy, Lenehan soberly describes Bloom as a rare cultured man with a commendable artistic nature.

[144]

Lenehan links M'Coy's arm and eagerly describes the return journey by horse-driven car through the Wicklow Mountains.

Mr Bloom is in a bookshop, looking through a selection of trashy novels. The owner throws two books on the counter, recommending both. Mr Bloom selects the one he thinks might be suitable for Molly. He reads a few pages, noting with interest an extract describing a lovely woman who spends the money of her jealous husband on beautiful gowns and underwear. Mr Bloom decides to take it.

Outside Dillon's auction rooms Dilly Dedalus waits for her father. Simon Dedalus arrives and gives out to her for not standing straight. He gives her a shilling and rejects a request for more with a tirade of abuse about the insolence of his daughters since their mother died. He gives her two pence for a bun and informs her that he will be home soon.

❧

Mr Kernan walks along James's Street, pleased with the good order for tea he has obtained for his employer Pulbrook Robinson. He attributes his good conversation and well-dressed appearance to his good fortune earlier with Mr Crimmins. As he admires his coat in the mirror of a hairdresser's shop he sees the windscreen of a passing motor car flashing in the sunlight.

Mr Kernan looks down at the place where Robert Emmet was executed, by the grisly method of being hanged, drawn and quartered. He tries to remember if Emmet was buried in Saint Michan's but recalls that the corpse of Emmet was brought at midnight for secret burial at Glasnevin. He is reminded that Dignam is now buried at the same graveyard.

Mr Kernan turns and walks down the incline of

Watling Street, on past the corner of the waiting-room for visitors to Guinness's Brewery. As he approaches Island Street he is reminded of the daring escape of Lord Edward Fitzgerald from Major Sirr. He thinks of the ill-fated rebellion and Ben Dollard's fine singing of the ballad about another hero who fought for Ireland in the same uprising. Mr Kernan rushes forward but is disappointed to miss the sight of the viceregal cavalcade passing Pembroke Quay.

Stephen Dedalus watches through a window as old Russell, the lapidary, polishes a gemstone. In Bedford Row he halts at a book-cart, wondering if he will find any of his school prize books that had been pawned. Stephen is greeted by his sister, Dilly, who has just purchased a French grammar. Stephen examines the book and warns her not to let Maggy pawn it. Inwardly, Stephen is overcome with pity for his shabbily dressed sister. He can do nothing to save her from misery without destroying himself in the process.

Father Bob Cowley and Simon Dedalus greet each other warmly outside the antique shop of Reddy and Daughter. Father Cowley reports that he is under siege at his house with two men trying to gain entrance. He acquaints Simon Dedalus with his opinion that the Jew Reuben J. Dodd is responsible for all his troubles. Father Cowley is presently waiting for Ben Dollard, who hopes to persuade the sub-sheriff, Long John Fanning, to call off his two bailiffs. Ben Dollard ambles towards the two men, greeting them with information that he has just consulted John Henry Menton. There is good news, because Father Cowley's landlord, Reverend Love, has previously distrained for rent. As a result Reverend Love's writ takes

The City Hall.   Dublin.

This is our one I dare-say it is dirty but antique so what matter? Of course it cant hold a candle to your magnificent (cant crith'ry)

[145]

John Wyse Nolan hurries down Cork Hill as Councillor Nannetti descends the steps of the City Hall.

precedence over that of Dodd's, which is now worthless. Ben Dollard links Father Cowley and walks forward, followed by Simon Dedalus.

Martin Cunningham and Mr Power walk out the gate of Dublin Castle conversing about the Dignam boy. Martin Cunningham is confident that the boy will be cared for as he has written to Father Conmee, outlining the whole case.

John Wyse Nolan hurries down Cork Hill as Councillor Nannetti descends the steps of the City Hall. Nolan informs Martin Cunningham that Bloom has contributed five shillings to the Dignam fund. The three men walk down Parliament Street where they see Jimmy Henry entering Kavanagh's wine rooms. Long John Fanning is standing in the door of Kavanagh's. Martin Cunningham fails to evince interest in the Dignam fund from either Fanning or Henry. They all move up the

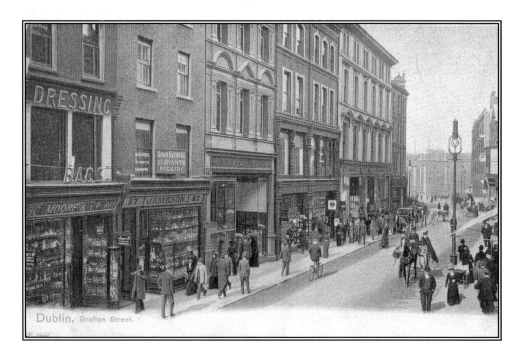

Cashel Boyle O'Connor Fitzmaurice Tisdall Farrell proceeds along Merrion Square, taking extreme care to walk outside the street lamps.

In Grafton Street he sees Blazes Boylan with a red flower in his mouth, listening to the ramblings of a drunken man.

stairs and turn as the clatter of hooves is heard. John Wyse Nolan returns to the doorway and watches dispassionately as the viceregal cavalcade passes through Parliament Street.

In the D.B.C. restaurant Buck Mulligan whispers to Haines that Parnell's brother is seated in a corner playing chess. Mulligan orders from the waitress and mentions that Haines missed the discourse on *Hamlet* by Stephen Dedalus. Haines expresses the view that Stephen may have a problem and wonders what it could be. Mulligan opines that the Jesuits drove Stephen mad with visions of hell and as a result he will never achieve the creativity required of a poet. Haines is mystified that Stephen should have a sense of eternal damnation, as there is no trace of hell in ancient Irish myth. Haines asks if Stephen has written anything for Mulligan's movement. Buck Mulligan sneers that Stephen will produce something in ten years. Haines, thoughtfully, replies that he would not be surprised if Stephen did eventually manage to write something.

Cashel Boyle O'Connor Fitzmaurice Tisdall Farrell proceeds along Merrion Square, taking extreme care to walk outside the street lamps. He halts at Wilde's corner and frowns at a poster proclaiming the arrival of Elijah at the Metropolitan Hall. He walks towards Clare Street and rudely brushes the tapping cane of a blind boy. The blind boy utters a volley of oaths after the departing eccentric.

Young Patsy Dignam walks along Wicklow Street, feeling the pork steaks he has just collected at Mangan's. In a window he looks at an advertisement for a boxing match between Myler Keogh and Sergeant-Major Bennett. He is disappointed to realize that the contest had taken place last May.

In Grafton Street he sees Blazes Boylan with a red flower in his mouth, listening to the ramblings of a drunken man. As he walks in Nassau Street, he meets other schoolboys and wonders if they have noticed that he is in mourning. His uncle Barney had promised to get the details of the funeral into the evening's newspapers, where everyone will see his name and his father's name. He remembers the closing of the coffin with his father inside and his mother crying in the parlour. He will never see his father alive again but he hopes that he is now safe in Purgatory because he was at confession on Saturday night.

After lunch William Humble, Earl of Dudley, Lady Dudley and entourage depart the Viceregal Lodge in

[148]

After lunch William Humble, Earl of Dudley, Lady Dudley and entourage depart the Viceregal Lodge in cavalcade.

FLY'S, LIMITED,   HOUSE PARTY AT THE VICE-REGAL LODGE, APRIL, 1904.   DUBLIN.

THEIR MAJESTIES' DEPARTURE FROM KINGSBRIDGE FOR KILKENNY, APRIL, 1904.

[149]

The viceregal cavalcade passes Kingsbridge Railway Station and proceeds along the quays.

cavalcade. At the lower gate of the Phoenix Park they are saluted by an obsequious policeman. The viceregal cavalcade passes Kingsbridge Railway Station and proceeds along the quays. The viceroy is well received as he makes his way through the city of Dublin.

As they pass Bloody Bridge Thomas Kernan waves, in vain, from across the river. At the Four Courts Richie Goulding is taken by surprise at the sight of the viceroy. Miss Kennedy and Miss Douce watch over the cross-blind of the Ormond Hotel. On Ormond Quay Simon Dedalus salutes by bringing his hat low and the viceroy returns the greeting. The Reverend Hugh C. Love salutes but is unobserved.

Lenehan and M'Coy watch from Grattan Bridge as the carriages pass by. Gerty MacDowell's view is spoiled by a tram and van stopped in front of her. John Wyse Nolan smiles coldly from the doorway of Kavanagh's wine rooms. Tom Rochford and Nosey Flynn watch the approaching cavalcade from Dame Gate. Tom Rochford, noticing Lady Dudley staring at him, takes his hands from his pockets and doffs his cap to her.

Printed and Published by Hely's, Limited, Dame Street, Dublin.

Photo by]   [*Lafayette*

HER EXCELLENCY COUNTESS DUDLEY.

Do you see the resemblance

Tom Rochford, noticing Lady Dudley staring at him, takes his hands from his pockets and doffs his cap to her.

From the windows of the D.B.C. restaurant Buck Mulligan and Haines look down at the cavalcade, while John Howard Parnell continues to study the chessboard. Dilly Dedalus, reading her French grammar in Fownes' Street, looks up to see the passing parade. John Henry Menton stares with his oyster eyes from the doorway of the Commercial Buildings. Under King William's statue Mrs Breen pulls her husband back from the hooves of the horses. Denis J. Maginni, the dancing professor, walks unobserved in Grafton Street. Blazes Boylan, hands in pockets, strides cheerfully along the provost's wall and forgets to give a salute.

Their Majesties at Ballsbridge, about to receive Address from Citizens' Committee.

[151]

From a hoarding the grinning fat lips of Eugene Stratton bid the cavalcade welcome to Ballsbridge.

His Excellency draws Lady Dudley's attention to the music coming from College Park, behind the wall of Trinity College. The cavalcade passes Cashel Boyle O'Connor Fitzmaurice Tisdall Farrell as he strides past Finn's Hotel. Hornblower salutes from the Lincoln Place entrance to Trinity College. In Merrion Square Patsy Dignam salutes, raising his new black cap.

The viceroy is on a journey to Ballsbridge where he will open the Mirus Bazaar, in aid of money for Mercer's Hospital. The cavalcade passes a blind boy and a man in a macintosh eating dry bread. From a hoarding the grinning fat lips of Eugene Stratton bid the cavalcade welcome to Ballsbridge. At Haddington Road two female cockle-pickers watch with amazement. On Northumberland Road the viceroy acknowledges infrequent salutes and a salute from Almidano Artifoni's trousers as he vanishes behind a closing door.

—14—

Sirens

Miss Douce and Miss Kennedy observe the viceregal cavalcade from a window of the public bar in the Ormond Hotel. Miss Kennedy likes Lady Dudley's clothes, while Miss Douce thinks that the gentleman with the tall hat in the second carriage admires and fancies her. They return to the bar for tea, served by the boots boy. They discuss Miss Douce's sunburn and laugh and giggle over an incident with a dirty old man at the Antient Concert Rooms.

Simon Dedalus strolls into the bar. He welcomes Miss Douce back from her holiday in Rostrevor and flirtatiously mocks her naughtiness in tempting men by sunbathing on the strand. Simon Dedalus continues with engaging banter and orders a whiskey and water.

Lenehan comes in, looks around and asks if Blazes Boylan was looking for him. He greets Simon Dedalus with news that he had been drinking with Stephen that day in both of Mooney's public houses. He adds that Stephen had received his wages and enthralled the company with his witty conversation.

Mr Bloom is in Daly's, where he selects writing stationery. In the distance Mr Bloom sees Blazes Boylan riding on a jaunting car over Essex Bridge towards Ormond Quay. He is struck by the amazing coincidence of seeing Boylan for a third time that day. He decides to risk following Boylan and hurriedly pays the shop assistant two pence for his stationery.

The blonde-haired Miss Kennedy reads a book silently. The sound of a

Grattan Bridge, Dublin

[152]

In the distance Mr Bloom sees Blazes Boylan riding on a jaunting car over Essex Bridge towards Ormond Quay.

tuning fork, left behind by the blind tuner, is heard from the saloon. Simon Dedalus plays the piano and begins to sing a love song. Miss Douce rebuffs an attempt by Lenehan to engage her in conversation. Blazes Boylan strides across the bar floor and is greeted by Lenehan. He orders a glass of ale for Lenehan and a sloe gin for himself. Blazes Boylan enquires if news of the big race has come in on the wire and they all answer that it is due in at four o'clock.

Mr Bloom arrives at the Ormond Hotel where he sees Boylan's car parked outside. Just then Richie Goulding appears carrying a legal bag. Mr Bloom decides to join Goulding for a meal in the Ormond, where he can observe Boylan and not be seen.

The bronze-haired Miss Douce exposes her obvious charms as she stretches for a bottle. Lenehan and Boylan watch her admiringly as she pours the drinks. The two men drink to the success of Sceptre in the Gold Cup. Blazes Boylan winks and tells Lenehan that he has a good bet on the horse for himself and a lady friend.

Pat, the waiter, shows Mr Bloom and Richie Goulding

WEATHER REPORTS. ILLUSTRATED. "Glass falling. Storms expected!"

P.V.B.

to a table near the door of the bar. The clock strikes four and Mr Bloom wonders if Boylan has forgotten his assignation with Molly.

Lenehan presses Miss Douce to perform her party piece of sounding the clock. Miss Douce checks that Miss Kennedy is gone and lifts her skirt above the knee. She bends, taunting her admirers, holding them in lustful suspense. Suddenly she lets her garter smack against her warm thigh, to shouts of encouragement from Lenehan. Blazes Boylan eyes Miss Douce with admiration then throws back his drink and leaves, followed by Lenehan.

Father Bob Cowley and Ben Dollard enter the bar and greet Simon Dedalus. Pat takes an order of whiskey for Richie Goulding and a cider for Mr Bloom. Ben Dollard calls on Simon Dedalus for a song. Mr Bloom hears the jingle of a jaunting car and realizes Boylan is on his way to Molly. Miss Douce turns away from the window, unable to understand why Boylan has left so suddenly.

In the saloon bar Ben Dollard, Father Cowley and Simon Dedalus laugh and reminisce about the night

[153]

Pat serves slices of liver to Mr Bloom and steak and kidney pie to Richie Goulding.

Blazes Boylan moves through
O'Connell Street, past the
statues of Sir John Gray,
Horatio Nelson and Father
Theobald Matthew.

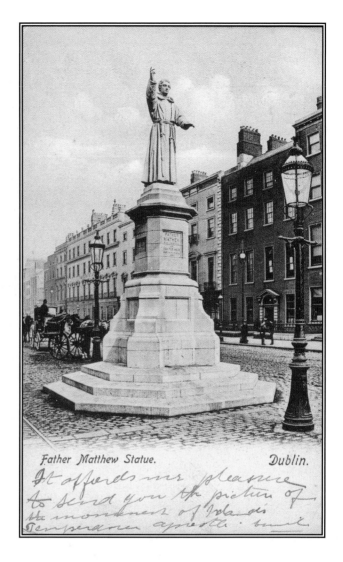

Father Matthew Statue.   *Dublin.*

*It affords me pleasure
to send you the picture of
the monument of Ireland's
Temperance apostle, &c.*

Dollard performed in concert with a pair of very tight
trousers supplied by the Blooms. They recall that Professor
Goodwin, Dollard's accompanist on the night, was inebriated, with hilarious consequences.

Pat serves slices of liver to Mr Bloom and steak and
kidney pie to Richie Goulding. They eat in silence. Blazes
Boylan's jaunting car hackney jingles along Bachelor's
Walk. Miss Kennedy serves two gentlemen with tankards
of stout and enticingly engages them in flirtatious conversation. Miss Douce warmly greets the arrival of George

DUBLIN.

Designed and Printed in Ireland   (Copyright) B. & N., Ltd., Dublin

Lidwell, a well-dressed solicitor. Father Cowley asks Simon Dedalus to sing 'M'appari' and offers to accompany him on the piano. Boylan's hackney jingles past Graham Lemon's and Elvery's Elephant House.

Richie Goulding mentions a memorable performance by Joe Maas in the old Theatre Royal, when Maas sang 'All is Lost Now'. Mr Bloom agrees with Goulding that it is a lovely air and reflects on its story of an innocent girl walking in her sleep to the villain's bedroom. Mr Bloom realizes that, for himself, it is also too late because Boylan is on his way.

Simon Dedalus begins to sing. Mr Bloom is struck by the coincidence that Simon Dedalus is singing Lionel's song from *Martha*, just as he is about to compose a letter to Martha Clifford. He remembers the first night he saw Molly at Mat Dillon's party in Terenure. They played musical chairs and laughed and danced together. As she sang for the company at Dillon's he turned the music pages, smelt her perfume and saw her beautiful bosom. Mr Bloom wonders why such a beauty with lovely Spanish

[155]

The hackney jaunting car jingles and jangles into Dorset Street.

eyes could have chosen him and concludes it must have been fate.

Simon Dedalus finishes singing to loud applause. Blazes Boylan moves through O'Connell Street, past the statues of Sir John Gray, Horatio Nelson and Father Theobald Matthew. Tom Kernan enters and joins the company in the bar. Richie Goulding is full of praise for the voice of Simon Dedalus. Mr Bloom inwardly reflects on how badly Simon Dedalus treats his brother-in-law, Goulding, all because of a family rift. Yet Goulding, surprisingly, praises and admires his singing. The hackney jaunting car jingles and jangles into Dorset Street. Miss Douce flirts with the suave George Lidwell while Miss Kennedy charms the two gentlemen drinking stout.

Mr Bloom decides to write to Martha Clifford. He uses a newspaper to conceal from Goulding what he is writing. Mr Bloom is unsure of what to say in the letter and decides to send her a postal order for a half-crown. He wonders why he engages in this foolishness and cautions himself against Molly finding out. Richie Goulding asks if Bloom is answering an advertisement and he answers affirmatively. Mr Bloom disguises some letters of his handwriting and signs off with a remark that he is very sad today. He reminds himself to buy a postal order and stamp and gets ready to leave for an appointment at Barney Kiernan's public house.

Miss Douce and George Lidwell listen in turn to a seashell, exchange flirtatious conversation about her holiday and swop intimate smiles. Father Cowley's fingers twinkle a tune on the piano. In Eccles Street Boylan alights from the car and knocks once on the door.

Ben Dollard is prevailed upon to sing 'The Croppy Boy'. Mr Bloom takes leave of Richie Goulding. He pays Pat for the meal and gives him a tip of two pence. Mr Bloom inwardly reflects on Ben Dollard's fall in life, with his once-prosperous business bankrupted with huge debts. Now the unfortunate Dollard is ruined by drink and lives in a cubicle in the Iveagh Home for destitute men. Mr Bloom lingers a while to listen to the words of the moving ballad. The line from the ballad that the hero is the last of his name and race reminds Mr Bloom that, because of Rudy's death, he too is in the same position.

Everyone listens intently as the ballad moves towards a brutal climax. Ben Dollard sings of the boy asking the priest for a final blessing. Then the priest reveals himself as a yeoman captain who curses the boy and grants him one final hour of life. Ben Dollard's mournful voice describes the execution of the boy at Geneva Barracks and his subsequent burial at Passage.

In the hallway of the Ormond Hotel Mr Bloom hears the cheers for Ben Dollard. He decides to post the letter to Martha Clifford and makes his way along the quay. An old whore in a tatty sailor's hat comes walking towards Mr Bloom. He knows her from a tawdry encounter in a lane, but worse still the woman knows Molly. Mr Bloom panics and stares in the window of Lionel Mark's antique shop as the woman passes by.

In the Ormond Hotel George Lidwell, Simon Dedalus, Bob Cowley, Tom Kernan and Ben Dollard clink their glasses before the temptresses, Lydia Douce and Mina Kennedy.

Mr Bloom looks at a picture of Robert Emmet, the gallant hero, in Lionel Mark's window. Gasses from the cider and burgundy have built up in his system. As he reads the final words of Emmet's speech from the dock he avails of the noise of a passing tram to break wind, loudly.

15

Cyclops

THE NARRATOR MEETS JOE HYNES in Stoneybatter and describes his near-blinding by the brush of a chimney-sweep. Joe Hynes invites the Narrator for a drink at Barney Kiernan's. They enter Barney Kiernan's to find the Citizen sitting in a corner with a mongrel dog called Garryowen. Joe Hynes orders three pints of Guinness, which are served by Terry, the barman.

The Citizen denounces the *Irish Independent* as a useless rag. He is angry that a paper founded by Parnell for working people should now include so many English names and addresses in the personal columns.

Alf Bergan, doubled with laughter, comes in the door and hides in the snug. He is amused by the postcard sent to Denis Breen. Now Breen is walking the streets of Dublin threatening to take a libel action and has called to see John Henry Menton and Long John Fanning. Joe Hynes enquires when Fanning is going to hang the prisoner in Mountjoy. The uproar over the hoax postcard awakens Bob Doran from a drunken stupor.

The Citizen wishes to know what Bloom, the damned Freemason, is doing walking up and down outside the door. Alf Bergan pays for his drink and produces a bundle of letters purporting to come from a hangman. Joe Hynes takes the letters. Bob Doran demands to know who they are laughing at. Alf Bergan is flabbergasted to learn that Dignam is dead. Once more an irritated Citizen draws attention to Bloom, while Alf Bergan remains still shocked at the news of Dignam's death. Bob Doran drunkenly refers to the

Guinness Brewery.   Locomotive Malt Waggon.

The Wrench Series, No. 8831

tragic death of Willy Dignam and weeps, as he holds Christ responsible for the death of the finest and noblest man that he has ever known.

Bloom comes in to enquire if Martin Cunningham is on the premises. Joe Hynes reads a letter of application for the job of hangman, written by a barber called Rumbold from Liverpool. The talk turns to capital punishment and the physical effects of hanging. Bloom declines the offer of a drink from Joe Hynes but accepts a cigar instead.

The Citizen and Joe Hynes converse about the Invincibles and other Irish revolutionaries. Bob Doran plays with Garryowen and feeds him a few biscuits from a tin provided by Terry. The Citizen and Bloom argue about Irish heroes like the Sheares brothers, Wolfe Tone and Robert Emmet.

The Narrator is mindfully scornful of Bloom, swanking with a big cigar in his mouth. He recalls Pisser Burke's story about Bloom when they were both resident at the City Arms Hotel. Pisser had recounted that Bloom was

[156]

Joe Hynes orders three pints of Guinness, which are served by Terry, the barman.

in the habit of playing up to an elderly resident in the hope of getting money in her will. On one occasion Bloom took the old lady's nephew on a drinking spree and brought him back drunk. According to Bloom this was to teach the young man the evils of drink, but nonetheless Bloom was verbally abused for his trouble by an enraged trio of women: the old lady, his wife and the owner, Mrs O'Dowd.

The Citizen glares angrily at Bloom and lifts his glass to drink to the memory of Ireland's dead heroes and Sinn Féin. Joe Hynes orders another round of drinks. Bloom declines his offer, explaining that he has only dropped in to meet Martin Cunningham about Dignam's insurance. Bloom adds that he has been invited by Cunningham to go to the Dignam home and begins to elaborate on the finer points of law relating to assignments on insurance policies. The Narrator is inwardly critical of Bloom's discourse on the nuances of law and remembers that Bloom only barely avoided arrest for selling questionable Hungarian lottery tickets because of friends in high places.

Bob Doran staggers over to ask Bloom to deliver his deepest sympathy to Mrs Dignam. He takes Bloom by the hand and drunkenly proclaims that there was never a finer person than poor Willy. Bob Doran weeps, shakes hands again and staggers out of the pub.

Terry delivers three more pints of Guinness and Joe Hynes hands one to the Citizen. Joe Hynes mentions the meeting of the cattle traders on the issue of foot-and-mouth disease. Bloom expresses his opinion on various remedies for disease in sheep and cattle. The Narrator thinks of Bloom as a know-all who at one time worked in a knacker's yard and was sacked by Joe Cuffe for giving cheek to a customer. Joe Hynes mentions the fact that Field and Nannetti are travelling by mail boat that night to raise the issue of foot-and-mouth disease in the House of Commons. He adds that Nannetti is under instructions from the Gaelic League to ask a question about the banning of Irish games in the Phoenix Park.

Bloom is disappointed to learn of Nannetti's imminent departure as he wanted to see him to discuss the Keyes advertisement.

Joe Hynes praises the Citizen for his work in the Gaelic sports revival and his athletic prowess as champion of Ireland in throwing the sixteen-pound shot. Alf Bergan recounts how Blazes Boylan made money, gambling on a boxing match, by spreading a rumour that one of the fighters was on the drink. He adds that Boylan is now organizing a concert in Belfast and Joe Hynes chips in that Mrs Bloom is one of the stars. Bloom confirms her appearance and declares that Boylan is an excellent organizer. The Narrator cynically reflects that Boylan, the son of a horse-dealing fraudster, is just the man to organize Molly Bloom.

J.J. O'Molloy and Ned Lambert come in and the conversation returns to Denis Breen. Ned Lambert announces that Breen has been advised by Corny Kelleher to have the handwriting on the postcard checked by a private detective. Joe Hynes accuses Alf Bergan of perpetrating the hoax while Bergan coyly rebukes Hynes for casting aspersions on his character.

J.J. O'Molloy expresses an opinion that an action might lie, if the message on the postcard implied that Breen was insane. Alf Bergan argues that insanity is obvious and J.J. O'Molloy opines that the truth of a libel is not a defence for publishing it. J.J. O'Molloy cites a test case in which a postcard was held to be adequate evidence of malice. He adds that Breen may have a case for libel.

Denis Breen and his wife pass the door, deep in conversation with Corny Kelleher. Joe Hynes asks about the Canada swindle case, heard earlier that day before the recorder, Sir Frederick Falkiner. J.J. O'Molloy replies that the case was remanded and explains that the fraud involved an offer in the newspapers of a passage to Canada for one pound. As a result a large number of people applied and were swindled when the offer failed to

Evicted tenant & his family

[157]

The Narrator inwardly reflects that the Citizen would be afraid to deliver a similar speech in Shanagolden, because the locals were still out to murder him for the foul deed of taking the land of an evicted tenant.

materialize. Alf Bergan and Ned Lambert agree that Falkiner is a decent judge who would swallow any hard-luck story. Alf Bergan remarks that Reuben J. Dodd was lucky not to be jailed by Falkiner for his suit against Gumley.

Bloom takes Joe Hynes aside to tell him not to worry about the debt of three shillings until the end of the month. He requests Hynes to have a good word with Myles Crawford about the Keyes advertisement and Hynes agrees to take care of the problem.

John Wyse Nolan and Lenehan arrive. Lenehan announces that Throwaway has won the Gold Cup at 20–1 and that Boylan lost a good bet on Sceptre for himself and a woman friend. John Wyse Nolan has news of a meeting in the City Hall about the Irish language, which spurs the Citizen to a savage tirade against the English nation.

An argument develops about law and history. The Citizen blames England for the depopulation of Ireland and the general ruin of trade and industry. John Wyse

Nolan is of the opinion that Ireland will soon be worse than Portugal if nothing is done to restore the forests of the country. The Citizen stresses the importance of Ireland's political and trade relationship with Europe prior to the English conquest. He foresees the glorious day when the first Irish battleship is seen on the high seas. The Narrator inwardly reflects that the Citizen would be afraid to deliver a similar speech in Shanagolden, because the locals were still out to murder him for the foul deed of taking the land of an evicted tenant.

John Wyse Nolan orders a drink for himself and Lenehan. The Citizen continues with his diatribe against the English. He denounces their terrible treatment of the Irish during the Famine, when millions fled the country in coffin-ships. The Citizen concludes his argument with the prophecy that the sons of these emigrants will return from America to avenge the wrongs perpetrated by the English against their country. John Wyse Nolan points out that the Irish fought for the Stuarts, French and Spanish, with nothing to show for their valiant bravery.

Joe Hynes calls on more drink for the Citizen and the Narrator. Bloom speaks excitedly to Nolan about persecution throughout history. He expounds on nations perpetrating hatred among nations. John Wyse Nolan asks him to explain the meaning of the word 'Nation'. Bloom answers that a nation is a group of people living together in the same place. The Citizen asks for Bloom's nationality, to which Bloom replies that he is Irish, born and bred. Contemptuously, the Citizen spits a ball of phlegm into the corner.

Bloom, cigar in hand, announces that he belongs to a race that is despised and persecuted. Even at the present time Jews are being robbed of what rightfully belongs to them. John Wyse Nolan is of the opinion that the Jews should oppose injustice with force and fight like men. Bloom argues against the use of force and expresses the belief that life is love, as opposed to insult and hatred.

St. Lawrence Gate.   Drogheda. Co. Louth.

[158]

The Citizen cites the infamy of the religious hypocrite Cromwell, who callously slaughtered the women and children of Drogheda.

Bloom tells Nolan of his appointment with Martin Cunningham and leaves.

The Citizen denounces Bloom as a preacher of cant while capable of robbing his neighbour at the same time. The Citizen cites the infamy of the religious hypocrite Cromwell, who callously slaughtered the women and children of Drogheda.

Lenehan informs the company that Bloom is gone out to collect his winnings on Throwaway, because Bantam Lyons had told him of Bloom's tip for the horse. Lenehan explains that Bloom was the only man in Dublin to back the horse because he had persuaded Lyons to back Sceptre. John Wyse Nolan praises Bloom for helping Sinn Féin and Arthur Griffith with the suggestion that they utilize their newspaper to expose the frauds and misdeeds of the British.

Martin Cunningham, Jack Power and the Orangeman Crofton come in, enquiring for Bloom. The general conversation is critical of Bloom, to the extent that Martin Cunningham calls on the company to be charitable. Ned

C.W.Faulkner & C.º London.E.C.

IRISH TERRIER.

"*Let you forget*"!!

[159]

The last they see is the jaunting car tearing round the corner with Garryowen in hot pursuit, hell-bent on ripping Bloom to pieces.

Lambert invites the three newcomers to have a drink and Cunningham accepts, adding they have time for one only.

Bloom returns and explains to Cunningham that he had gone around to the courthouse in search of him. The Narrator is of the silent opinion that the Jew is telling lies and was too mean to buy a drink with his winnings of five pounds. The Citizen makes menacing remarks about Bloom. Martin Cunningham, sensing danger, orders Power, Crofton and Bloom out of the pub and onto the jaunting car. He instructs the jarvey to take off.

The Citizen, cursing and spitting, rises to his feet and makes for the door with Joe Hynes and Alf Bergan trying in vain to pacify him. He shouts for three cheers for Israel after the departing Bloom. Bloom shouts back that Mendelssohn, Marx, Mercadante, Spinoza and Christ, the Citizen's God, were Jews. The Citizen is outraged and returns to grab the biscuit tin. He charges out the door, with Alf Bergan clutching his elbow and Ned Lambert and J.J. O'Molloy weak with laughter. The jarvey manages to drive away as the Citizen unleashes the biscuit tin and a volley of oaths after the departing Bloom. The last they see is the jaunting car tearing round the corner with Garryowen in hot pursuit, hell-bent on ripping Bloom to pieces.

~16~

Nausicaa

THE SUN IS SETTING on Sandymount Strand where three girls, Cissy Caffrey, Edy Boardman and Gerty MacDowell, are sitting on the rocks in their favourite place. On this occasion they are accompanied by Cissy's four-year-old twin brothers, Tommy and Jacky, together with Edy's eleven-month-old baby brother. From the nearby Star of the Sea Church the sound of prayer in adoration to Mary is heard. The girls watch carefully as the twins get up to all kinds of innocent mischief.

Gerty MacDowell, a beautiful example of Irish maidenhood, sits quietly on a rock near her friends. She has a frail, graceful figure, pale skin and deep blue eyes. Her clothes are the very latest style and her underwear is blue, because blue is her favourite colour. Gerty is slightly annoyed with her friend, Edy Boardman, for suggesting that the ardour of her boyfriend, Reggy Wylie, has cooled. Gerty knows that it was a simple matter of a lover's quarrel, not helped by the fact that Reggy is now confined at home by his father to study for a prize in the Intermediate Examination. She dreams of marriage to Reggy and remembers his attempted kiss at Stoer's party.

Gerty is shocked to hear Cissy Caffrey say that she might give Tommy a smack on the bottom for boldness, because a gentleman nearby may have heard a rude word.

The voices of prayer and the sound of the organ come wafting over the evening air. Reverend John Hughes SJ is conducting the men's temperance

Star of the Sea Church,   Sandymount.

HELY'S, LIMITED, DUBLIN.

[160]

From the nearby Star of the
Sea Church the sound of
prayer in adoration to Mary
is heard.

retreat with the Holy Rosary, a sermon and Benediction. As Gerty listens to the Litany of Our Lady, she reflects on her unhappy home life caused by her father's intemperate drinking. She loves her father and fondly remembers him singing with Mr Dignam at her mother's birthday party. Now poor Mr Dignam is dead from a stroke and her mother warned her father that this was a lesson for him about the evils of alcohol consumption.

One of the twins kicks his ball in the direction of the gentleman in black. The gentleman throws the ball back to Cissy but it rolls down the slope and comes to rest under Gerty's skirt. Gerty kicks and misses, to the amusement of Edy and Cissy. She blushes, lifts her skirt and gives the ball a good kick back to the twins.

Gerty takes a closer look at the sad face of the gentleman close by. She looks out to sea, realizing that he was looking at her with a meaning that etched into the depths of her soul. She guesses by his dark eyes and pale, intelligent face that he is a foreigner, the exact image of Martin Harvey, the famous actor. Gerty can see that he is in deep mourning by his sorrowful face. She is pleased

MARTIN HARVEY

[161]

She guesses by his dark eyes
and pale, intelligent face that
he is a foreigner, the exact
image of Martin Harvey, the
famous actor.

that something reminded her to wear transparent stockings because this is a situation that she had always
dreamed about. Her heart goes out to him as the husband
she has dreamed of, not caring if he is a sinner or a rogue.

The twins quarrel and play. The Litany draws to a close
and the choir begins to sing the Tantum Ergo. Gerty
removes her hat, cognizant of his admiring glances. She
puts her hat back on, in such a way that she can catch the
look in his eyes. Gerty swings her foot faster realizing
that she has roused his basic instincts. She blushes the
colour of a red rose.

Edy Boardman notices that Gerty is distracted and offers
her a penny for her thoughts. Gerty smiles and remarks

LEAP YEAR.
Buttonholed.

[162]

Gerty winces but responds speedily that she can have anybody she likes because it is leap year.

that she was wondering whether it was late. Cissy Caffrey walks over to the gentleman and boldly asks him the correct time. He apologizes as his watch has stopped but surmises that it must be after eight o'clock, as the sun has set.

Gerty observes the gentleman winding his watch, putting it away, then replacing his hands in his pockets. She feels the irritation of her period coming on as his dark eyes are fixated upon her with a look of wilful admiration for her alone.

Edy and Cissy are talking about the time and want Gerty to leave. Edy asks if Gerty is heartbroken about being ditched by her boyfriend. Gerty winces but responds speedily that she can have anybody she likes because it is leap year. Edy and Cissy make preparations to leave. As a steeple bell rings out from the church, Canon O'Hanlon gives the Benediction from the altar.

Gerty sits in the twilight and sadly reflects that the years are quickly evaporating. She is not afraid of competition from other girls, with one exception – the consequence of an accident on her way down Dalkey Hill, which she has always attempted to conceal.

The Obelisk, Victoria Hill, near Dalkey

– the consequence of an accident on her way down Dalkey Hill, which she has always attempted to conceal.

Canon O'Hanlon locks the door of the tabernacle and the temperance retreat is over. Just then, the fireworks from the Mirus Bazaar light up the sky. Edy, Cissy and the children rush down the strand calling to Gerty to follow. She remains and exchanges glances with the man whose face by now is full of silent passion. They are alone. His hands are moving and his face is distorted. She leans back, one knee in her hands and reveals her lovely legs and blue underwear.

The children shout as the fireworks explode in the heavens. They all fall silent as a huge firework makes its way skyward over the trees and explodes in a blast of

He sees the intermittent
flashes from the Bailey
Lighthouse afar off.

Bailey Lighthouse,   Howth Head.

light and stars. The onlookers gasp with excitement and
fall silent as the sparking lights gradually fade away.

Gerty glances shyly at the gentleman. Mr Bloom
leans against a rock, castigating himself for his misconduct before the eyes of an innocent girl. He senses that
there is forgiveness in her eyes, although he has sinned
grievously. It would remain a secret between them both.

Cissy Caffrey calls for Gerty and she waves her handkerchief in reply. Gerty rises to leave, wondering if she
will ever meet the gentleman again. She decides they
will meet and until then she will dream about the
encounter. They exchange a last lingering look at each

other. She rises and gives him a kind of forgiving smile. She walks very slowly along the strand because Gerty MacDowell is lame.

As Gerty limps away Mr Bloom reflects that her defect is much worse in a woman. However, he is glad he was unaware of her affliction while looking at her. He remembers the way she took off her hat to display her hair, which brings to mind the time he sold the combings of Molly's hair for ten shillings. The question of whether Boylan gives money for favours comes to mind and he decides that Molly would be worth at least a pound. Mr Bloom is struck by the coincidence of his watch stopping at half past four, the time he surmises Molly and Boylan made love. Mr Bloom adjusts his damp shirt and concludes that the aftermath of his experience is unpleasant.

In the distance he sees Gerty and her companions moving about in excitement at the sight of another exploding rocket. Mr Bloom is confident that Gerty will throw a last look at him, which she does, before disappearing behind the rocks. He is thankful for the experience and feels there was a type of mental telepathy between them. He is saddened by the thought that a young girl's beauty only lasts for a few years, to fade inevitably with childbirth and the never-ending drudgery of married life. He is reminded to pay a visit to Mrs Purefoy at the lying-in hospital.

He sees the intermittent flashes from the Bailey Lighthouse afar off. Thoughts of Howth and the rhododendrons flicker through his mind. He fondly recalls the charades at Luke Doyle's and the six Dillon girls playing with Molly at Mat Dillon's party in 1887.

Night is slowly falling as the nine o'clock postman completes his final round. Mr Bloom feels old and tired as the events of the day flow through his mind. He wonders if either himself or Gerty will return to the same spot but concludes it is unlikely that they will ever meet again. Mr Bloom drifts gently into a half-dreaming sleep.

~17~

Oxen of the Sun

MEN OF WISDOM know that they have an obligation to reproduce their own species. The Celts held the art of medicine in great esteem and their doctors laid down various remedies to cure the sick. They set up special homes for the care of expectant mothers, so that a woman at her most vulnerable time would be removed from danger. This facility was provided for rich and poor alike and is a praiseworthy undertaking for any nation.

Mr Bloom, a wandering Jew, stands outside the house of Horne where seventy beds are maintained for expectant mothers. Mr Bloom is brought to Holles Street by compassion for all mankind. Nurse Callan admits the wanderer and blesses herself, as lightning flashes outside. Mr Bloom knows Nurse Callan as his former landlady; he was a tenant in her house some nine years ago. He enquires after Mrs Purefoy and Nurse Callan informs him that she is in the throes of the most difficult childbirth that she has ever witnessed. However, she adds that Mrs Purefoy's three days of suffering will soon be over.

A junior doctor called Dixon comes through the door. He knows Mr Bloom, having treated him for a bee sting at the Mater Hospital. Dixon invites Mr Bloom to a room where a group of revellers are engaged in merry-making. Dixon pours out a drink for Mr Bloom, which he pretends to drink but later empties into a neighbour's glass. Nurse Callan comes to the door and pleads for silence because of the impending childbirth.

The participants in the revelry are Dixon, Lynch, Madden, Lenehan,

THE VATICAN GARDENS: THE POPE AND CARDINALS

Crotthers, Stephen and Punch Costello. Of these, the most inebriated is Stephen, who clamours for more drink.

A debate arises about the decision to be taken in the event of a threat to the life of both mother and child. They all agree that in such circumstances the life of the mother should be saved. Madden recounts a case where a mother was allowed to die because of her husband's religious beliefs. Stephen makes a cynical observation that the baby and mother now glorify God with one in Limbo and the other in Purgatory. He heaps criticism on the Catholic Church for its teachings on contraception and birth. Mr Bloom is asked for his opinion and shrewdly comments that the Catholic Church gains financially from the dual event of the birth of a child and the death of a mother. However, inwardly Mr Bloom is deeply concerned about Mrs Purefoy and is reminded of Rudy's death eleven days after his birth. He is sorry for Stephen who appears to be ruining his life in the company of wastrels and women of ill-repute.

Stephen fills all the glasses and proposes a toast to the

[165]

Stephen fills all the glasses and proposes a toast to the Pope.

Pope. He shows the company his coins and notes from Deasy and claims the money is in payment for a song that he has written. Stephen delivers a sermon on the thorny question of whether the Virgin Mary conceived knowingly or unknowingly. He argues that she is either of divine substance if she knew God or of human substance if she did not. Stephen declares that the concept of pregnancy without pleasure and birth without pain is unacceptable to him.

Punch Costello bangs the table and strikes up a bawdy ballad about a pretty wench impregnated by a jolly adventurer. Nurse Quigley comes to the door and angrily calls for silence. Dixon, in jest, asks why Stephen has not entered the priesthood. Lenehan mentions the stories circulating about Stephen's attempts to soil the virtue of innocent young girls. The laughter increases as the conversation turns to the rites of wedlock and fornication. Stephen launches himself into a blasphemous sermon about sex, betrayal and the meaning of birth and life.

A loud crack of thunder explodes, causing Lynch to tell Stephen that he has offended God. Stephen is frightened and drinks another slug for courage as the thunder rumbles overhead. Mr Bloom moves to calm Stephen by explaining that thunder is merely a natural phenomenon. Stephen is not consoled because in his heart he knows that his saintly youth has been lost to the carnal attractions of women. The company denounces Heaven in preference for carnal pleasures, which may be freely indulged while protected from plague and childbirth by a contraceptive.

This wretched group stands deceived because the thunder was, in fact, the voice of an angry God who will soon punish them for their abuses and sins.

It is raining heavily in Duke's Lawn, Merrion Green and Holles Street. In Merrion Square Buck Mulligan, coming from George Moore's, encounters Alec Bannon, newly arrived from Mullingar. Buck Mulligan invites Bannon to join him for a drinking session at the maternity hospital.

LIVERPOOL. LANDING STAGE.

Lenehan refers to a letter in the evening paper about the killing of cattle because of foot-and-mouth disease. Mr Bloom is worried about the slaughter of animals that he had seen that morning being driven to the Liverpool boats. He is unable to credit that the situation is so critical, having considerable experience in the cattle trade when he worked for Joe Cuffe. Stephen allays Mr Bloom's fears with news that a doctor is coming from Moscow with a cure for the disease.

Buck Mulligan appears in the doorway, accompanied by Alec Bannon. He distributes cards with an inscription describing himself as a fertilizer and brooder based on Lambay Island. He proposes to purchase Lambay Island from Lord Talbot of Malahide to set up a fertilizing farm. His services would come free to all classes, from the lowly kitchen maid to a lady of high degree.

Alec Bannon talks to his neighbour about his good luck in meeting a young girl down in Mullingar. He expresses sorrow at not having a contraceptive while with her but knows where he can obtain a French version for

[166]

Mr Bloom is worried about the slaughter of animals that he had seen that morning being driven to the Liverpool boats.

their next meeting. The conversation turns to the dangers and advantages of using or not using a contraceptive. This noble and enriching topic is cut short by a ringing bell.

Nurse Callan enters the room and tells Dixon that the woman has given birth to a boy. Dixon rebukes the company for their riotous behaviour and leaves to take care of Mrs Purefoy. Mr Bloom marvels, in his own mind, at how these students can behave like drunken louts yet suddenly change by the acquisition of a degree into respectable doctors.

This man, Bloom, is an alien who has no right to criticize. He is an ungrateful traitor who forgets the civil rights and other benefits conceded to him. He has sullied the bedroom of a respectable woman and cast doubt on her virtue. This old lecher has made a carnal attack on his housemaid that fortuitously was repulsed by a cleaning brush. He has been castigated by Mr Cuffe for giving cheek to a farmer. It is wrong for Bloom to preach while still practising in middle age the nasty habit of young boys. This hypocrite should keep his advice for his own problems, particularly his neglected wife.

In a loud clamour of voices the students discuss the far-ranging problems of medicine. Punch Costello reminds Stephen of their days at Clongowes when Father Conmee was rector. Neither of them know anything about their old school friends. Stephen urges Costello not to worry, as he can call them back to life at any time through his writings. Vincent Lynch casts doubt on Stephen's ability as a writer but wishes him well. However, Lynch expresses the hope that one day Stephen will produce a masterpiece.

Madden and Lenehan whinge about their losses in the Gold Cup, both having backed Sceptre. Lenehan describes the running of the race, with Throwaway beating Sceptre on the run to the finishing line. Lenehan lauds Sceptre as a great filly whose equal will never be seen again. A debate of immense importance ensues, with each participant aware of the cruciality of their contribution.

Meanwhile Mrs Purefoy offers a prayer in thanksgiving.

Castle from the Lawn, Clongowes Wood College,   Co. KILDARE.

ing finished yet. I am counting the days till the 21st June. The Exams commence next week Berna

dear Mlle Bossier, Would you please post your cards so that they would reach me on Sunday when I get the post myself, as sometimes my cards get lost or mislaid

if they come when I am not in... You will be thinking I am a great bother.

The Castle.   Dublin.

[167]

Punch Costello reminds
Stephen of their days at
Clongowes when Father
Conmee was rector.

[168]

Her new baby will be named
after an important cousin who
works at Dublin Castle.

Her only desire now is to have her husband with her at the bedside to share in her happiness. Her new baby will be named after an important cousin who works at Dublin Castle. She may now rest in peaceful contentment and so may her husband, Doady. God knows that Doady has also done his duty and in due course will receive his heavenly reward.

Mr Bloom looks at Stephen and is inwardly saddened by Stephen's penchant for harsh words and the crudities of life. He recalls a beautiful May evening among the grove of lilac trees at Roundtown. The game of bowls on the well-cut lawn was watched by the Dillon sisters, Floey, Atty and Tiny, in company with a dark friend. Stephen, a little boy of five, was standing on an urn, nervously glancing at times towards his watchful mother.

In the outer room the company falls silent. As the thunderstorm breaks, Stephen shouts the name of Burke's public house. Most of them follow Stephen into the hallway and out the door. Mr Bloom lingers a while with Nurse Callan to send his good wishes to the new mother. The revellers proceed down the street shouting and speaking incomprehensibly.

In Burke's pub drinks are ordered amidst a welter of noise and confused conversation. Bantam Lyons is seen. Stephen orders absinthe for everyone except Mr Bloom, who chooses wine. Alec Bannon realizes that Mr Bloom is the father of his girlfriend. The man in the macintosh, known as Bartle the Bread, is seen drinking bovril. This man was once a prosperous citizen but is now in penury because of his love for a married woman who is dead. The subjects of Dignam's death, Jenatzy, the racing driver and the Russo-Japanese conflict are shouted in garbled confusion.

The landlord calls time and the revellers leave the pub. One of them vomits. Stephen and Lynch decide to go to the red-light district. They all disperse in noisy and drunken disarray.

∽18∽

Circe

STEPHEN AND LYNCH make their way through the filth and squalor of Mabbot Street amidst a welter of screams and oaths. They pass close to two inebriated solders, Private Carr and Private Compton. An elderly procuress offers sex from a doorway. She spits contemptuously in the wake of Stephen and Lynch and shouts a derogatory reference to penniless Trinity medical students. A drunken labourer lurches, staggers and grips the rails for support.

A breathless and panting Bloom passes under the railway bridge in Talbot Street. He enters Olhausen's, the pork butchers, and buys a warm pig's foot and a cold sheep's foot, wrapped separately. He emerges, still gasping from a stitch in his side, and attempts to cross the road. He narrowly escapes injury from passing cyclists and a sand-strewer. Jacky Caffrey, chased by brother Tommy, runs full force into Bloom, leaving him shocked and weak. Bloom checks his valuables, mindful of the ruses utilized by pickpockets.

An apparition of Rudolph Bloom materializes, dressed as an elder of Zion. He castigates his son Leopold for wasting money on drink and visiting places of ill-repute. His mother, Ellen Bloom, appears in pantomime garb and whines about a boyhood misdemeanour. Molly Bloom stands before him dressed in Turkish attire, complete with yashmak. She chastises him in Moorish and he apologizes for forgetting her lotion at Sweny's the chemist.

The elderly procuress grabs his sleeve and offers a virgin for ten shillings.

Bloom checks his valuables,
mindful of the ruses utilized
by pickpockets.

Gerty MacDowell limps towards him, exhibiting her blood-stained clothes. She slobbers and paws Bloom, accusing Bloom of being a dirty old, perverted, married man. Gerty tells him that she loves him for what he did and limps away into the night.

The spectre of Mrs Breen in a man's overcoat now threatens to expose Bloom to Molly for being in the streets of sin. Bloom assuages the situation by reminding her of the good old days at Georgina Simpson's party, when she was the pretty Josie Powell. Denis Breen, attired as a Hely's advertising man, shuffles past them in slippers, followed by a jeering Alf Bergan. Mrs Breen gives Bloom a look of encouragement and asks for a kiss. He pretends to be shocked at the idea of Molly's best friend behaving like that. Richie Goulding becomes visible, bearing his legal bag imprinted with a skull and cross-bones. Bloom is about to reveal a secret between himself and Mrs Breen when she fades away.

A whining dog follows Bloom as he marches towards the dangerous part of the red-light district. A woman urinates like a cow as she stands in an archway. A group of men, employed by Derwan's the plasterers, listen to their foreman recount the story of a man who defecated into a bucket of porter. Bloom excuses himself for being suddenly taken short and forced to use the bucket of porter.

Bloom trudges along towards the distant lights of a street. He reflects on the drunken confusion at Westland Row and wonders why he is following Stephen and Lynch. Bloom considers Stephen to be the best of those at the maternity hospital party and worries about Stephen losing his money.

Two policemen grab Bloom and demand his name and address. He tells them that he is Doctor Leopold Bloom, the dental surgeon. A business card falls from his hat revealing Bloom as Henry Flower of no fixed address and he is ordered to the police station.

A weeping Martha Clifford accuses Bloom of being a false deceiver. She threatens to tell her brother, the full back for Bective Rugby Club, about Bloom's deceit. Bloom accuses Martha Clifford of being drunk and attempts to explain his innocence to a jury. He declares himself to be a respectable, married man of impeccable character. His wife is the daughter of a general called Tweedy, famous for his heroism at Rorke's Drift. Bloom elaborates on his important connections with the press and invites telephonic verification of his alibi. Myles Crawford materializes, telephone in hand, and shouts vulgar abuse down the line.

A TELEPHONE TRAGEDY.
(in 6 Acts)

ACT. VI. (5 minutes later)
REALISATION! (Cut off!)

August 15th '04

P.V.B.

[170]

Myles Crawford materializes,
telephone in hand, and shouts
vulgar abuse down the line.

Philip Beaufoy comes to the witness box and accuses
Bloom of plagiarism. He denounces the ghastly fouling
of his article and also accuses Bloom of having a disrep-
utable private life.

The court crier calls a new witness, Mary Driscoll, a
scullery maid. Mary Driscoll steps forward carrying a
bucket and a scouring brush. She gives evidence that
Bloom made advances on her when his wife was out
doing the shopping. He had held her with subsequent
bruising in four places and, furthermore, he had med-
dled with her clothing. Bloom rebuts the evidence with
a claim of counter-assault. Mary Driscoll responds that
she did not use her scouring brush on Bloom but merely
gave out to him for his misconduct. To sustained laughter
in court, she adds that Bloom told her to keep silent
about the incident.

Bloom takes the witness box and enters a plea of not
guilty. He delivers an incomprehensible speech, which is
greeted by further laughter. Professor MacHugh rises to
cross-examine Bloom on the issue of defecating in a bucket in Beaver Street. Bloom admits the offence, claiming

Bloom takes the witness box and enters a plea of not guilty.

IN COOURT.

COUNSEL: "What's your name?"
WITNESS: "The same as me Father's."
COUNSEL: "And what is your Father's name?"
WITNESS: "The same as mine."
COUNSEL: "But what is both your names?"
WITNESS: "Sure there both alike."

agonizing bowel trouble in mitigation. There is uproar in court as Bloom mumbles inaudibly.

J.J. O'Molloy, in barrister's attire, rises to plead for Bloom. He argues that his client is a poor foreign immigrant who is only trying to make an honest living. The alleged intimacies are common in his client's native land and in any event there was no attempt at carnal knowledge. J.J. O'Molloy submits that Bloom, of Mongolian descent, is not responsible for his actions and is in fact quite insane.

Bloom, in the attire of a low-type oriental sailor, begins to lilt in pidgin English. Bloom is shouted down

[172]

The Honourable Mrs Mervyn Talboys appears dressed as a man, complete with hard hat, boots, waistcoat and hunting whip.

VESTA TILLEY.

and O'Molloy rebukes the audience for annoying his client. J.J. O'Molloy indicates that he will call evidence to show that a hidden hand is operating against Bloom. He calls on Bloom to do the decent thing and Bloom offers to pay a penny in the pound. J.J. O'Molloy assumes the deathly features of a sick John F. Taylor and asks to be excused as he has just come from a sick bed. He then acquires the attributes of Seymour Bushe and pleads that Bloom be afforded the holy benefit of the doubt. Bloom offers to supply the court with the very best of references.

Mrs Yelverton Barry, a society lady, accuses Bloom of sending her an anonymous letter in which he made improper suggestions. Mrs Bellingham alleges similar misconduct, including an exhortation in writing from Bloom that she commit adultery with him as soon as possible. The Honourable Mrs Mervyn Talboys appears dressed as a man, complete with hard hat, boots, waistcoat and hunting whip. She claims that Bloom had seen her at a polo match in the Phoenix Park and subsequently sent her indecent photographs. Moreover, he had urged her to misbehave with officers, to foul his letter indecently and to give him a vicious whipping.

A number of respectable Dublin women display indecent letters sent by Bloom. Mrs Talboys threatens to scourge Bloom and he cringes for mercy. She rebuffs his pleadings, calls him a cuckold and orders his trousers to be taken down.

A fog lifts to reveal the faces of twelve jurors: Martin Cunningham, Jack Power, Simon Dedalus, Tom Kernan, Ned Lambert, John Henry Menton, Myles Crawford, Lenehan, Paddy Leonard, Nosey Flynn, Charley M'Coy and the Narrator. The court crier denounces Bloom as a well-known criminal, cuckold and a public danger to the people of Dublin. Sir Frederick Falkiner sentences Bloom to be hanged. Long John Fanning calls for a hangman and Rumbold agrees to do the job for five guineas.

Bloom denies a charge of bomb-making, claiming Dignam's funeral as an alibi. Paddy Dignam displays himself as a putrefying, decaying corpse and delivers a speech on the reasons for his death. John O'Connell issues a burial docket and Father Coffey performs a brief burial service. Paddy Dignam calls for a prayer and slides down a coal hole followed by a fat, old rat. Tom Rochford executes a daring act and disappears down the same hole.

Bloom stands before Mrs Cohen's brothel, where he is accosted by a young prostitute called Zoe Higgins. She fondles him and bites his ear. Bloom caresses her breasts and enquires if she is a Dublin girl. Zoe replies that she is English and asks him for a cigarette. Bloom lectures her on the evils of cigarette smoking.

Bloom changes to a political agitator, dressed in working man's apparel. He delivers a lengthy speech on the history and evils of cigarette smoking. He becomes an alderman of Dublin and addresses the electors, to prolonged applause. The political dignitaries of Dublin, including the lord mayor, shake his hand and offer congratulations. The streets of Dublin are lined by a huge crowd, held back by troops of various regiments. A procession of enormous size makes its way along the route, headed by John Howard Parnell. Leaders of Church and State take precedence, trailed by serried ranks from every strata of Irish society. In royal attire and mounted on a milk white steed, Bloom appears under the arch of triumph and is rapturously received by the cheering crowd. The Bishop of Down and Connor presents Bloom to the mob as the undisputed King of Ireland. Dr William Alexander, Archbishop of Armagh, entreats Bloom to uphold law and mercy in his judgments. Bloom puts his right hand on his private parts and solemnly swears to do so. Cardinal Michael Logue, Archbishop of Armagh, pours hair oil on Bloom's head, declaring him to be anointed.

In Christ Church, Saint Patrick's, George's Church and Malahide, bells ring out in celebration. Lords of the realm step humbly forward to pay homage. Bloom raises his hand for silence. He announces the appointment of his loyal horse as Grand Vizier and repudiates his wife in favour of the beautiful princess, Selene. His former legal wife is removed by the police and the arrival of Princess Selene is greeted with cheers. John Howard Parnell hails Bloom as a fitting successor to his brother.

Bloom promises his people a golden age of prosperity and grandeur. A man in a macintosh denounces Bloom as a notorious arsonist. Bloom orders him to be shot. Money and gifts are distributed to the assembled citizenry. A mêlée develops and women crowd round to touch the

An Popt Ʒaeðealaċ—An ċeað Ceim Súðailte.
The Irish Jig - Leading off Double.

He performs astonishing feats of juggling and dances an acrobatic Highland Fling.

end of his apparel. Bloom moves among the crowd, kissing babies, shaking hands and playing with children. He performs astonishing feats of juggling and dances an acrobatic Highland Fling. Bloom refuses three shillings proffered by Joe Hynes and engages in further deeds of mercy and charity.

He opens a court of conscience where he dispenses free advice and judgments to all comers. The curator of the National Museum, Kildare Street, materializes with statues of naked women. Mrs Riordan describes Bloom as a nasty person and tears up her will. Nosey Flynn calls for

Nosey Flynn calls for a tune
and Bloom obliges.

Irish Piper. *With best wishes & kind remembrances from ...*

a tune and Bloom obliges. Lenehan denounces Bloom as a plagiarist. Alexander J. Dowie accuses him of hypocrisy and debauchery. The mob howls for Bloom's blood, shouting that he is worse than Parnell. Bloom pleads innocence and blames his brother, Henry, who lives in Dolphin's Barn.

Bloom calls Dr Malachi Mulligan, a medical specialist in matters of sex, to give evidence on his behalf. Mulligan pronounces Bloom to be a bisexual deviant who has recently escaped from an asylum. He outlines a wide variety of peculiar ailments afflicting Bloom including premature baldness from indulging in the schoolboy

The Irish Emigrant.

I'm sit-ting on the stile Ma-ry.

[175]

Bloom acquires the hat, shoes, stick and bundle of an Irish emigrant and speaks about leaving home in a mock Connemara brogue.

habit of self-abuse. Mulligan pronounces Bloom a virgin while Bloom holds his hat over his genitalia.

Dr Madden, Dr Crotthers and Dr Punch Costello give further testimony about Bloom's medical condition. Dr Dixon describes Professor Bloom as a perfect woman and appeals for clemency on the grounds that Bloom is about to produce a baby. There is general uproar and a feeling of compassion for Bloom. Bloom expresses a wish to be a mother. Eight of Bloom's children of different colours materialize and are appointed to the highest positions of public trust and company management.

A voice from the crowd asks if Bloom is the Messiah

while another calls for a miracle. Bantam Lyons asks him to prophesy the winner of the Saint Leger horse race. Bloom performs a series of miracles including hanging from Nelson's Pillar by his eyelids. The Papal Nuncio traces Bloom's lineage in direct descent from Moses to Virag and pronounces him God.

Anonymous accusations are levelled against Bloom and he is stoned by the crowd. Mastiansky and Citron denounce Bloom as a false Messiah and he is handed over for death by burning to the Dublin Fire Brigade. As the flames rise higher Bloom calls on the daughters of Erin not to weep for him. The daughters recite a litany of Bloom while a choir sings a heavenly chorus. Bloom falls silent, shrinks and is reduced to ashes.

Zoe Higgins remarks that Bloom is talking too much. Bloom acquires the hat, shoes, stick and bundle of an Irish emigrant and speaks about leaving home in a mock Connemara brogue. Zoe offers Bloom a short time with her for ten shillings. She invites him to see the new pianola in the music room and promises to remove her clothes. Zoe leads him by the hand up the steps, through the hall and into the music room. Lynch is seated with legs crossed on the hearth rug. Kitty Ricketts, a pale-faced prostitute, sits on the table. Stephen is standing near the pianola. Florry Talbot, a blonde, fat prostitute, is lying spread out on the sofa.

Florry Talbot mentions that she has read in the newspaper about the forthcoming visit of an Antichrist. A gramophone blares and a rocket explodes to proclaim the arrival of Elijah in the form of an American preacher, Alexander J. Dowie. A voice warns of a second coming and entreats the occupants of the music room to join the side of the angels. Elijah calls on his three sisters to confess their sins. Kitty Ricketts confesses to a weak moment with a plumber on Constitution Hill. Zoe Higgins declares she did it for fun, while Florry Talbot attributes her downfall to drink.

Zoe asks for a cigarette and Lynch throws one on the

Porte St Martin

BLANCHE MIROIR

[176]

The door of the music room
opens and Bella Cohen, an
enormous brothel keeper,
enters.

table. As she stretches for a light, Lynch playfully lifts
her skirt to expose the bare flesh above her garters. The
standing Bloom watches with a faint smile of desire.

Lipoti Virag, Bloom's grandfather, arrives down the
chimney and bows. He introduces himself and asks if
Bloom had noticed the injection mark on her thigh,
exposed by lack of underwear. Virag lectures Bloom on
various kinds of medical remedies. He chides Bloom for
silly projects, like studying the problems of religion and
attempting to square the circle for a prize of one million
pounds. Virag mentions Bloom's preoccupation with
female underwear.

Henry Flower, dressed in a mantle and sombrero, reveals himself. He carries a dulcimer and sings in a sweet voice to his own accompaniment. Henry caresses a decapitated female head and murmurs lovingly while playing a lute. Virag yawns, removes his head and exits with it under his arm, together with Henry, his harp slung over his shoulder.

A man is heard making his way down the stairs and taking his coat and hat from the stand in the hall. Bloom overhears the man talking with prostitutes at the door and wonders if he could be Boylan. The noise of high heels, clicking and clacking on the stairs, is heard.

The door of the music room opens and Bella Cohen, an enormous brothel keeper, enters. She is dressed in a yellow gown and cools herself with a black fan. Her sweating heavy face features a growing moustache. Bella introduces herself with a vulgar reference to her sweating and waves her fan for coolness. She glances round the room, her beady eyes fixing on Bloom.

The Fan flirts with Bloom and observes that he is married. Bella draws near, still winnowing her fan. A cringing Bloom begs for domination and explains that he is tired, old and abandoned. The Fan asks Bloom to be hers and points down to an unfastened bootlace.

Bella raises her gown and lifts a fat foot to the edge of a chair. An old Bloom applies himself to fixing the laces of her boot. Bloom recalls a boyhood yearning to be a fitter at Mansfield's shoe shop, where he could lace up the shoes of the beautifully small-footed ladies of Clyde Road.

Bella replaces her foot on the floor and begins to develop masculine features. Bello orders Bloom to the floor with a barrage of insults. Bloom, now female, grunts and roots at Bello's feet. Bello grinds a heel into Bloom's neck and threatens a wide variety of dire punishments. Bloom escapes under the sofa and is coaxed out, only to receive a savage hair pulling and other tortures. Bloom screams in pain and Bello orders the girls to hold him down.

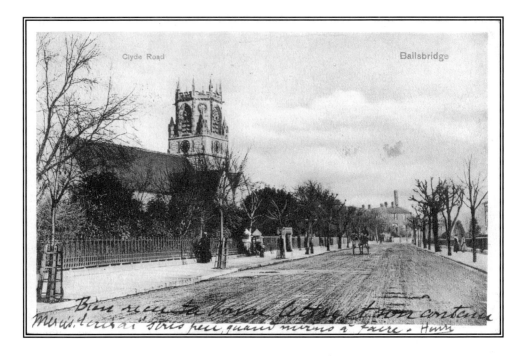

Clyde Road

Ballsbridge

Mrs Keogh, the brothel cook, comes through the door and offers to help. They all hold Bloom down and Bello squats on his face, smoking a cigar. Bello bemoans his losses on Guinness's shares and viciously puts out his cigar in Bloom's ear. Bello bestrides Bloom, squeezes his testicles and orders him off for a horse ride. A sweating Bloom confesses that he is now a woman. Bello announces that Bloom's longings have been fulfilled and in future he will wear clothes and underwear similar to the other girls of the house.

Bloom, assuming the features of a gaudy blonde actress, admits to wearing Molly's clothes as a joke when they lived in Holles Street. Bello pours scorn on Bloom's excuses, reminding him of when he dressed up and posed in Miriam Dandrade's underwear. Bloom blames Gerald for his conversion to the love of corsets, acquired when Bloom played the role of a female in a play at High School.

Bello assumes ownership of Bloom and allocates him a variety of menial duties to be executed around the brothel. He will be beaten for any mistakes and offered to

[177]

Bloom recalls a boyhood yearning to be a fitter at Mansfield's shoe shop, where he could lace up the shoes of the beautifully small-footed ladies of Clyde Road.

[178]

Mrs Keogh, the brothel cook, comes through the door and offers to help.

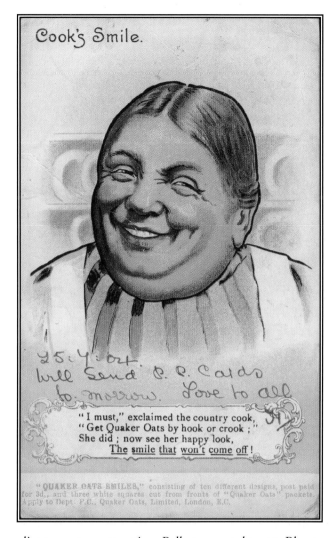

Cook's Smile.

"I must," exclaimed the country cook,
"Get Quaker Oats by hook or crook;"
She did; now see her happy look,
The smile that won't come off!

"QUAKER OATS SMILES," consisting of ten different designs, post paid for 3d., and three white squares cut from fronts of "Quaker Oats" packets. Apply to Dept. P.C., Quaker Oats, Limited, London, E.C.

clients as a new attraction. Bello teases and taunts Bloom about his lack of sexual prowess, compared to Boylan's virility. Bloom, now reverted to male features, begs his wife Molly for forgiveness. Bello reminds him that everything has changed in the twenty years that he has slept like Rip Van Winkle. Milly Bloom materializes and informs Bloom that he has grown old. Bello tells him to make a will and die. Jewish friends gather to lament his passing.

The Yews of Poulaphouca murmur about a High School excursion when Bloom left his companions, to abuse himself alone, in their quiet glade by the waterfall.

Bloom excuses himself on the precocity of youth, when the slightest temptation was enough to set him off. He cites Lotty Clarke, viewed in her night clothes through his father's opera glasses, as an example. No one could possibly resist Lotty as she rolled down hills or climbed trees. In any event Bloom argues that he was only gratifying a desire at a time when girls were uncooperative.

Bella Cohen asks who was playing the piano. Bloom requests Zoe for a return of his talisman. Zoe rolls up her slip and removes Bloom's potato from the top of her stocking. Bella angrily castigates the free show of flesh and enquires who is paying. Stephen takes out a banknote and indicates that he is paying for all three. Bloom settles a dispute over the money by paying for himself and returning a pound note to Stephen. At Bloom's request Stephen hands over his money for safekeeping.

Zoe reads Stephen's hand and finds courage written on it. Lynch smacks Kitty twice on the bottom. Father Dolan springs from the pianola to ask if the lazy, scheming boy who broke his glasses wants a flogging. Father Conmee, a mild and kind rector, materializes to tell Father Dolan that Stephen is a good little boy. Zoe examines Bloom's hand and sees a nagged and downtrodden husband.

Blazes Boylan and Lenehan trot past in a hackney car. Boylan leaps from the car and asks Bloom if the wife is out of bed. Bloom, in hotel attendant's uniform, tells Boylan she is in her bath and Boylan throws him sixpence for a drink. Boylan allows Bloom to watch through the keyhole while the lovemaking is described in detail by Mina Kennedy and Lydia Douce.

Private Carr, Private Compton and Cissy Caffrey walk by, singing 'My Girl's a Yorkshire Girl'. Zoe borrows two pence and puts them in the pianola. Professor Goodwin, in formal concert dress, staggers across the room and sits on the piano stool. The pianola plays 'My Girl's a Yorkshire Girl' in waltz time, as Stephen and Zoe dance around the room. Professor Maginni performs an intricate display of dancing movements while Professor Goodwin thumps the air and then collapses on the stool. Stephen and Zoe whirl about the room, causing Zoe to fall in a chair from giddiness.

Kitty, Florry and Lynch join the dance while Stephen grabs his ashplant and high kicks in the middle of the room. The dance moves to a climax. The voice of Simon Dedalus is heard urging Stephen to think of his dead mother's family. The pianola comes to the end of the tune and the couples separate. Stephen whirls alone, staggers and stops in his tracks.

Through the floor of the room there rises the leprous rotting corpse of Stephen's mother. From a tower Buck Mulligan proclaims that she is merely dead. The mother introduces herself as the once lovely May Goulding, now dead. Stephen is terrified as his mother approaches, mouthing a warning that his death is also inevitable. A horror-stricken Stephen tells her that cancer killed her, not him, and that Mulligan had offended her memory. She reminds Stephen of the love song he had sung on her deathbed. Stephen begs her to tell him whether she now has knowledge of the word that is known to every man. She urges Stephen to pray and repent because of hell's fire. Stephen rejects her pleadings because he refuses to serve the Catholic Church. In her moment of agonizing death she calls on Jesus to have mercy on Stephen.

Stephen smashes the chandelier with his ashplant and runs from the room. There is a general rush for the door and Bloom returns for Stephen's ashplant. Bella wishes to know who is paying for the broken lamp and Bloom responds that she has taken enough money from Stephen. He points out that only a part of the lamp had been broken and in any event she should look after the Trinity students who are good customers of her business. Bella angrily castigates the antics of Trinity students who merely come around for free entertainment after the boat race.

HIS MAJESTY'S ARRIVAL AT PUNCHESTOWN. APRIL, 1904.

From the doorway Zoe shouts that a row has started. Bloom throws a shilling on the table for the damage and hurries out of the building. Corny Kelleher arrives in a hackney car in company with two gentlemen in search of ladies of the night. At the corner of Beaver Street Bloom finds Stephen in the middle of a noisy, argumentative crowd. Private Carr asks Cissy Caffrey if Stephen had insulted her. Cissy explains that Stephen had attempted to proposition her while the soldiers were away urinating. Private Carr threatens to hit Stephen for insulting Cissy while Bloom urges Stephen to leave. Stephen mentions King Edward and Private Carr takes umbrage to an imagined insult to his King.

King Edward materializes in an archway wearing a white jersey, a badge of the Sacred Heart and other important insignia. He carries a plasterer's bucket in one hand and calls for a fair fight while wishing both contestants the best of luck. King Edward shakes hands with the combatants and their immediate supporters, to the applause of the assembled crowd.

Stephen continues to annoy the soldiers with smart

[179]

King Edward shakes hands with the combatants and their immediate supporters, to the applause of the assembled crowd.

[180]

The Citizen, with a shillelagh in his right hand, screams for God to slit the throats of the English dogs who hanged the leaders of Ireland.

INJUSTICE TO IRELAND.

Is it there,yez are, ye two-faced Lyin' Blaguard wid yer mane Blarney about the Sun; no Sun ivir riz anywhere, afore it did in Ould Ireland! England afore Ireland! nivir!! Hurroo!!!

remarks as Bloom attempts to placate them. Kevin Egan of Paris makes an appearance dressed in a Spanish shirt and the hat of a Peep-O-Day-Boy. He greets Stephen in French, while a rabbit-faced Patrice Egan peeps out from behind his father. The Citizen, with a shillelagh in his right hand, screams for God to slit the throats of the English dogs who hanged the leaders of Ireland. The Croppy Boy, with a hangman's rope around his neck, steps forward declaring that he bears no hatred for any living person and loves his country above his King. Rumbold, the hangman, pulls the rope and The Croppy Boy expires.

Cissy Caffrey pleads for someone to intervene and stop the impending fight. Private Carr threatens to wring the neck of anybody insulting his King. Bloom rushes to Lynch and asks him to call Stephen away. Lynch argues that Stephen will not listen to him and leaves the scene with Kitty Ricketts. Stephen calls the departing Lynch a traitorous Judas. Private Carr gives Stephen a punch in the face. Stephen staggers, falls and lies stunned on the ground.

Two policemen arrive on the scene. Bloom argues for Stephen in the face of allegations by the soldiers that Stephen started the fracas. Corny Kelleher joins the onlookers and Bloom asks him to have a word with the policemen. The second policeman greets Kelleher by name. Corny Kelleher excuses Stephen on the grounds of over-celebrating a big win on the Gold Cup. The policemen accept Kelleher's explanation and move away. Bloom explains that he is in the area on his way home through Gardiner Street. Corny Kelleher offers to take Stephen home but Bloom promises to look after him.

Bloom attempts to revive Stephen but he groans and turns over on the ground. Bloom stands over the body, holding Stephen's hat and ashplant. The ghostly figure of an eleven-year-old boy emerges from the dark shadows reading a book. The astonished Bloom calls out the name of his dead son, Rudy.

~19~

Eumaeus

Mr Bloom helps Stephen to tidy himself and hands over the hat and ashplant. Stephen is a little unsteady on his feet and asks for a drink of some kind. Mr Bloom suggests a visit to the nearby cabman's shelter. Mr Bloom and Stephen walk along Beaver Street and turn left towards Amiens Street. They pass the North Star Hotel and the impressive entrance to the terminus of the Great Northern Railway.

Mr Bloom gently lectures the still slightly inebriated Stephen on the dangers of visiting places of ill-repute and the over-indulgence of alcohol. He mentions the timely arrival of Corny Kelleher which, possibly, saved Stephen from a night in the Bridewell police station and a court appearance the following day. Mr Bloom criticizes the fact that all of Stephen's medical friends, with one exception, had abandoned him. Stephen ruefully remarks that this exception, Lynch, turned out to be a Judas.

They walk along the rere of the Custom House and go under the Loop Line Bridge. They see a fire burning in front of a box, housing a night-watchman of the Dublin Corporation. Stephen recognizes the man inside the box as Gumley, a former friend of his father, but chooses to avoid an encounter with him.

From under the arches of the Loop Line Bridge a shadowy figure greets Stephen. Stephen ascertains that the man is Lord John Corley, much the worse for drink. Corley acquired his unmerited title through a rumour that

Published by Stewart & Woolf, London, W. C.
Printed in Saxony Series No. 109.

Great Northern Railway Terminus.

Dublin.

Was at Prush on Saturday meeting a cousin. Saw a friend of yours – I expect you had a big day at B. Castle I didn't write. my cycle was away on monday. Cannot have it so much now. I could meet you any day this week – Would Thursday do? Have you been to Prush yet. Could you not go down some day. Sure it will be good. I will do you something. Thanks very much for invitation. I am

Custom House and Quays, Dublin

[181]

They pass the North Star Hotel and the impressive entrance to the terminus of the Great Northern Railway.

[182]

They walk along the rere of the Custom House and go under the Loop Line Bridge.

his grandmother, a Talbot, was related to the Lords Talbot of Malahide. As a result the debauched and down-and-out Corley was jokingly referred to in conversation as Lord John Corley. Corley spins Stephen a hard luck story and looks for help by way of money for lodgings or a job. Stephen tells him there will be a job available in the morning at Mr Garrett Deasy's school in Dalkey. Stephen recommends a cheap dosshouse in Marlborough Street for Corley to spend the night and gives him a half-crown. Corley assumes that Stephen's companion is a friend of Boylan and asks Stephen to put in a good word for a job with Boylan's firm. The two men part company and Stephen rejoins the waiting Mr Bloom. He passes on Corley's request for the job of carrying a sandwich-board for Boylan, which is politely ignored by Mr Bloom.

Mr Bloom enquires where Stephen hopes to spend the night. He rules out a long walk to Sandycove because there's no certainty that Mulligan and Haines would let him in after the fracas at Westland Row Railway Station. Mr Bloom asks Stephen why he left the family home and Stephen glibly replies that it was to find misfortune. Mr Bloom refers to Simon Dedalus as a gifted man who takes great pride in his son, Stephen. He suggests that Stephen stays the night at his father's house, inwardly bearing in mind that Mulligan and Haines had deliberately abandoned Stephen at the railway station. There is no response to the suggestion from Stephen, as he mentally pictures the squalor of family life during his last visit.

Mr Bloom warns Stephen not to trust Mulligan as a friend or confidante. He would not be surprised if Mulligan had added a drug to Stephen's drink for some ulterior motive. However, he has learned that Mulligan is a good sporting all-rounder with a great medical career ahead of him. Mr Bloom mentions Mulligan's outstanding bravery in saving a man from drowning at Skerries or Malahide. He is unable to understand why such a man could behave so badly towards Stephen,

Skerries. *The Shanty. Bush. R!. Dublin.* The Harbour.

Awfully windy + showery, so we are settling down to eew + to read for the day. Jerdia.

The Wrench Series. No. 9913. Mealley, Fancy Depôt, Skerries.

other than through jealousy. Mr Bloom concludes that in any event Mulligan is simply picking Stephen's brains.

The two men enter the cabman's shelter alleged to be run by the former Invincible, Fitzharris, known as Skin-the-Goat. They find seats in a corner, watched by the stares of a motley collection of customers. Mr Bloom orders a cup of coffee and a bun for Stephen, which is served by the keeper.

A sailor with a red beard, who had been watching the new arrivals, bluntly asks Stephen for his surname, to which Stephen replies Dedalus. The sailor fixes a pair of bloodshot, boozy eyes on Stephen and asks if he knows a man called Simon Dedalus. Stephen acknowledges that he has heard the name. Turning to address the other customers of the shelter, the sailor earnestly remarks that he has seen Simon Dedalus shoot two eggs straight off the tops of two bottles, using his deadly left hand, propped over the shoulder. The whole company watch and wait in silent anticipation as the sailor demonstrates the two shots, one after the other. He concludes the tale

[183]

Mr Bloom mentions Mulligan's outstanding bravery in saving a man from drowning at Skerries or Malahide.

by saying that he saw Simon Dedalus perform that trick about ten years ago, when the sharpshooter was on a world tour with Hengler's Circus.

The sailor introduces himself to his audience as W.B. Murphy from Carrigaloe, Queenstown Harbour. He has a wife down there, waiting seven years for his return. The sailor announces that he arrived in Dublin at eleven o'clock that morning on board a three-masted sailing ship and produces a grubby document showing his discharge from service.

Several members of his audience query Murphy about the countries and sights that he has seen in his travels throughout the world. Murphy reels off a series of places and amazing episodes. With his own eyes he has seen a crocodile bite off the barb of an anchor and the cannibals of Peru who eat the corpses of men and the livers of horses. Murphy produces a postcard from his inside pocket, sent to him by a friend, and pushes it across the table for all to see. All eyes focus on the postcard view in expectation of unbridled savagery. It is a large group of primitive Bolivian Indians, mainly scantily clad women and children, who squat, suckle, sleep and otherwise harmlessly pose in front of a shanty made of twigs. For effect, Murphy adds that they chew all day on the leaves of the coca plant and the women cut off their breasts when child-bearing age is over. The postcard holds the audience spellbound for a considerable time. Mr Bloom casually turns the postcard to reveal the name of the addressee, Mr Boudin, resident in Santiago, Chile.

Murphy turns to the subject of a killing he witnessed in Trieste, perpetrated by an Italian smuggler on his partner in crime. He produces a knife that he claims is similar to the one used in the murder. He holds the knife up in full view at the ready position to strike. The murder took place in a brothel where one partner waited behind a door and buried his knife to the hilt in the back of his unsuspecting colleague. Murphy glances round the room, snaps the blade closed and puts the knife back in his pocket.

An unidentified customer innocently suggests that it was suspected for a time that foreigners using knives had perpetrated the Phoenix Park murders, later attributed to the Invincibles. Mr Bloom and Stephen instinctively glance towards the keeper, Skin-the-Goat, who acts as if he does not understand a word of what has been said about the murders.

The door opens and an old prostitute peers into the room, looking for business. Mr Bloom is taken aback but does not show it. It is the same woman he encountered earlier that day on Ormond Quay. Unfortunately Mr Bloom had had a previous dalliance in a lane with this semi-idiotic woman, who knows his wife from seeing them walking together. Mr Bloom is relieved when Skin-the-Goat orders her to leave. Mr Bloom expresses surprise to Stephen at why any man would risk his health with a wretched woman of that kind. Stephen responds that the buying and selling of souls practised in this country is far worse and, in any event, the woman buys dear and sells cheap, contrary to good merchandizing.

Murphy makes his way out of the shelter, pauses to take his bearings and takes a long swig from a bottle of rum. Mr Bloom watches as Murphy stares up at the arches and ironwork of the Loop Line Bridge. Murphy urinates loudly, disturbing a horse in the hackney cab rank, which in turn wakens Gumley. Gumley has landed the temporary position of night-watchman through the humanitarianism of Pat Tobin. Gumley is a man from a decent family who has lost his way in life through an inability to overcome his fondness for alcohol.

Murphy returns and regains his seat while Skin-the-Goat abuses England for draining the wealth and resources out of Ireland. Skin-the-Goat expresses his advice that all Irishmen should stay at home and cites Parnell's opinion that Ireland could spare none of her sons. Murphy takes offence to this statement and says that the Irish provided the best soldiers and military leaders. In his opinion the Irish Catholic peasant was

Bridges & Custom House.
Dublin.
Marie, I have heard thee
in thy soliloquy; may I cross the Bridge.

[184]

Mr Bloom watches as Murphy stares up at the arches and ironwork of the Loop Line Bridge.

the cornerstone of the British Empire. Mr Bloom inwardly reflects that the Irish fought more often on the side of the English than against them. He feels that Skin-the-Goat, the alleged Invincible, should be avoided. Only fools would get involved in revolutionary activity, as there was a good chance of betrayal by people like Peter or Denis Carey. Yet Mr Bloom retains a certain grudging admiration for a man who has the courage to fight physically for his political convictions. He reminds himself that Fitzharris, alias Skin-the-Goat, merely drove the escape car for the Invincibles and did not participate in the actual crime itself. This fact was pleaded in court and saved his skin. Mr Bloom reflects that Skin-the-Goat would have been better off to die naturally or by a rope, rather than repeatedly giving farewell performances like some fading actresses.

The argument between Murphy and Skin-the-Goat reminds Mr Bloom of the similar discussion he had heard in Barney Kiernan's. He explains to Stephen how he silenced the offender on that occasion by disclosing that Christ was a Jew. Mr Bloom declares himself to be against violence of any kind. As a patriotic Irishman, he wants everyone to enjoy a decent standard of living through honest endeavour and work. Stephen wishes to be excluded from work but Mr Bloom reassures him that writing literature should rank *pari passu* with manual labour.

Mr Bloom finds a copy of the *Evening Telegraph* and glances through the contents, which include the Russo-Japanese War, the Gordon Bennett motor-car race, the Canada swindle case, Throwaway's victory in the Gold Cup, the New York ship disaster, Deasy's letter on foot-and-mouth disease and the funeral of Patrick Dignam. He reads out the full account of Dignam's funeral for Stephen and is slightly annoyed at the misspelling of his own name. However, he is greatly amused by the inclusion of Stephen and M'Coy who did not attend and M'Intosh who does not exist. Stephen takes page two to read the text of Deasy's letter while Mr Bloom reads an account of the running of the Gold Cup. Mr Bloom notes that Lenehan's version of the race was rubbish and that the selection of Bantam Lyons was among the also-rans.

While Mr Bloom and Stephen are distracted, the others express a variety of opinions about Parnell: the return of Parnell will be announced one morning in the newspaper; there was an alleged sighting of Parnell by a soldier in South Africa; he should have committed suicide or disappeared for a time after his betrayal by trusted party members; Parnell was not dead and the coffin was filled with stones; he should never have taken on the priests. Mr Bloom listens to the various recollections and inwardly ponders the death, downfall and betrayal of the great leader. He concludes that once Parnell had lost possession, it was almost impossible to return to his former position and reputation.

Skin-the-Goat launches a verbal attack on Kitty O'Shea, blaming her for hammering the first nail in Parnell's coffin. Mr Bloom reflects on the story of

BAILE ÁTHA CLIATH. Museum Stáire Nádúrdha 7 Íomhaigh Tighearna Pluncoet.

(314)

[185]

Mr Bloom maintains that his wife could easily have posed for the statues of Grecian goddesses that he had seen earlier that day in the National Museum.

Parnell and Kitty O'Shea, which had aroused extraordinary curiosity at the time. The newspapers made plenty of money by reporting all the intimate details of the affair. However, Mr Bloom considers that the matter was a simple scenario of a failed marriage, which Parnell had stumbled across and then fell victim to the obvious charms of a beautiful woman. The tragedy of Parnell was the attack of the Catholic Church and the stab in the back by the tenants for whom Parnell had tirelessly fought throughout his political life.

Mr Bloom mentions to Stephen that Kitty O'Shea was possibly of Spanish ancestry and Stephen facetiously replies that she was the daughter of the King of Spain. Mr Bloom produces a faded photograph, lays it down on the table and asks Stephen if he considers the subject to be Spanish-looking. Stephen gazes at the photograph of a beautiful woman, displaying a generous bosom, standing near a piano. Mr Bloom informs Stephen that the portrait is of his wife, the well-known singer, Madame Marion Tweedy. The photograph was taken about eight years ago and is a good likeness of her facial

THE LOW—BACKED CAR.
Oh, I'd rather own that car, sir,
   With Peggy by my side,
Than a coach and four, and gold galore
   And a lady for my bride;
For the lady would sit fornenst me.

[186]

The driver watches the two men walk up Gardiner Street and just sits silently in 'The Low-Backed Car'.

expression but does not do justice to her figure. Mr Bloom maintains that his wife could easily have posed for the statues of Grecian goddesses that he had seen earlier that day in the National Museum.

A sudden fear overcomes Mr Bloom at the thought that Molly might be gone when he arrives home. However, he is consoled by the recollection that all was well at home that morning and that his fears are merely a fleeting bout of irrationality. Mr Bloom is delighted to be in the company of a well-educated young man and awaits a suitable opportunity to invite Stephen to his house. Mr Bloom pays the bill of four pence and both men leave the shelter.

Although refreshed by the night air, Stephen is still a trifle weak and wobbly, so Mr Bloom links his arm and leads him forward into the night. They pass the sleeping Gumley and proceed arm in arm through Beresford Place. They discuss music, with Mr Bloom expressing a particular liking for the operas *Don Giovanni* and *Martha*. One of his particular favourites is Lionel's song from *Martha* which, by a strange coincidence, he had heard that day in the Ormond Hotel, perfectly rendered by Stephen's father. Stephen professes a liking for the songs and music of Shakespeare's era.

They encounter a road sweeper and its driver being dragged along the streets by an old horse. Mr Bloom informs Stephen that his wife would enjoy meeting him, as she loves all kinds of music. Stephen begins to sing a ballad in German. Mr Bloom feels that Stephen has a fine tenor voice and, with proper training, could succeed as a professional singer. At the same time there is no reason why he could not continue writing. Mr Bloom is of the opinion that Stephen should break with Mulligan, who tends to criticize and deprecate Stephen in his absence. The old horse deposits three steaming lumps of manure on the street. They walk in the direction of Gardiner Street as Stephen concludes the singing of the ballad. The driver watches the two men walk up Gardiner Street and just sits silently in 'The Low-Backed Car'.

～20～

Ithaca

ON THEIR HOMEWARD JOURNEY Bloom and Stephen discuss a
wide variety of subjects, including music, literature, politics,
medicine and religion. Bloom discovers that they share common
likes and dislikes. They both enjoy the impression of art as
opposed to pictorial reality. They prefer continental life to that of an island
and share a common disbelief for many doctrines of religions and politics.
Stephen disagrees with Bloom's philosophy on social issues while Bloom
opposes Stephen's theories about literature.

When they arrive at 7 Eccles Street Bloom is annoyed to discover that
he has forgotten the key. Bloom climbs over the railings, drops to the base-
ment and opens the scullery door. He reappears and allows Stephen in the
front door.

In the kitchen Bloom lights the fire, puts on the kettle and washes his
hands with the bar of lemon soap. Stephen declines an invitation to wash
because of his dislike for water. Bloom surveys the kitchen dresser and, particularly, notes an empty jar of Plumtree's Potted Meat, a basket with one
pear and a half-full bottle of port. Two mutilated betting tickets, resting on
the dresser, remind him of the number of times during the day that he had
received intimations of the result of the Gold Cup. Predictions of the result
were given to him at Barney Kiernan's, Davy Byrne's, Graham Lemon's,
O'Connell Street and Sweny's of Lincoln Place. Bloom concludes that
there are problems in the interpretation of random omens and portents.

Bloom is the only son and heir born to Rudolph and Ellen Bloom, while Stephen is the eldest surviving son and heir of Simon and Mary Dedalus.

Lawrence, Publisher, Dublin.

THE BIRTH OF AN HEIR.

Och! Paddy, wake up, don't be dhramin'
Joy, agrah, from your eye should be sthramin'
Arrah, whist, to the SMALL STRANGER schramin'
"I'M HEIR to the BYRNES and O'TOOLES."

So am I, are you

However, he is pleased at having lost nothing and brought profit to others.

Bloom serves two cups of Epp's Cocoa, which they drink in silence. Bloom believes that he differs from Stephen in four crucial aspects: name, age, race and religion. He calculates that he is sixteen years older than Stephen and remembers their two previous meetings. The first was in 1887 at Mat Dillon's, Roundtown, and the second in 1892 at Breslin's Hotel, Bray, with Stephen's father and granduncle. In the course of their conversation about times past they discover a mutual link to Mrs

Riordan. This woman had stayed with the Dedalus family for three years and thereafter at the City Arms Hotel when the Bloom family were resident there. Bloom remembers Mrs Riordan as a wheelchair-bound widow of fairly limited means who he sometimes took for summer evening walks. Stephen's memories of the dead woman are of a lamp burning before a statue of the Blessed Virgin and her green brush in honour of Charles Stewart Parnell and the maroon brush in honour of Michael Davitt.

Neither men refer to their racial origins but feel free to discuss their parents. Bloom is the only son and heir born to Rudolph and Ellen Bloom, while Stephen is the eldest surviving son and heir of Simon and Mary Dedalus.

Bloom was baptized on three occasions. The first was by a Protestant clergyman, next by three men under a pump in Swords and, finally, by Reverend Charles Malone CC in the Church of the Three Patrons, Rathgar. Coincidentally, Stephen was also baptized by the same priest in the same church.

Bloom attended nursery school and High School and likes to boast that his education was completed in the university of life. Stephen paved his way through all grades of the education system, culminating with an arts degree from the Royal University.

Stephen represents the artistic mind, while Bloom is more inclined to the scientific. Bloom advances some of his ideas for novel inventions and theorizes on the many unexploited ideas in the field of advertising.

Stephen relates his parable of Palestine, which leads to a discussion about Jews and Judaism. They make comparisons between the Hebrew and Irish languages and note the persecution and suffering endured by both nations. The aspirations of both races are similar, with the Jews seeking a restoration of their nation in Palestine while the Irish look for Home Rule. Bloom invites Stephen to sing a ballad about a little boy who is murdered by a

St. John's Church, Sydney Parade

[188]

Bloom asks Stephen if he has heard of Mrs Emily Sinico, killed in a tragic accident at Sydney Parade Railway Station on 14 October 1903.

Jew's daughter. Bloom smiles as the story unfolds but is perturbed by the reference to the Jew's daughter being dressed in green as it reminds him of Milly. He reflects on Milly's birth, childhood nightmares and growth through adolescence to the position of acquiring a new male friend in Mullingar.

Bloom proposes that Stephen should spend the night at his home and reflects on the advantages that could accrue from an extended stay. Stephen would have a secure home to pursue his literary endeavours. Bloom himself would be pleasantly stimulated by an intelligent companion. Molly would lose interest in Boylan and improve her Italian pronunciation. There would also be the interesting possibility of marriage between Stephen and Milly.

Bloom asks Stephen if he has heard of Mrs Emily Sinico, killed in a tragic accident at Sydney Parade Railway Station on 14 October 1903. As a consequence of a short negative answer by Stephen, Bloom decides not to explain his absence at the funeral of Mary Dedalus on 26 June 1903, that date being the vigil in commemoration of his own dead father, Rudolph Bloom.

ROTUNDA HOSPITAL.
DUBLIN.

Stephen declines the offer of accommodation and Bloom returns Stephen's cash, held for safe keeping. They discuss specific arrangements and locations for reciprocal instruction between Molly and Stephen in Italian and voice training. Bloom is inwardly sceptical that the proposals will ever come to fruition because the past can never be rectified or the future predicted. He remembers sitting alone at a performance of Albert Hengler's Circus in the Rotunda, Rutland Square, when a clown informed the audience that Bloom was his father. In 1898 he had etched three notches on a florin in the assumption that it would eventually return to his possession. The clown was not his son and the florin never returned.

Bloom is frustrated and depressed by the obstacles he faces in his desire to amend social conditions and put an end to international animosity. He resists the urge to speculate on the changes that might be achieved by the intervention of a superior being. Stephen telepathically conveys to Bloom that he has proceeded as a rational human being from the known into the abyss of the unknown.

[189]

He remembers sitting alone at a performance of Albert Hengler's Circus in the Rotunda, Rutland Square, when a clown informed the audience that Bloom was his father.

Bloom exits the house carrying a lighted candle, followed by Stephen bearing his hat and ashplant. As they emerge from the dark passage into the garden they are greeted by a clear night sky, full of shining stars. Bloom thinks of the immensity and age of the universe, weighed against the puny lifespan of man. He considers the question of whether other planets are inhabited and if these people are redeemed by God. Bloom reasons to himself that aliens would also succumb to the vanities of life. Logic tells him that Heaven does not exist and in any event it is an impossibility to proceed from what is known to that which is unknown.

At Stephen's invitation the two men urinate and watch as a star precipitates across the sky. The bells of George's Church ring out as the two men take leave of one another.

The loneliness of the moment causes Bloom to reflect on the names of his friends and companions who have died in different ways and in different places. As he enters the front room he experiences a painful bang on the head due to the relocation of furniture in his absence. Among other things the piano had been switched with the sideboard. He notices the exposed keyboard of the piano and a copy of the words and music of 'Love's Old Sweet Song' on the music rest.

Bloom lights a cone of incense and surveys the wedding presents on the mantelpiece. He settles some books that were improperly arranged on the bookshelves, sits down and removes his collar and tie. The budget for 16 June 1904 is compiled by him in precise detail and balanced to the penny.

Bloom fantasizes about purchasing a house with extensive gardens in a well-to-do area of suburban Dublin. He contemplates a series of intellectual pursuits and recreational activities. Bloom considers the possibility of becoming a gentleman farmer, producing hay and rearing pigs, cattle and sheep.

As a member of the landed élite, Bloom foresees him-

"The Decent cot that tops the neighbouring hill." *Irish Farmyard* 7739

self entering parliament. He aspires to the highest levels of honesty and integrity and recalls his history of truth and rectitude. At High School Bloom expressed disbelief in Protestantism, the faith of his father following his conversion from Judaism by the Society for Promoting Christianity among the Jews. Bloom formally abjured Protestantism in favour of Roman Catholicism in advance of his marriage. He has publicly supported the land reforms of Michael Davitt and the Home Rule fight of Charles Stewart Parnell.

Bloom unlocks a drawer containing a collection of sundry memorabilia, including three typewritten letters addressed to Henry Flower and Martha Clifford's name and address written in secret code. He adds the new letter from Martha Clifford, collected that day in Westland Row, to his collection.

Bloom opens a second drawer, which contains personal and financial family details. There is a birth certificate bearing his full name, Leopold Paula Bloom, an endowment policy, a deposit account passbook with the Ulster

[190]

Bloom considers the possibility of becoming a gentleman farmer, producing hay and rearing pigs, cattle and sheep.

My Dear Ada, 16/4/04 thanks very much for your last letter & P.C. this will remind you of the Sundays we came here. How is Your Collection. I have 716 now. My Niece had a Baby girl last week they are well. Dawson S[t] apris will write you soon. Love: Edie

Interior of Royal Hospital, Kilmainham, Co. Dublin

[191]

A fear of destitution and poverty overcomes Bloom, particularly the prospect of ending his days as a mendicant inmate of the Royal Hospital, Kilmainham.

Bank, College Green, a certificate for £900 worth of Canadian Government Stock at 4 per cent interest, a receipt for a grave at Glasnevin and a change of name notice from Virag to Bloom, executed by his father. He sees an envelope addressed to himself, which evokes memories of words in his father's final letter. His father expressed the wish to be with his wife in death and for his son Leopold to be kind to his dog, Athos.

Feelings of sadness and remorse weigh on Bloom as he reflects on the disrespect he had shown in the past for his father's religious beliefs and practices. He takes some consolation for the sad memories of his dead father in the insurance policy, the deposit account and the stock certificate. A fear of destitution and poverty overcomes Bloom, particularly the prospect of ending his days as a mendicant inmate of the Royal Hospital, Kilmainham. He sees death or departure to foreign countries as the means of preventing such a situation arising.

In his mind Bloom summarizes the main events of the day, allocating each a Jewish religious rite or historical

Oh be careful and
always get there first
What price this
" P "
" Pussy "

He wont be happy till he gets it ᶜ¹ ²·⁷ ⁵⁷·⁵⁷·⁵ .

significance. He ponders the enigma of M'Intosh's real name and casually lists the minor blemishes of an otherwise perfect day. Bloom puts out the light and makes his way to the bedroom. He halts at a portrait of Molly's dead father, Drum Major Brian Cooper Tweedy of the Royal Dublin Fusiliers. In the bedroom he sees Molly's clothes and personal possessions scattered on an old trunk. Bloom removes his clothes and puts on a long white nightshirt. He takes a pillow and places it at the end of the bed and climbs in.

As he extends his legs he becomes gradually aware of his wife's presence, the imprint of a male other than himself and a few crumbs of meat, which he removes. Bloom compiles a series of twenty-five men who are perceived by him to be a part of Molly's interesting and varied sex life. Each of these men appear on the scene imagining themselves to be first but are in fact just one in an endless series. The named men on Bloom's list are Lieutenant Mulvey, Penrose, Bartell d'Arcy, Professor Goodwin, Julius Mastiansky, John Henry Menton, Father Bernard Corrigan, Maggot O'Reilly, Mat Dillon, Val

[192]

Bloom removes his clothes and puts on a long white nightshirt.

Dillon, Chris Callinan, Lenehan, Ben Dollard, Simon Dedalus, Pisser Burke, Joe Cuffe, Wisdom Hely, John Hooper, Dr Francis Brady, Father Sebastian and Blazes Boylan. The anonymous admirers or suitors are a farmer from the Dublin Horse Show, an Italian who plays a hand-organ, a man in the Gaiety Theatre and a boot-black from outside the General Post Office.

Bloom thinks of Boylan as a boastful bounder of questionable business ability and integrity. He is jealous and envious of Boylan and considers some form of ret-ribution, either by physical or legal means. However, he forms an opinion that it is better to accept the situation rather than seek victory or vindication. On a universal scale he concludes that the affair between Boylan and Molly is insignificant and matters very little.

Bloom becomes excited by the close presence of Molly's bottom and kisses each cheek in turn. His action causes Molly to question him about his day. Portraying himself in a good light, Bloom relates a series of lies, truths and wilful omissions about his activities. He dwells at length on Stephen Dedalus, the teacher and author who was accidentally concussed while perform-ing a difficult gymnastic exercise. As Molly listens, she is aware that full sexual intimacy with Bloom has not occurred for more than ten years. Bloom reflects that close mental communication with Molly has broken down since the onset of Milly's puberty. He is unhappy that both women now act in concert to cross-examine him on the activities of his day-to-day life.

Molly and Bloom recline on opposite ends of the bed. Bloom is tired from his wanderings and drifts wearily into a deep sleep.

— 21 —

Penelope

MOLLY LIES AWAKE IN BED pondering why Poldy had asked her to serve him breakfast in bed. He had not made such a request since their days at the City Arms Hotel, when he was trying to impress the old bitch, Mrs Riordan, who never left them a penny in her will. She is certain that he has made love during the day and has told her a series of lies about meeting Hynes and Menton. Molly remembers Menton, the baby-faced, oyster-eyed solicitor and his impudence to her on one occasion. Poldy has probably involved himself with some slut, because the other day she caught him writing a letter that he suspiciously hid when she came into the room.

There was the time in Ontario Terrace when he took a shine to their servant girl, Mary. Mary had encouraged and tempted him with a falsely padded bottom. Poldy spoiled servants and took Mary's part on the issue of the missing oysters, arguing that there was no proof of Mary's guilt. Molly is certain that he was up to something with Mary, which came to a head when she found garters in the girl's room. She recalls that Mary was very angry when she gave her a week's notice to quit.

Molly speculates that Poldy could not last long without sex and remembers the last time he performed intimacy of a kind with her. It was the night Poldy, Boylan and herself walked along the river Tolka when Boylan and herself secretly exchanged hand squeezes. She knows that Poldy suspects the affair but will not give him the pleasure of finding out for certain.

She fantasizes about paying a young boy to make love to her and thinks of the way she would seduce him by letting him see her new garters. Molly thinks that Poldy should give up sex at his age and reflects on his less than normal sexual practices with her. One should be able to indulge in long passionate kissing with a man without the benefit of marriage. She is reminded of an embarrassing confession to Father Corrigan when she told him that she was touched on the canal bank instead of her bottom.

Boylan had smacked her on the bottom as he left and, although she laughed at the time, she dislikes his familiarity. They had both fallen asleep after the port and potted meat but were suddenly awakened by a loud peal of thunder. They had made love several times during the afternoon, which makes her wonder if Boylan's enormous genitals are attributable to consuming oysters. The thought of having another child by Poldy and not by Boylan seems a pleasant idea.

Molly supposes that Poldy's encounter with Josie Powell and thinking about herself and Boylan caused his sexual arousal. Georgina Simpson's party comes to mind where Poldy and Josie Powell were flirting and dancing. She discounts Poldy's feeble excuse that he did not wish to see Josie as a wallflower. However, even if he is back with Josie, she would have little difficulty enticing him back with her feminine charms. Molly wonders what Josie is like now with a crazy husband to look after.

She is grateful that Poldy, for all his faults, is neat and tidy in his ways and has polite manners. The thought of how different men are to women brings to mind Boylan's attraction to the shape of her feet. Before their first formal introduction, Boylan had seen her having tea and buttered bread with Poldy in the Dublin Bakery Company tea rooms and had feasted his eyes on her feet as she walked to the toilet. She wonders why women's feet are attractive to Boylan and, for that matter, to Poldy.

Molly recalls Bartell d'Arcy, the tenor who Poldy was fond of ridiculing. D'Arcy had kissed her on the choir stairs immediately after she had sung Gounod's 'Ave Maria'. She has a good mind to show Poldy the exact location of the kiss, just to show him that he does not know everything about her.

In their courting days Poldy took a peculiar obsession with her underwear and drawers. He begged her to lift her petticoat in the street and threatened to kneel down in the rain. She lifted them a little and touched his trousers with her hand to keep him from disgracing her in a public place. The night in Dolphin's Barn when he kissed her heart comes to mind, but he was never able to kiss like Lieutenant Gardner.

Molly thinks of Boylan and their impending concert tour to Belfast. It is pleasing that they will be completely on their own, as Poldy will be in Ennis for the anniversary of his father's death. She wonders what would happen if she never came back and eloped with Boylan, who is able to get people on the stage. Her last concert, a year ago in St Teresa's Hall, Clarendon Street, reminds her of little bitches like Kathleen Kearney acquiring singing contracts through influence. She recalls how Poldy landed her a part in the 'Stabat Mater' by posing as a composer, only to be subsequently exposed by the Jesuits as a plagiarizing Freemason.

Molly is unhappy that Poldy has recently become interested in Sinn Féin and Arthur Griffith. She detests the mention of politics since her boyfriend Lieutenant Stanley Gardner died of enteric fever in the Boer War. On the evening at the canal lock when they kissed goodbye, Gardner had called her his lovely Irish beauty.

She hopes that Boylan will buy her a present in Belfast and wonders if he likes her. Boylan was very angry during the afternoon when he found out that he had lost twenty pounds on Lenehan's tip, half of which was on for her. Molly reflects on the sponger, Lenehan, who made advances to her on the way home from the Glencree Dinner. During that dinner Val Dillon, the lord mayor, had stared at her with lewd glances.

A good example is Lily Langtry, the mistress of the Prince of Wales, who was beautiful at forty-five.

"What honour to be born on Fortunes hill?
The merit is to climb it."

MRS. LANGTRY.   Photo by Lafayette

Molly speculates about what kind of underwear Boylan would like her to wear and remembers that many of the Gibraltar girls wore none. She resolves to give up her bottle of stout at dinner because her belly is getting too big. She is unhappy about their financial situation, always having to skimp and save. By her own estimation she will be thirty-three in September, and many women retain their beauty well into their forties. A good example is Lily Langtry, the mistress of the Prince of Wales, who was beautiful at forty-five.

Molly considers that Poldy should give up his job as

Lithographic Department, Hely's, Limited, Acme Works, Dame Court, Dublin.

a canvasser for the *Freeman's Journal* and find a regular job. He could still be with Joe Cuffe were it not for his stubborn attitude. Poldy had sent her to Cuffe in an attempt to retrieve the situation but, although Cuffe took a fancy to her bosom, he was sorry that he was unable to reinstate Poldy. Molly believes that Boylan made her breasts a bit firmer by sucking on them and admires their beauty in comparison to the ugliness of male sex organs. She reflects on the general view that women are beautiful and is reminded of the time Poldy suggested that she pose in the nude for a picture by a strange rich man. That was at the time when he had lost his job at Wisdom Hely's and she was performing at the Coffee Palace.

   She remembers how full her breasts were when she was feeding Milly. Poldy had said there was enough for two babies and suggested that an extra pound a week could be earned as a wet nurse. One morning Penrose, a pale-faced student who stayed nearby with the Citrons, nearly caught her washing her breasts, but she

[194]

That was at the time when he had lost his job at Wisdom Hely's and she was performing at the Coffee Palace.

managed to grab a towel in time. At that time her breasts were hard and painful so she asked Poldy to suck them. He thought her milk superior to that of cows and wanted some in his tea. She could write a book about Poldy if she could remember half of his weird antics. She wishes Boylan or anybody was in the bed to make love to her. The torrid events of the afternoon with Boylan pass through her mind and she counts the days until Monday's assignation with him.

The whistle of a distant train reminds her of 'Love's Old Sweet Song'. Gibraltar comes to mind and her friend, Hester Stanhope, who had sent her such a lovely dress from Paris. Hester and her older husband, Wogger, became good friends. Wogger was very fond of her and brought her along to the bullfights at La Linea. Molly recalls the day that the Stanhopes left Gibraltar and her tearful parting with Hester. Hester left an incorrect forwarding address, perhaps because Wogger had taken a fancy to her.

Life in Gibraltar was sometimes quite boring after the departure of the Stanhopes. It was a military routine, interspersed with long dull conversations between her father and Captain Grove about famous military campaigns. She received very few letters, except those she posted to herself. Perhaps Boylan will send her a longer letter the next time if he is really interested in her. At least Boylan has brought badly needed excitement into her life.

Molly recalls the morning when their housekeeper, Mrs Rubio, handed her a letter from Mulvey seeking an appointment. She spent the entire day deciphering the message through the handwriting and the language of stamps. Mulvey was the first man to kiss her under the old Moorish Wall in Gibraltar. She never knew what kissing meant until the young boy's tongue was in her mouth and she was responding with her knee.

On the day before Mulvey left Gibraltar they lay together on the rocks overlooking a secluded cove. Molly recollects the hot passion of the moment, which she contrived to fall short of full intimacy, because she was afraid

Strawberry Beds. *Mar 5/04. This is a picture of the Dublin. Strawberry Beds in Phoenix Park, where we once went & had Strawberries & Cream. Love. Jennie.*

The Wrench Series. No. 1705.

of unwanted pregnancy. Harry Mulvey and herself had faithfully promised to renew their love when he returned to Gibraltar. After Mulvey sailed away on board *H.M.S. Calypso*, she thought of him all the time on the high seas. Mulvey had given her a Claddagh ring as a memento, but she had presented it to Gardner for luck before he left for South Africa. The ring probably brought him bad luck because he died of fever in the war against the Boers.

Another train whistle again brings to mind 'Love's Old Sweet Song' and her forthcoming concert. She can't wait to appear on stage to show Kathleen Kearney and the other bitches that the soldier's daughter outshines the local Irish talent. These daughters of cobblers and publicans would drop dead if they could have seen her walk down the Alameda Esplanade in Gibraltar on the arm of an officer. She knew more about men and living at fifteen than these failures will know at fifty. Gardner had once told her that no one could resist her beautiful smiling mouth and teeth.

Molly hopes that Poldy is not going to get involved

[195]

The idea of a nice picnic at the Strawberry Beds comes to mind, with everybody contributing five shillings.

with medical students who will lead him astray. It is bad enough Poldy coming in at an unearthly hour but he had the cheek to wake her up and order eggs for breakfast. She decides to do some early morning shopping for fish and some meat. The idea of a nice picnic at the Strawberry Beds comes to mind, with everybody contributing five shillings. She remembers an infamous outing to Bray when Poldy asserted his expertise to the boatman and, subsequently, nearly drowned the two of them through incompetence at the helm. It was fortunate that they were saved by a stranger who was standing on the slip with Pisser Burke. She hates Pisser from their time at the City Arms Hotel where Pisser spied on them and always turned up when they were fighting.

The house is lonely now without Milly and she wonders if Poldy deliberately sent her to Mullingar because of her liaison with Boylan. Poldy and Milly have become very cosy and friendly of late. However, she knows that it is to her Milly would turn if anything went wrong. Milly is now keenly interested in flirting with boys and smoking cigarettes. Molly dislikes Milly exposing her legs in public and Milly's aversion to being touched by her own mother. Milly had rebuked her in the Theatre Royal for crushing the pleats of her skirt. Molly remembers being touched several times by a strange man during a performance of *Trilby*, starring Beerbohm Tree at the Gaiety Theatre.

The unexpected arrival of her monthly period annoys Molly because it might interfere with next Monday's tryst with Boylan. She deplores this regular inconvenience to women but, at least, Boylan has not made her pregnant. This always seems to arrive at the wrong time, like it did on the special night with Poldy in their presentation box at the Gaiety Theatre. That was the night a well-dressed gentleman in a box above used opera glasses to stare down at her bosom.

Climbing out of bed, she sits on the chamber-pot thinking of the smooth whiteness of her thighs and the

Mr. Beerbohm Tree

3019. 5. *How do you like this old Chap*

[196]

Molly remembers being touched several times by a strange man during a performance of *Trilby*, starring Beerbohm Tree at the Gaiety Theatre.

loud noise of urination. Molly is reminded of the beautiful letters that Poldy sent her during their courting days in which he praised the beauty of her body. The words excited her so much that she fondled herself several times a day, although she never admitted this to Poldy.

At their first meeting they had stared at one another for a long time, possibly because she had the Jewish looks of her mother. The Doyles had told her that Poldy was a potential parliamentary candidate. She castigates herself for being such a fool as to believe his rubbish about Home Rule and the Land League.

She rises from the chamber-pot, puts on a sanitary

towel and climbs back into bed. Molly reflects on the lack of progress they have made over sixteen years and their large number of rented accommodations since marriage. When things were going well Poldy always stuck his foot in it, like he did at Thom's, Hely's, Cuffe's and Drimmie's. He was lucky not to be jailed over the lottery tickets and was prone to giving impudence. The next thing will probably be his dismissal from the *Freeman's Journal* because of his association with Sinn Féin or the Freemasons.

As the bells of George's Church strike two o'clock Molly is reminded of Poldy's late homecoming. She resolves to check his shirt in the morning for an emission and search his pockets for the hidden contraceptive. She wonders if he made love to Josie Breen but decides he would be afraid to do it with a married woman.

Her thoughts turn to the list of mourners at Dignam's funeral that she had seen in Boylan's newspaper. She is critical of their propensity for drink and resolves to keep Poldy out of their clutches. The deceased Paddy Dignam was an amusing little drunk who attended the Glencree Dinner. Molly recalls the memorable night when Ben Dollard borrowed formal clothes for a professional concert that were far too small, much to the hilarious amusement of his audience. Simon Dedalus was a flirtatious man who always turned up drunk for concerts and mixed his verses. He had a glorious voice and on one occasion they joined in singing a beautiful duet. Eleven years ago she had met Stephen with his parents and, earlier, as a lovely little boy at Mat Dillon's party.

In the cards that morning she had foreseen a union with a dark stranger. She would not be too old for Stephen and, if he came to stay, he might write poetry about her. At her age it would be lovely to have an intelligent and handsome poet to discuss matters of interest. She wonders what to do about Boylan, who lacks manners and refinement. Molly is critical of the vulgar manner in which Boylan exposed his private parts to her, hoping to

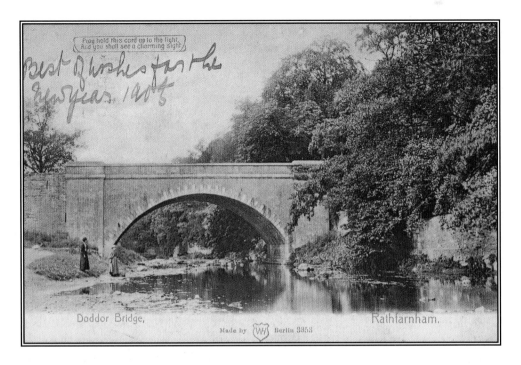

Doddor Bridge,   Rathfarnham.

Made by (W/) Berlin 3353

be admired. She should not be blamed for being still young and is critical of Poldy for his coldness towards her. The only time he embraces her is in his sleep and then it is her bottom he kisses. A woman needs to be constantly embraced to keep her young. Any man will suffice as long as you love or are loved. In the past she had considered picking up a sailor on the quays for casual sex against a wall on a dark night. On another occasion she had thought of making love to a handsome dark-eyed gypsy from the camp in Rathfarnham. She reasons that this is exactly what all men do themselves.

Molly thinks of the wild life Stephen is living and wonders why people who have a fine son are not happy. She recalls the death of her son Rudy and acknowledges the fact that she will never have another. It was their first death and, since then, things have never been the same between herself and Poldy.

She reflects on the names of people and places in Gibraltar and tries out a few words in Spanish. The idea of speaking Spanish to Stephen and learning Italian in

[197]

On another occasion she had thought of making love to a handsome dark-eyed gypsy from the camp in Rathfarnham.

[198]

She recalls the day that Poldy had said the sun was shining for her alone, as they lay among the rhododendrons on Howth Head.

Rhododendrons. Howth Castle, Demesne. Co. Dublin.

cocpeel you home.

yours. David.

10033 H.

turn pleases her. She imagines bringing Stephen his breakfast in bed and the excitement of having him stay. If he wanted to read in bed during the morning, Poldy could just as easily make breakfast for two as for one. Molly resolves to buy a pair of red slippers, a semi-transparent gown and a snappy dress jacket.

Poldy will be given a final chance, so she decides to get up early and serve his tea and eggs. She will sing, be generally happy about the house and allow him a view of her underwear as she dresses to go out. She has a good mind to tell Poldy everything because it is his fault that his wife is a wanton adulteress. He will be allowed a degree of sexual intimacy, then she will ask him for money to buy underwear. She will leave him behind wondering where she has gone and lusting after her.

She will rise early and order flowers to be delivered from Lambe's, just in case Poldy arrives home with Stephen. Her thoughts turn to nature and the beautiful countryside, with flowers of every shade and hue. She recalls the day that Poldy had said the sun was shining for her alone, as they lay among the rhododendrons on Howth Head. She responded to his long kiss and led him on to ask for more. At first she did not reply but then her eyes told him to ask again. She drew him down so that he could sense her breasts and smell her perfume. His heart was pounding as she yielded with a final word of yes.

~22~

Wandering Characters, 16 June 1904

O N 16 JUNE 1904 James Joyce fielded hundreds of fictional characters, old and new, on a one-day outing through the streets of Dublin and environs. Thousands of other names are included in this immense catalogue of historical, literary and contemporary characters which, at times, can be quite bewildering. There is the added difficulty of implied knowledge about some of the leading characters that have featured prominently in Joyce's earlier work. For example, the character of Stephen Dedalus is particularly vague without the benefit of a previous reading of *A Portrait of the Artist as a Young Man*. Significantly, Stephen's secondary education at Belvedere College is ignored in *Ulysses*, while Clongowes Wood features prominently throughout.

For the purpose of portraying these interesting characters only their history and activities, as documented in *Ulysses*, are taken into consideration. Joyce utilized numerous lists, locations and events, of which the following serve our purpose: the funeral of Patrick Dignam, Mr Bloom's list of suitors, the wanderers of 16 June 1904, Davy Byrne's, the Ormond Hotel, Barney Kiernan's, Burke's, the National Library of Ireland, the cabman's shelter, and Bella Cohen's brothel and environs.

The Funeral of Patrick Dignam

The theme of death permeates *Ulysses* and is particularly exploited in the 'Hades' episode. The funeral cortège of Patrick Dignam leaves the family home at 9 Newbridge Avenue, Sandymount, in a procession of three horse-drawn carriages. The cortège crosses four waterways, the Dodder, Grand Canal, Liffey and Royal Canal, on the journey to Prospect Cemetery, Glasnevin. After the religious ceremony in the chapel, thirteen characters (death's number) assemble to witness the burial of Patrick Dignam: Leopold Paula Bloom, Bernard Corrigan, Martin Cunningham, Simon Dedalus, Patrick Aloysius Dignam, Joseph Hynes, Cornelius Kelleher, Thomas Kernan, Edward J. Lambert, John Henry Menton, M'Intosh, John O'Connell and Jack Power.

The following characters are among the dead remembered in the thoughts and conversations of the living: Ellen Bloom, Rudolph Bloom, Rudy Bloom, Mary Dedalus, Patrick Dignam, Robert Emmet, Daniel O'Connell, Charles Stewart Parnell and Emily Sinico.

Leopold Paula Bloom, alias Henry Flower, is known as Poldy to his wife and usually called Mr Bloom by James Joyce. He was born on 6 May 1866 at 52 Clanbrassil Street, Dublin, the only son of a Jewish father and a Christian mother. After a spell at Mrs Ellis's nursery school, Mr Bloom was enrolled as a day-pupil at High School, 40 Harcourt Street, a well-respected educational establishment for Protestant boys. He left High School in 1880 and thereafter educated himself by reading books of an informative nature, most notably on astronomy and history. He constantly exercises his highly inquisitive mind with visits to museums and libraries, and seems well-informed on most subjects. His innate cunning and patience enable him to overcome the vicissitudes and difficulties presented by life.

Mr Bloom was baptized a Protestant, which faith he

HOUSE PARTY AT LISMORE CASTLE, MAY 1904.

[199]

This house party at Lismore Castle features two real-life characters from *Ulysses*, King Edward and the lord lieutenant of Ireland, William Humble, Earl of Dudley.

formally abjured in favour of Catholicism immediately prior to his marriage. Nowadays he professes atheism on the grounds of his own logical reasoning that it is impossible to prove the existence of Heaven or God, there being no way of proceeding from the known to the unknown. Mr Bloom is loosely employed as an advertising canvasser for the *Freeman's Journal* newspaper, having previously held a variety of positions at Joseph Cuffe's cattle superintendents, Drimmie's insurance agents, Hely's stationers and printers, and Thom's printers. It is said that he lost several of these jobs for being a know-all with a propensity for putting his foot in it.

In 1888 he married Madame Marion Tweedy, the concert singer. They had two children, Milly and Rudy. Rudy died in 1894, eleven days after birth, and this tragedy, combined with his father's suicide, is a never-ending source of grief to Mr Bloom. Although reasonably well-off, with cash, stocks and income, Mr Bloom is always on the lookout for means of making extra money. However, irregularities with his Hungarian lottery tickets scheme landed him in trouble with his Freemason lodge. At one

Fisher Folk.

10033 D.

Howth. Co. Dublin.

My dear Friend
I like so much the
new series of parisian Cards, with
plenty of room for a kind message
from you. Best of hand shakes
from your friend by the sea
Millicent.

27. 9. 04.

time he was thought of as a future member of parliament and is recognized for his support of Parnell and the Sinn Féin movement. While he has garnered a reputation for tightness with money, he is known for helping those down on their luck and for contributing generously to the Dignam fund. Mr Bloom is fair, kind and considerate to his fellow man and opposed to all forms of bigotry and violence. He is aware that his wife is having a torrid affair with her business manager, Blazes Boylan, and accepts the situation with pragmatism and philosophy. Mr Bloom consorts with prostitutes and engages in a secret risqué correspondence with a young girl called Martha Clifford. He is not adverse to the odd bout of onanism and has acquired a fetish for women's feet and underwear.

Bernard Corrigan is the brother-in-law of the deceased Patrick Dignam and known as Uncle Barney to his nephew, Patsy Dignam. He travels to Glasnevin in the second mourning coach and carries the wreath to the graveside. Not to be confused with Father Bernard Corrigan, Molly Bloom's confessor.

[200]

These fishermen would have interested John Millington Synge, but not James Joyce. The main characters of *Ulysses* are drawn from the familiar middle-class background of his former day-to-day life in Dublin and environs.

Martin Cunningham is a decent, charitable individual who works in Dublin Castle and is married to an alcoholic wife. He is closely associated with the collection for Dignam's family and in sorting out the problems of insurance and young Patsy Dignam's future. Cunningham has arranged to meet Mr Bloom at Barney Kiernan's in the afternoon so that they can travel together to the Dignam family home about the insurance. He arrives with Jack Power and Crofton just in time to rescue Mr Bloom from the wrath of an irate Citizen.

Simon Dedalus is a widower with no visible means of support other than by borrowing or pawning. He lives in Cabra with his four daughters, Boody, Dilly, Katey and Maggy. Simon is proud of his only son, Stephen, but fears that Buck Mulligan is a bad influence on him. At Dignam's funeral he weeps for his dead wife, May, a member of the Goulding family, whom he loathes and constantly criticizes. A shortage of money for food at the table does not prevent him doing the rounds of drinking establishments with his middle-class friends, most of whom are as reduced in circumstances as he is himself. At the Ormond Hotel Simon orders a whiskey, flirts with the barmaids and sings 'M'Appari' for his friends. Molly Bloom remembers his flirting ways and the glorious tone of his voice, which is probably why he appears on the list of her suitors.

Patrick Aloysius Dignam, known as Patsy, is the eldest son of the deceased and, strangely, is the only member of Dignam's family, other than his Uncle Barney, to attend the burial at Glasnevin. The well-wishers' decisions to board Patsy at the Artane Industrial School while seeking a job for his younger sister at Todd's, the Dublin merchandiser, is an enigma only explained if we assume that Patsy is either a little wayward and in need of correction or a young orphan requiring a useful trade. Special guidance, education and job training for wayward or

Dublin. O'Connell's Monument. *July 8·1904*
My dear Mrs George I am sending
you these cards & I hope you will like
them I am very sorry that I could

The 'Hades' episode concerns death and the memory of the dead, a theme that permeates *Ulysses.* Within sight of this O'Connell Monument, Prospect Cemetery, Glasnevin, thirteen mourners pay their final respects to Patrick Dignam.

orphaned Catholic boys was provided since 1870 by the Christian Brothers, Artane, and not at the O'Brien Institute for Destitute Children, Marino. After the funeral Patsy is sent on an errand to Mangan's for pork steaks. As he wanders through Wicklow Street, Grafton Street and Nassau Street, he ponders the ramifications of his father's death and salutes the viceregal cavalcade.

Joseph Hynes is the newspaper reporter responsible for the account of Dignam's funeral in the *Evening Telegraph* on 16 June 1904. He is a strong nationalist and instigates a visit to Parnell's grave after Dignam's burial. At Barney

Kiernan's Hynes buys drink generously for all the company yet has ignored several hints from Mr Bloom about a debt of three shillings.

Cornelius Kelleher, known as Corny, is the manager of the funeral establishment of Messrs H.J. O'Neill & Son, 164 North Strand Road, the firm contracted to conduct the proceedings of the Dignam funeral. There is reasonable evidence to support the suspicions of several characters that Corny is a police informer. In the 'Circe' episode Corny is instrumental in saving Stephen Dedalus from arrest by two policemen.

Thomas Kernan works as an agent for Pulbrook Robertson, the tea merchants. Today he has made a good business deal, which he attributes to his well-dressed appearance and entertaining conversation. Walking near Guinness's Brewery, Kernan is unlucky to miss the progress of the viceregal cavalcade but does see the flash of the only moving motor car in *Ulysses*. At the Ormond Hotel Kernan celebrates his good fortune with his friends and asks Ben Dollard to sing his favourite ballad, 'The Croppy Boy'.

Edward J. Lambert, commonly called Ned, works for a seed merchant in St Mary's Abbey. In the 'Wandering Rocks' episode he conducts Reverend Hugh C. Love on a tour of this historic building associated with Silken Thomas. Lambert, an amusing character, lampoons Dan Dawson's speech in the offices of the *Evening Telegraph* and leaves with Simon Dedalus for a drink at the Oval pub. He turns up again at Barney Kiernan's, this time with J.J. O'Molloy, where the row between Mr Bloom and the Citizen paralyzes him with laughter.

John Henry Menton, the solicitor and commissioner for oaths and affidavits, has offices at 27 Bachelor's Walk. Menton attends the Dignam burial in his capacity as a former employer of the deceased. As the mourners exit Prospect Cemetery Mr Bloom points to a dent in Menton's hat and is snubbed for his pains. The enmity between the two men dates from Mat Dillon's party in Roundtown, where Mr Bloom not only beat Menton at bowls but won the heart of Marion Tweedy, fresh from Gibraltar. Menton still fancies Molly Bloom and wonders why a beautiful woman like her would marry a coon like Bloom. He appears on the list of suitors but Molly has scant regard for Menton, with his peculiar eyes and gross impudence.

M'Intosh is a mysterious character sometimes called Bartle the Bread. He turns up as an unidentified stranger at Dignam's burial wearing a brown macintosh and appears among the mourners in the *Evening Telegraph* as M'Intosh, due to a misunderstanding between Mr Bloom and Hynes. M'Intosh is seen during the 'Wandering Rocks' episode and makes an appearance at Burke's pub. There are several hints that M'Intosh may be the man who loves a deceased woman, probably Mrs Emily Sinico.

John O'Connell, the caretaker of Prospect Cemetery, Glasnevin, greets the mourners at Dignam's funeral and recounts an amusing story of two drunken Dubliners on a visit to the graveyard. O'Connell supervises the burial and receives the official papers from Corny Kelleher.

Jack Power, a government employee at Dublin Castle, travels in the first mourning coach with Martin Cunningham, Simon Dedalus and Mr Bloom. Power is a handsome and courteous individual who is reputed to maintain a non-carnal relationship with a barmaid at either the Moira or Jurys. During the journey to Glasnevin, Power rescues Mr Bloom from uncomfortable references to Blazes Boylan with flattering remarks about Molly Bloom's singing career. Power introduces the sub-

[202]

The village of Finglas is mentioned several times during the 'Hades' episode. Prospect Cemetery and the house where the Childs murder took place are located on the Finglas Road. Mr Bloom's mother and son, Rudy, are buried in the family plot on the Finglas side of the cemetery.

[203]

A Dublin jaunting car or hackney car, complete with a customer and cabman in control. The Glencree Dinner revellers hired one of these, as did Blazes Boylan for his visit to Molly Bloom. In the background is the National Library of Ireland, location for the entire proceedings of 'Scylla and Charybdis'.

FIONNGLAISE, sráid-bhaile i n-aice Baile Átha Cliath.

(259)

A City Jaunting Car, Dublin

Last lap, old Reg. Hope to be with you all tomorrow afternoon about 6. or half-past. This is not a bad photo. is it? The place is the library. A.E.C.D.

Castle Street, Dalkey, Dublin   Published by Richardson, Lei

Hope your & our Mother have enjoyed your holiday - das "Whit"? — V. H H

ject of suicide and is subsequently embarrassed to learn that Bloom's father committed suicide. At Barney Kiernan's Power joins in the rescue of Mr Bloom from the attack of the Citizen.

Ellen Bloom, née Higgins, the mother of Leopold Bloom, lies buried with her grandson, Rudy, in the family plot on the Finglas side of Prospect Cemetery. Raised as a Christian, she married a Jewish immigrant to Ireland called Rudolph Bloom and subsequently gave birth to only one child. This son constantly thinks of his dead mother and ponders the gruesome truth that his father, Rudolph, poisoned himself through grief shortly after the death of his beloved wife, Ellen.

Rudolph Bloom was the late proprietor of the Queen's Hotel, Ennis, County Clare. Born a Hungarian Jew, he changed his name from Virag to Bloom by deed poll.

[204]

The entire 'Nestor' episode takes place at Mr Garrett Deasy's school in Dalkey. Stephen reappears immediately after this episode on Sandymount Strand; it is a matter of conjecture whether he took a train or a Dalkey tram.

He was converted to the Irish Protestant Church by the Dublin branch of the Society for Promoting Christianity among the Jews. On 27 June 1886 Rudolph Bloom ingested aconite poison at his own hotel. He left his money and a suicide note addressed to his son, Leopold, in which he explained his wish to join his wife in death. The message included an exhortation that his son be kind to his faithful dog, Athos. It seems likely that Rudolph is buried in Ennis, as his only son Leopold visits Ennis each year on the anniversary of his father's tragic death.

Rudy Bloom, the infant son of Leopold and Molly Bloom, died on 9 January 1894, eleven days after his birth. His death marked a watershed in the married life of the Blooms, with Molly forming a distaste for intimacy with her husband after the tragedy. Rudy is constantly in the minds of both parents, particularly Mr Bloom, who fantasizes and hallucinates about his dead son.

Mary Dedalus, known as May, is the sister of Richie Goulding and the deceased wife of Simon. She died a long, lingering death from cancer and was buried on 26 June 1903 in Prospect Cemetery. The sight of her grave moves Simon Dedalus to tears and he declares that he will soon be with her in the grave. Almost a full year after her death her son Stephen is still wearing black attire in mourning, notwithstanding the fact that he had refused her dying request to kneel and pray at her deathbed. Stephen is dominated and haunted by her memory in his thoughts, dreams, conversations and fantasies.

Patrick Dignam died of apoplexy induced by excessive drinking, leaving a poverty-stricken wife and five children. Dignam is fondly remembered for his geniality but particularly for his weakness for alcohol, which cost him his job with John Henry Menton. His insurance policy is heavily mortgaged and there is little cash. Fortunately a good number of his friends are rallying strongly on the day to help the family. Dignam attended the Glencree Dinner.

Robert Emmet, the gallant Irish hero, was hanged, drawn and quartered for leading an abortive rebellion in 1803. In a famous speech from the dock Emmet requested that his epitaph should not be written and his grave remain unmarked until Ireland took her place among the nations of the earth. After Dignam's burial Mr Bloom walks alone among the graves and speculates where Emmet may have been secretly buried. Coincidentally Mr Bloom subsequently sees a copy of Emmet's speech in the window of Lionel Marks' antique shop. The memory of Emmet and the men who died for Ireland lives strongly in the minds of many of the characters in *Ulysses*.

Daniel O'Connell, known as the Liberator, is another deceased Irish political legend remembered in the 'Hades' episode. The stature of O'Connell among the Irish people is reflected in the finest and tallest memorial in Prospect Cemetery. Interestingly the mourners at Dignam's funeral have little to say about O'Connell, other than to refer briefly to the fact that his body is in the tomb while his heart is buried in Rome.

Charles Stewart Parnell, the disgraced Protestant leader, idolized by many of the characters of *Ulysses*, is also buried in Prospect Cemetery. After Dignam's burial several mourners break off to visit the fallen hero's grave at the instigation of Joe Hynes. Parnell's ruin and downfall as leader of the Irish Home Rule Party was caused by his adulterous liaison with Kitty O'Shea, later to become his wife. The husband of Kitty O'Shea took a divorce action, during which the intimate boudoir details of Parnell and his mistress were splashed all over the newspapers. Mr Bloom and other characters are highly critical of the public declaration against Parnell by the Catholic clergy and the way the majority of his former

[205]

Irishtown is adjacent to Sandymount Strand and the home of Richie and Sara Goulding, Stephen's uncle and aunt. The Dignam cortège swerves to avoid the tram tracks near Watery Lane, Irishtown, where Mr Bloom observes Stephen walking nearby. Stephen subsequently decides not to pay a call on his uncle and aunt at Strasburg Terrace, Irishtown.

[206]

This picture, taken from Seapoint, of a much-travelled railway line, looks south towards Monkstown. Out of view, the tracks proceed north along the curve of the sea, turning landwards when in sight of Cock Lake, Sandymount Strand. The next stop is Sydney Parade Railway Station, where Mrs Emily Sinico was accidentally killed in 1903.

Hely's, Limited.]   "ST. MATTHEW'S NATIONAL SCHOOLS, IRISHTOWN."   *[Printers, Dublin.*

View of Salthill Hotel, Monkstown, Co. Dublin.

13-5-04

Trust you feel rested by now — We drove into Dublin after luncheon and have just returned. It rained of course — Let me know where you reach Lancs. Hope you put my name on the bike ∞

supporters turned against him for the relatively minor sin of adultery.

Emily Sinico was accidentally killed at Sydney Parade Railway Station on 14 October 1903 and was buried at Prospect Cemetery. Mr Bloom attended her funeral and remembers her tragic death as he wanders among the dead. Mrs Sinico appears to be of deep interest to Mr Bloom as he raises the question of her death with Stephen Dedalus, who indicates that he did not know her.

Mr Bloom's List of Suitors

Of the many lists of names that appear in *Ulysses*, none is more interesting than the series of twenty-five men compiled by Mr Bloom in the 'Ithaca' episode. This is generally called the list of Molly's suitors, because of the obvious Homeric allusion to the suitors who waited for the hand of Penelope in marriage. While the hopeful Greeks adequately fit the definition of suitors, Mr Bloom's men fall into the more wide-ranging categories of admirers and lovers, some of whom are would-be happy contenders for the hand in marriage of the lovely, if not notorious, Madame Marion Tweedy.

Four men in this series are anonymous: the farmer, an organ-grinder, a bootblack and a stranger. It is reasonable to assume that the farmer took a fancy to Molly Bloom on a visit to the Horse Show at Ballsbridge. The organ-playing street performer and the bootblack outside the General Post Office would have been less than masculine had they failed to admire the beautiful songstress strolling through the streets of Dublin on the arm of her husband. Two strange gentlemen admired Molly Bloom in the Gaiety Theatre. One used crowding in the pits during a performance of *Trilby* as an excuse to foist his unwelcome touches on her. The other used opera glasses to ogle her from above, on the special and only occasion that the

The Duke of Devonshire.   The Marquis of Londonderry.
H.R.H. The Duke of Connaught.   H.M. The King.   His Excellency The Lord Lieutenant.

HELY'S, LIMITED.   PHŒNIX PARK RACES, APRIL, 1904.   DUBLIN.

[207]

The sport of kings is much enjoyed by the characters of *Ulysses*. The main sporting event of 16 June 1904 was the Gold Cup at Ascot, won by outsider Throwaway. The shock result is badly received in Dublin by everyone except Mr Bloom, who neither lost or won on the race.

Blooms had a box at the theatre, courtesy of Michael Gunn. It is always unwise to make Freudian assumptions about Mr Bloom, particularly in matters of sexual selection. However, the evidence points to the gentleman of fashion, complete with strong opera glasses, pivotally poised above the bosomy beauty, as the Gaiety stranger selected by Mr Bloom as the fifteenth suitor.

The names of the following make up the list: Lieutenant Harry Mulvey, Penrose, Bartell d'Arcy, Professor Goodwin, Julius Mastiansky, John Henry Menton, Father Bernard Corrigan, Alderman Robert O'Reilly, Matthew Dillon, Valentine Blake Dillon, Christopher Callinan, T. Lenehan, Benjamin Dollard, Simon Dedalus, Andrew Burke, Joseph Cuffe, Wisdom Hely, Alderman John Hooper, Dr Francis Brady, Father Sebastian and Hugh E. Boylan.

Lieutenant Harry Mulvey, born in Cappoquin, County Waterford, was a British naval officer attached to *H.M.S. Calypso*. Mulvey first saw Marion Tweedy in the Calle Real, Gibraltar, and later arranged an assignation by letter.

H.E. Cardinal Vannutelli.   His Grace The Archbishop of Dublin.

PROCESSION ON THE WAY TO THE CATHEDRAL.

Sackville St.   Dublin.

He was the first man to exchange intimate kisses with Marion. They spent a final day of passion, short of full intimacy, on the rocks overlooking a fir-tree cove. Although they exchanged vows to renew their love when Mulvey returned, she never saw him again.

Penrose was a delicate-looking student who stared through the windows in the hope of an erotic glimpse of Molly when the Blooms had lodgings with the Citrons in Lombard Street West. Poor Penrose's peccadillo seems to have arisen when the breastfeeding of Milly was in full flow. On one occasion the half-naked mother foiled the luckless voyeur with a last-gasp snatch of a towel.

Bartell d'Arcy is a well-known professional tenor who sang at the Glencree Dinner. He earned his colours as a suitor by kissing Molly on the choir stairs following her rendering of 'Ave Maria'. Mr Bloom dislikes d'Arcy intensely and speaks disparagingly of his conceit and waxed moustache.

Professor Goodwin, the elderly piano accompanist, is renowned for his outlandish performances when under the influence of alcohol. He has accompanied Molly Bloom and Ben Dollard in concert and attended the Glencree Dinner.

Julius Mastiansky was a Jewish friend of Molly and Leopold Bloom in the early days of their married life. The mild and quiet Mastiansky spent many pleasant evenings with the newlyweds, chattering and playing his zither in their parlour. Mrs Mastiansky reddened the cheeks of the young bride with intimate details of her husband's bizarre bedroom preferences.

Father Bernard Corrigan, a Catholic priest, was at one time a confessor to Molly Bloom. His appearance on Mr Bloom's list of suitors owes much to Molly's confession to him that she had been touched by a man. When Father Corrigan asked where, Molly, much to her subsequent embarrassment, told him it was on the canal bank.

Alderman Robert O'Reilly appears to be the only candidate for the suitor, merely named Maggot O'Reilly. In 'Lestrygonians' Mr Bloom recalls Alderman O'Reilly's drunken escapade at the Glencree Dinner of 1894, when he emptied his port into his soup and slurped noisily before the appropriate signal to start. Significantly, this sole recollection of an O'Reilly, other than on his list, occurs during rapid random thoughts exclusively featuring suitors, successively as follows: Widsom Hely, Val Dillon, Alderman Robert O'Reilly, Professor Goodwin, Penrose and Bartell d'Arcy. In the absence of any other hard evidence, it seems reasonable to deduce that the proverbially 'drunk as a maggot' or 'maggoty drunk' alderman of Glencree infamy is none other than suitor Maggot O'Reilly.

Matthew Dillon, generally called Mat, hosted the well-remembered party in the lilac garden of his home at Medina Villa, Kimmage Road, Roundtown, in June 1887. A few of his five daughters were friendly with Marion Tweedy, then freshly returned from Gibraltar. It was at Dillon's party that the darkly handsome Leopold Bloom was introduced to his future wife. Among the other guests were John Henry Menton and Simon and May Dedalus with their young son, Stephen.

Valentine Blake Dillon, known as Val, is a brother of Mat and the former lord mayor of Dublin who attended the 1894 Glencree Dinner in that capacity. Val Dillon certainly deserves to be on the list of suitors or admirers because, at the well-remembered dinner, much to Molly's disgust, he stared and leered at her with his dirty-looking eyes.

Pro Cathedral, Marlborough Street.

HELY'S, LIMITED, DUBLIN.

[210]

The Cathedral of St Mary or the Pro-Cathedral was located on the fringes of the red-light district described in 'Circe'. In 'Eumaeus' Stephen suggests a cheap dosshouse in Marlborough Street as a possible place for Lord John Corley to spend the night.

Christopher Callinan features on Mr Bloom's list of suitors, perhaps because he once shared a lift home from the Glencree Dinner with the Blooms and Lenehan. His main claim to fame is that he is a brother-in-law of Ignatius Gallaher, a legendary journalist with the *Freeman's Journal* who developed an ingenious code to transmit news of the Phoenix Park murders by the Invincibles to the *New York World.*

T. Lenehan, more commonly called just Lenehan, is a tipster for the *Sport* newspaper. He is a man about town, gambler, raconteur, sponger and ubiquitous in drinking sessions. Lenehan boasts of a furtive sexual encounter with Molly Bloom on the way home from the Glencree Dinner. At the Ormond Hotel Lenehan flirts with the barmaids and joins with Blazes Boylan in a toast to their anticipated winnings on Sceptre in the Gold Cup at Ascot. Lenehan is one of the main causes of the row at Barney Kiernan's, revealing that Mr Bloom had a substantial windfall on the outsider, Throwaway. Lenehan

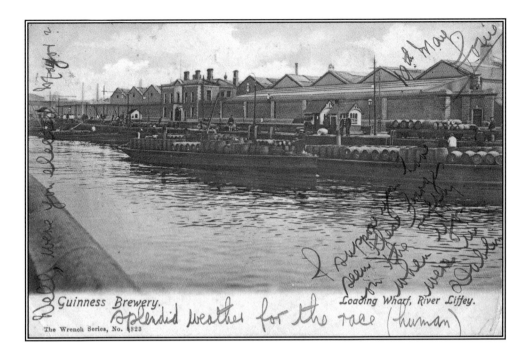

Guinness Brewery.   Loading Wharf, River Liffey.

The Wrench Series, No. 4923

Splendid weather for the race (human)

turns up at the medical students' drinking party at the maternity hospital, Holles Street and needless to say is with them again in Burke's public house.

Benjamin Dollard, or Ben to his friends, is a gout-ridden, bankrupted businessman with massive unpaid debts. Drink is the cause of his ruin and he now lives in the Iveagh Home for down-and-out men. Ben is a singer of professional concert standard, having performed with Bartell d'Arcy at the Glencree Dinner and with Professor Goodwin on the memorable occasion of the tight pants. He joins his good friend, Simon Dedalus, for a drink in the Ormond Hotel and gives a wonderful rendition of 'The Croppy Boy'.

Andrew Burke, nicknamed Pisser, stayed at the City Arms Hotel when the Blooms were resident there. Pisser spied on the activities of the Blooms and always turned up when they were having a row. It was Pisser who spread the rumour about Mr Bloom playing up to Mrs

[211]

The barges filled with barrels of export stout are being loaded for transport down the Liffey to the Dublin docks. The characters of *Ulysses* rarely refer to Guinness by name, preferring to order wine of the country, Ardilaun's, etc.

Riordan in the hope of getting into her will. Molly Bloom hates Pisser and recalls the time he turned up like a bad penny on the pier in Bray to witness the rescue of the Blooms from a boating fiasco.

Joseph Cuffe is a superintendent of cattle sales, with offices at 5 Smithfield, reasonably adjacent to the Dublin Cattle Market. Mr Bloom worked for Cuffe as a clerk but was sacked for what Molly described as pigheadedness. Molly visited Cuffe in a failed attempt to have her husband reinstated. On that day Cuffe graduated to Mr Bloom's list with his unabashed admiration for Molly's bosom.

Wisdom Hely is a prominent printer, stationer and owner of Messrs Hely's Ltd, 89, 90 & 91 Dame Street, Dublin. Mr Bloom worked for Hely as a blotting-paper salesman, and on one occasion was rebuffed by Hely on an issue of advertising. Hely believes in advertising because, on 16 June 1904, five men parade around the streets of Dublin with the five letters of Hely's boldly emblazoned on their five tall hats.

Alderman John Hooper is an old friend of the Blooms who gave them an embalmed owl as a wedding present.

Dr Francis Brady was Molly Bloom's doctor at the time Milly was being weaned. Mr Bloom obtained a belladonna prescription from the old doctor to ease the soreness of Molly's breasts.

Father Sebastian, the mystery priest from Mount Argus, appears on the list for no apparent reason.

Hugh E. Boylan, known as Blazes, is a well-known man about town, impresario, advertiser, gambler, ladies' man and Molly Bloom's present lover. Like most of Dublin, Mr Bloom knows of the affair and regards Boylan as a cheating, boastful cad. Boylan has arranged by letter to call at the Bloom's house to finalize details of his forth-coming promotion in Belfast, featuring Molly, John McCormack and other celebrities. It is obvious that the main objective of his visit is an afternoon of torrid love-making assisted, no doubt, by an earlier feed of oysters at the Red Bank restaurant. Boylan has a good bet on Sceptre for himself and Molly, and toasts the horse's anticipated victory at the Ormond Hotel. After flirting with the barmaids, Boylan departs the hotel for Eccles Street on a jingling hackney car and is secretly observed by a hapless Mr Bloom.

[212]

The picturesque windmill of Skerries, eighteen miles from the capital, is where Buck Mulligan is reputed to have rescued a man from drowning. There are many references in *Ulysses* to the small fishing villages of Skerries, Malahide and Howth, all to the north of central Dublin.

The Wanderers of 16 June 1904

The 'Wandering Rocks' episode shows a large number of major and minor characters criss-crossing and mingling on the streets of Dublin for about an hour on the after-noon of 16 June 1904. The episode itself is divided into nineteen separate stories featuring most of the main characters. These moments of time in different lives are interspersed with sudden flashbacks to other happenings. In the main these flashbacks refer to the progress of Father John Conmee's walk to Artane and the viceregal cavalcade's journey to Ballsbridge.

[213]

Mr Bloom was employed by Hely's Limited, Dame Street, as a traveller for blotting-paper and a collector of outstanding accounts.

The following feature prominently in the stories of the nineteen subsections: Father John Conmee, Cornelius Kelleher, Marion Bloom, The Dedalus Girls, Hugh E. Boylan, Stephen Dedalus, Miss Dunne, Edward J. Lambert, Reverend Hugh C. Love, J.J. O'Molloy, Tom Rochford, Nosey Flynn, T. Lenehan, C.P. M'Coy, Leopold Paula Bloom, Simon Dedalus, Tom Kernan, Father Bob Cowley, Benjamin Dollard, Martin Cunningham, Jack Power, Malachi Mulligan, Haines, Cashel Boyle O'Connor Fitzmaurice Tisdall Farrell, Patrick Aloysius Dignam, William Humble (Earl of Dudley) and Lady Dudley.

Skerries.

How do you stand Lizzie? I can't know. She is the greatest little Lizzie I ever met. Don't mind her if she says she is enjoying herself —

She tells the most awful lies I ever heard — What do you think of the view? — It is one of the principal views in the whole place. Joined in love by "Our Sister." Yours very sincerely, Snetta C.

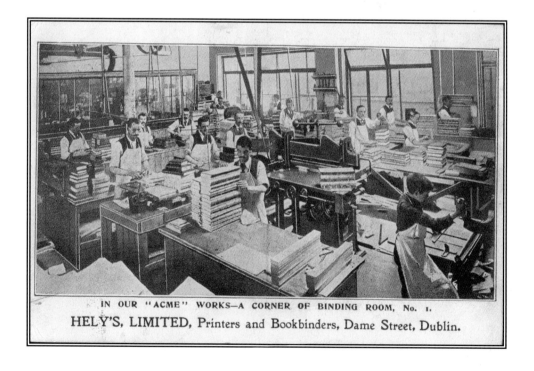

IN OUR "ACME" WORKS—A CORNER OF BINDING ROOM, No. 1.

HELY'S, LIMITED, Printers and Bookbinders, Dame Street, Dublin.

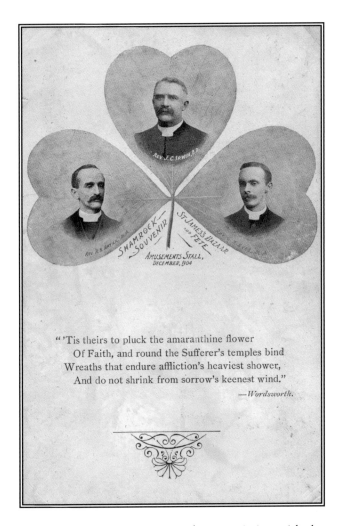

The following are mentioned in association with the progress of the viceregal cavalcade in the nineteenth subsection of the 'Wandering Rocks' episode: Thomas Kernan, Richard Goulding, Mina Kennedy, Lydia Douce, Simon Dedalus, Reverend Hugh C. Love, T. Lenehan, C.P. M'Coy, Gertrude MacDowell, John Wyse Nolan, Tom Rochford, Nosey Flynn, Malachi Mulligan, Haines, John Howard Parnell, Dilly Dedalus, John Henry Menton, Denis Breen, Josephine Breen, Professor Denis J. Maginni, Hugh E. Boylan, Cashel Boyle O'Connor Fitzmaurice Tisdall Farrell, Hornblower, Patrick Aloysius Dignam, M'Intosh and Almidano Artifoni.

Father John Conmee SJ is the superior of St Francis Xavier's Church, Gardiner Street, and was the rector of Clongowes Wood College when Stephen Dedalus and Punch Costello were students. A charitable and kind man, today Father Conmee is on an errand of mercy to the Artane Industrial School in the expectation of boarding young Patsy Dignam with the Christian Brothers, presumably to learn a good trade. Father Conmee is also a writer with a particular interest in the romance of early history.

Marion Bloom, wife of Leopold Bloom, is the well-known concert soprano who performs under her maiden name of Madame Marion Tweedy. She was born in Gibraltar on 8 September 1870. Her father, Brian Tweedy, was a drum major in the Royal Dublin Fusiliers and her mother, Lunita Laredo, was a Spanish Jewess. She is shortly to make an important appearance in Belfast on the same concert bill as J.C. Doyle and John McCormack. This major concert tour is being organized by Blazes Boylan, her newly acquired business manager and lover.

A letter has arrived from Boylan on the morning of 16 June 1904, advising that he will be calling at 4 p.m. that afternoon with a programme for the concert. Molly is aware that Poldy has some idea about their affair but will not let him have the satisfaction of finding out for sure. Molly claims to have known more about men and life at fifteen than all her singing rivals combined will know at fifty. Her assertion is given substance by her torrid descriptions of the afternoon's lovemaking with Boylan, which have the hallmark of a woman well-versed in extramarital activity.

Although there is no evidence of full sexual relations with anybody other than Boylan and her husband, she seems willing enough to take Stephen Dedalus as a lover. A certain amount of sly innuendo circulates among the characters about her sexual reputation. While Poldy numbers her suitors at twenty-five, she accounts for a little over half that number in her end-of-day reverie and, of these, many are merely admirers. Interestingly, her husband knows nothing about her handsome boyfriend, Lieutenant Stanley Gardner, fondly remembered for his unsurpassed kissing ability.

Full sexual relations with Poldy ceased approximately eleven years ago. Her affair with Boylan has not helped her relationship with Poldy. Molly is critical of her husband's peccadillos and his inability to hold down a regular job. Her thoughts constantly return to sex and her forthcoming assignations with Boylan. He does not feature prominently in her future plans, which may include an affair with Stephen Dedalus or a rekindling of her old passion with Poldy. It is Poldy who is last on her mind, in those final pre-sleep seconds, and the day when she surrendered herself to him for the first time among the rhododendrons of Howth.

The Dedalus Girls, Boody, Dilly, Katey and Maggy, make several appearances in the subsections of the 'Wandering Rocks' episode. Dilly collects money from her father for food and later meets her brother, Stephen, who agonizes over her poverty-stricken appearance. Maggy stays at home in Cabra boiling clothes and preparing a meal of bread and pea soup obtained from Sister Mary Patrick. Katey and Boody are critical of their father's improvidence.

Stephen Dedalus, known as Stevie to himself and Kinch to Buck Mulligan, was born in 1882, the only son of Simon and May Dedalus. Stephen was baptized a Catholic at the Church of the Three Patrons, Rathgar, his godmother being Miss Kate Morkan, 15 Usher's Island. He was educated at the Jesuit boarding-school of Clongowes Wood, Sallins, County Kildare and at University College, 86 Stephen's Green North. In 1902 he received a bachelor of arts degree from the Royal University, the examining body. Shortly after graduation

[215]

In 1903 Madame Marion Tweedy made a concert appearance at St Teresa's Hall, Clarendon Street. Her husband has a distinct aversion to Carmelite nuns because of the difficulty in collecting money on their outstanding accounts when he worked for Wisdom Hely.

Carmelite Church, Clarendon Street.

Stephen left Dublin for Paris where he became part of the bohemian life there, studied at her famous libraries and formed a friendship with the exiled Irish revolutionary, Kevin Egan.

In 1903 he returned from Paris at his father's request because his mother was dying from cancer. By then a lapsed Catholic, Stephen refused his mother's last wish that he kneel and pray at her bedside, on the stubborn principle that he could not serve a religion in which he did not believe. Today, almost a year after her death, Stephen still wears black in mourning for his dead

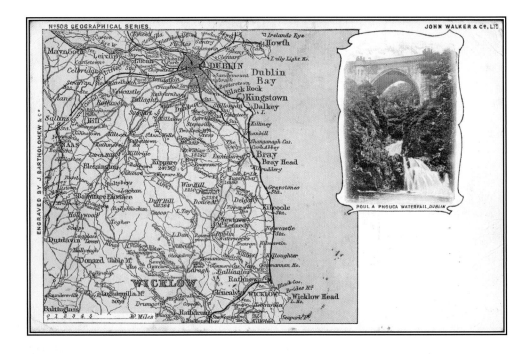

No 508 GEOGRAPHICAL SERIES.

JOHN WALKER & Co, Ltd

ENGRAVED BY J. BARTHOLOMEW & Co

POUL A PHOUCA WATERFALL, DUBLIN

mother. He agonizes all day about her grisly death, his loneliness, alienation and the poverty of his family.

Stephen regards himself as a poet with aspirations to produce a great literary masterpiece at some future date. He works as a part-time teacher in Dalkey and has rented accommodation nearby at the Martello tower in Sandycove with Haines and Buck Mulligan. After breakfast Stephen sets off on a day of extraordinary experiences, the pinnacle of which is a drunken visit to a brothel, followed by a fight in which he is knocked unconscious and ultimately rescued by Mr Bloom. Aloof and somewhat critical of his contemporaries, he is acutely aware of his exclusion from Dublin literary circles, evidenced by not being invited to George Moore's soirée and his omission from the forthcoming anthology of young Irish poets by George Russell. By day's end he has resolved to break with Mulligan, not to return to the family home or the Martello tower and to give up his job as a teacher.

[216]

Although not named on this map of Wicklow, the Glencree Reformatory is located about midway up the Glencree River. It would seem that the Blooms, Lenehan and Chris Callinan took the more arduous journey over the Featherbed on their way home from the Glencree Dinner, rather than the relatively easier route via Enniskerry and the Scalp.

Miss Dunne works as a secretary for Blazes Boylan and seems to spend her day reading trashy novels and thinking about her social life. We learn from Miss Dunne's typing that the day in question is 16 June 1904.

Reverend Hugh C. Love, a young Protestant clergyman, is engaged in writing a book on Irish history. While researching his project in St Mary's Abbey, he is assisted by Ned Lambert. Reverend Love has served a writ for non-payment of rent against his tenant, Father Bob Cowley which, as it transpires, inadvertently saves Father Cowley from the bailiffs of Reuben J. Dodd.

J.J. O'Molloy, sometimes called Jack, is a down-at-heel barrister ruined from gambling and high living. Judgments have been registered against him in *Stubb's Gazette* and he is inundated with writs and garnishee orders from a host of creditors. Today he is on a doomed errand to borrow money from Myles Crawford at the offices of the *Evening Telegraph*. At one time O'Molloy was regarded as one of the cleverest junior barristers in Ireland but now conducts a diminishing practice. In Barney Kiernan's O'Molloy dispenses unpaid legal advice on a variety of subjects, including the Denis Breen post-card hoax and the Canada swindle case.

Tom Rochford is famous for the rescue of a man who was in danger of being smothered from sewer gas. Rochford has invented a machine which shows the act in progress at music halls at any given time, which he demonstrates to Nosey Flynn, M'Coy and Lenehan. Rochford is a customer of Davy Byrne's pub, where he discusses the Gold Cup with Bantam Lyons and Paddy Leonard.

Nosey Flynn is a habitual frequenter of Davy Byrne's pub where he sits in his nook, ready to engage all comers in conversation. Although Mr Bloom is wary of Flynn's

Rotunda, Dublin.

question about the organizer of Molly's concert, he considers Flynn to be without guile.

C.P. M'Coy, known as Charley or plain M'Coy, is an assistant to the coroner, Louis Byrne, at the Dublin Morgue. M'Coy was at one time an advertising canvasser for the *Freeman's Journal* but lost this job for the alleged misappropriation of the proceeds of advertisements. M'Coy asks Mr Bloom to include his name on the list of mourners at Dignam's funeral because of a drowning case at Sandycove. Mr Bloom is subsequently amused to see M'Coy's name in the *Evening Telegraph* listed among those present at Dignam's funeral. M'Coy's wife, Fanny, is another concert soprano with a forthcoming engagement.

Father Bob Cowley is a defrocked or non-practising Catholic priest and friend of Simon Dedalus and Ben Dollard. Father Cowley is being pursued by the bailiffs on foot of a writ issued against him by Reuben J. Dodd.

[217]

At this point Dignam's funeral cortège was overtaken by another hearse carrying the coffin of an illegitimate child. Dignam's cortège and later Boylan's hackney car took a right bearing up the steep incline of the Rotunda, Rutland Square. Mr Bloom attended a performance of Albert Hengler's famous circus at this venue.

[218]

Actors and actresses feature throughout *Ulysses*, including Martin Harvey, Beerbohm Tree, Lily Langtry and Marie Kendal. They had a celebrity status similar to film stars and pop idols of the present day. Although love is a theme of *Ulysses*, the beautiful, popular and aptly named Miss Mabel Love is, unfortunately, omitted.

Ben Dollard ascertains that Dodd's writ is worthless because Father Cowley's landlord, Reverend Love, has a prior claim. Father Cowley joins the fun in the Ormond Hotel where he accompanies his two friends, Simon Dedalus and Ben Dollard, on the piano.

Malachi Mulligan, known as Buck, lives with Haines and Stephen Dedalus in rented accommodation at the Martello tower. A plump medical student and writer of blasphemous and scurrilous compositions, Mulligan is, nonetheless, accepted in Dublin literary circles. Mulligan is expected to have an excellent career in medicine and is admired for his bravery in rescuing a drowning man. The relationship between Mulligan and Stephen is uneasy and quarrelsome, with Stephen mainly on the receiving end of Mulligan's taunts and jibes. Simon Dedalus regards Mulligan as a very bad influence on his son's life while Stephen considers Mulligan an enemy and resolves to completely break with him. Mr Bloom warns Stephen not to trust Mulligan because he believes that Mulligan's so-called friendship is motivated by envy or the opportunity to pick Stephen's brains.

Haines, the English friend of Buck Mulligan, is a writer with an interest in Gaelic culture. During the night of 15 June 1904, Haines rants and raves in his sleep about shooting a black panther, which annoys Stephen to the point of threatening to leave the tower. The next day Haines visits the National Library, buys a few books and meets Mulligan at the D.B.C. restaurant, Dame Street, from where they view the progress of the viceregal cavalcade.

Cashel Boyle O'Connor Fitzmaurice Tisdall Farrell is a street character and eccentric who strides about the city in a peculiar fashion, taking particular care to walk outside lampposts.

William Humble, Earl of Dudley, is the viceroy and lord lieutenant of Ireland. Today he travels in cavalcade from the Viceregal Lodge in the Phoenix Park on the way to open the Mirus Bazaar in aid of funds for Mercer's Hospital. Nearly all the characters of *Ulysses* give him a cordial and respectful reception as his cavalcade passes through the streets of Dublin at an easy trot.

Lady Dudley accompanies her husband in the first carriage of the cavalcade. Her stare forces Tom Rochford to take his hands out of his pockets and doff his cap to her.

DUBLIN. THE MUSEUM.

[219]

Mr Bloom's view from Molesworth Street at the end of the 'Lestrygonians' episode. He takes action to avoid contact with Blazes Boylan, turns sharply right and into the National Museum, Kildare Street, barely visible on the extreme right. On the extreme left is the National Library of Ireland.

Today Lady Dudley is the subject of a court case before Sir Frederick Falkiner, arising from a political postcard sold to her by one of the hawkers outside the Viceregal Lodge.

Richard Goulding, known as Richie, is a cost drawer attached to the legal firm of Collis and Ward. Richie and his wife, Sara, live in Irishtown and are the uncle and aunt Stephen intended to visit when walking on Sandymount Strand. Simon Dedalus detests his in-laws, although Richie has no such hatred for Simon. He has dinner at the Ormond Hotel with Mr Bloom, who suspects Richie of perpetrating the Denis Breen postcard hoax. Richie suffers from poor health, attributable to a misspent youth.

Mina Kennedy, the blonde barmaid of the Ormond Hotel, is not quite as attractive to men as her siren colleague Miss Douce. Mina is attracted to Blazes Boylan, who ignores her in preference to Miss Douce. Nonetheless, this temptress, usually addressed as Miss Kennedy, has her own coterie of ardent admirers.

Photo by] September 17" 1904   DUBLIN HORSE SHOW, 1904.   Yr ...   [Lafaye
HIS EXCELLENCY THE LORD LIEUTENANT IN THE ENCLOSURE.
hope you had a good passage and arrived safely.

HELY'S, LIMITED,   KING EDWARD VII. AT PUNCHESTOWN, APRIL, 1904.   DUBLIN.

[220]

This real-life character of *Ulysses*, Lord Lieutenant William Humble, Earl of Dudley, is doing the rounds at the most important event in the Dublin social calendar.

Lydia Douce, the bronze-haired barmaid and other siren of the Ormond Hotel, is flirtatious and attractive to men, particularly in view of her freshly acquired holiday suntan. She performs a party piece on demand that involves lifting her skirt and smacking her elastic garter against her thigh. Miss Douce is quite surprised that her charms failed to keep Blazes Boylan at the Ormond Hotel.

Gertrude MacDowell, called Gerty, is the object of Mr Bloom's lust on Sandymount Strand. She is a beautiful young girl of twenty-one whose only impediment is a limp incurred through an accident on Dalkey Hill. Gerty has an unhappy home life, caused by her father's drinking. She daydreams of marriage to her presently estranged boyfriend, Reggy Wylie. Gerty is not shy in exposing her blue underwear to the voyeuristic stranger and seems cognizant of the effect of her exhibitionism. In the afternoon Gerty is in central Dublin on an errand, and in the evening she visits Sandymount Strand with friends, Edy Boardman, Cissy Caffrey and three children.

[221]

According to the characters of *Ulysses*, King Edward has a weakness for gambling and women. Here we see his graciousness pandering to both vices at Punchestown races.

John Wyse Nolan is one of a group who visit the wine rooms of James Kavanagh during the progress of the viceregal cavalcade. Nolan is a staunch nationalist with a hatred of the British establishment, as evidenced by his contemptuous stare at the viceregal cavalcade. He turns up at Barney Kiernan's with news of a meeting in the City Hall about the Irish language and expresses strong patriotic views in his conversations.

John Howard Parnell is the Dublin City Marshall and brother of the deceased political leader, Charles Stewart Parnell. With his family connections, it is not surprising that this Parnell continues playing chess at the D.B.C. restaurant and ignores the passing viceregal cavalcade. Mr Bloom considers that John Howard and the rest of the surviving Parnell family are all a bit mad.

Denis Breen, the half-mad husband of Josie Breen, spends his day traversing the streets of Dublin in search of a solicitor to take an action for libel. Breen is outraged at the receipt of an anonymous postcard bearing a four-letter coded message, the meaning of which Breen and others seem to understand but is, strangely, never revealed to the reader.

Josephine Breen, once the lovely Josie Powell, is the wife of Denis, friend of Molly Bloom and erstwhile girl-friend of Mr Bloom from his younger days. Mr Bloom meets her in Westmoreland Street and is shocked by her dowdy appearance and how badly Josie has aged since the time they played charades at Luke Doyle's party in Dolphin's Barn.

Professor Denis J. Maginni is a professor of dancing seen walking in Grafton Street during the viceregal cavalcade. He is famous for his colourful and zany attire.

Hornblower, the gate-lodge porter at the rear entrance to Trinity College, Lincoln Place, salutes Mr Bloom in the morning and the viceregal cavalcade in the afternoon.

Almidano Artifoni is the absent-minded music teacher who urges Stephen Dedalus to pursue a professional singing career. Both Artifoni and Stephen converse in Italian outside Trinity College in an episode of 'Wandering Rocks'.

Davy Byrne's

Drinking sessions in licensed premises are part of Dublin life and ideal locations for characters to meet and exchange conversation, hurl abuse and get drunk. As many of Joyce's characters have a fondness for drink, it is not surprising that we are privy to four sessions in

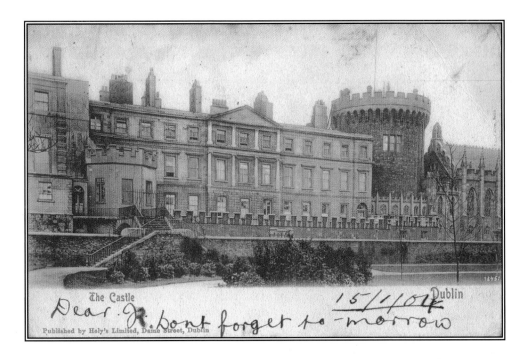

The Castle   Dublin
Dear R. dont forget to morrow   15/1/04
Published by Hely's Limited, Dame Street, Dublin

[222]

Dublin Castle, town residence of the lord lieutenant and seat of British rule in Ireland since the days of Queen Elizabeth I. Many civil service positions in Dublin Castle were filled by the Dublin middle classes, not least Martin Cunningham and Jack Power.

ascending degrees of drunkenness. The first session takes place at Davy Byrne's of Duke Street, where six characters exchange polite conversation: Davy Byrne, Leopold Paula Bloom, Nosey Flynn, Paddy Leonard, Frederick M. Lyons and Tom Rochford.

Davy Byrne is the owner of the pub bearing his own name at 14 Duke Street. Like most good landlords, he looks after his customers and indulges in polite and unobtrusive conversation. Byrne is rather stingy with free drink and, according to Mr Bloom, stands a drink only in leap years.

Paddy Leonard is another habitué of Davy Byrne's who arrives with Tom Rochford and Bantam Lyons. Leonard forces Bantam Lyons to reveal the source of his tip for the big race and Bantam points to the departing Mr Bloom as the man who gave him the information.

Frederick M. Lyons, generally known as Bantam, is the

man who misconstrues Mr Bloom's words about throwing away a newspaper to be a tip for Throwaway in the Gold Cup. Despite his avowed intention in Davy Byrne's to have five shillings on Throwaway, Bantam is put off backing the winner by Lenehan.

The Ormond Hotel

Nearly all of the 'Sirens' episode takes place in the Ormond Hotel where drinking, flirting, music and song combine for the general enjoyment of all concerned. Among the interesting characters closely associated with this drinking session are: Leopold Paula Bloom, Hugh E. Boylan, Father Bob Cowley, Simon Dedalus, Lydia Douce, Benjamin Dollard, Richard Goulding, Mina Kennedy, Tom Kernan, T. Lenehan and George Lidwell.

George Lidwell is a solicitor and another of the many characters in *Ulysses* associated with the legal profession. Although Lidwell listens attentively to the singing, the suave solicitor is far more preoccupied with his flirtatious liaison with the lovely Lydia Douce.

Barney Kiernan's

The 'Cyclops' episode is set in Barney Kiernan's pub and is recounted by a nameless man, generally called the Narrator. It is a typical Dublin drinking session involving talk about topical events, religion and politics. In direct proportion to drink consumed there is a deterioration in conversation and attitude, inevitably leading to an almighty row. The participants in this session are: Alf Bergan, Leopold Paula Bloom, Citizen, Crofton, Martin Cunningham, Bob Doran, Joe Hynes, Edward J. Lambert, T. Lenehan, J.J. O'Molloy, Narrator, John Wyse Nolan and Jack Power.

[223]

This postcard bears a Dalkey postmark, 10 am, 16 June 1904, the time Stephen Dedalus leaves Mr Garrett Deasy's school in Dalkey, at the end of the 'Nestor' episode. The unsigned message to a Mrs Fisher of London reads: 'I have put a dot over No 3. The island is the place with the tower on it.' The tower in question is not the Martello tower, Sandycove, but another tower on Dalkey Island. A drowning off Dalkey Island features prominently in *Ulysses*. The sender has marked No. 3, Sorrento Terrace, Dalkey, and the wall on the left hides Vico Road where some of Stephen's well-off pupils live in fashionable splendour.

Sorrento Terrace and Dalkey Island.   Co Dublin.

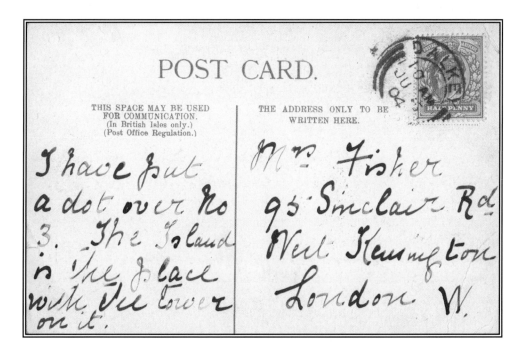

POST CARD.

THIS SPACE MAY BE USED
FOR COMMUNICATION.
(In British Isles only.)
(Post Office Regulation.)

THE ADDRESS ONLY TO BE
WRITTEN HERE.

I have put
a dot over No
3. The Island
is the place
with the tower
on it.

Mrs Fisher
95 Sinclair Rd
West Kensington
London W.

DUBLIN SKETCHES.

Hewth Harbour   Designed and Printed in Ireland.   (Copyright) B. & N., Ltd., Dublin

Alf Bergan, the sub-sheriff's assistant, is a regular customer of Barney Kiernan's. Prior to his arrival Bergan mistakenly believes he has seen Patrick Dignam and is badly shaken by news of Dignam's death. Mr Bloom strongly suspects that Bergan is implicated in perpetrating the postcard hoax on Denis Breen.

Citizen is a fixture at Barney Kiernan's and is today accompanied by Giltrap's dog, Garryowen. He is the one-time champion of Ireland at putting the sixteen-pound shot. This one-eyed bigot is a fanatical Irish nationalist, incapable of any point of view but his own. However, he is highly praised for his contribution to the revival of Gaelic sports. Citizen's anti-British and anti-Jewish feelings inevitably lead to a major row with Mr Bloom, much to the amusement of customers and street onlookers.

Crofton, the Presbyterian Orangeman, is an ex-employee of the Collector General's Office, Dublin Castle, and

[224]

This lady could well be Molly Bloom, in typical Edwardian attire, looking at a scene in Howth, the favourite haunt of the Blooms in their courting days.

[225]

A typical Edwardian street character whose expression is etched with the stoic impassivity, acquired through a life of hardship. Joyce liked to boast that none of his characters were worth more than £100, which is more or less true. However, most of them were middle class: lawyers, teachers and other professionals down on their luck, mainly through improvidence and drink.

Vendor of eggs.

arrives at Barney Kiernan's in the company of Martin Cunningham and Jack Power.

Bob Doran is a brother-in-law of Jack Mooney, whose mother kept a boarding-house in Hardwicke Street. Doran staggers around Dublin during the morning in the course of what is described as one of his drinking sprees. By afternoon he has fallen into a drunken sleep at Barney Kiernan's. When he awakens, Doran indulges in a maudlin eulogy of his dear, dead friend, Willy Dignam and staggers out in search of pastures new.

Judge's Smile.

"We cannot," says the judge, "dispense
With wholesome grains of common sense;
We find for Quaker Oats," and hence
The smile that won't come off! 13.

[226]

Sir Frederick Falkiner,
Freemason, judge and
recorder of Dublin, is held
in high esteem by the
characters of *Ulysses*.

Narrator is the title generally given to the nameless one who narrates the 'Cyclops' episode of *Ulysses*. For a living, he collects bad and doubtful debts. The Narrator is inwardly scornful of his drinking companions, particularly Mr Bloom, who he regards as a know-all and a cuckold.

Burke's

A visit to Burke's pub is the culmination of the 'Oxen of the Sun' episode. Most of the characters have the advantage

WEATHER REPORTS, ILLUSTRATED.   "Dull and Gloomy!"

P.V.B

[227]

In 'Nestor' the ugly and dull-witted boy, Sargent, is given a hard time by headmaster Garrett Deasy. However, he is helped and treated kindly by Stephen, who is mindful that the boy was at least loved by his own mother.

of a good head of steam, acquired during a particularly heavy session of drinking in a room at the maternity hospital, Holles Street. When their drunken behaviour is factored in to the normal crescendo of closing time in a Dublin pub, the conversation at Burke's is almost unintelligible. Because of this, there is a degree of uncertainty about the names of those who participated in this session, but the best estimates are: Alec Bannon, Leopold Paula Bloom, Francis Costello, J. Crotthers, Stephen Dedalus, Dr Dixon, T. Lenehan, Vincent Lynch, Frederick M. Lyons, M'Intosh, William Madden and Malachi Mulligan.

Alec Bannon from Mullingar, County Westmeath, is a young student and friend of Buck Mulligan. Bannon is presently engaged in a sexual relationship with the fifteen-year-old Milly Bloom, who works for a photographer in Mullingar. Mulligan brings him along to the medical students' party.

[228]

In a letter to her father, Milly Bloom mentions a favourite song of her new boyfriend, Alec Bannon, and Blazes Boylan, in praise of lovely seaside girls. This postcard was published in Vienna and posted with a comment on the latest swimwear for seaside girls: 'If this had been the fashion when some people I know were at Skerries, there would have been more bathing.'

Francis Costello, known as Punch, is a medical student and erstwhile schoolboy companion of Stephen Dedalus at Clongowes Wood College. Costello sings a number of bawdy ballads at the drinking party.

J. Crotthers, from Scotland, is another of the medical students who behave badly, yet turn out in the end to be pillars of society.

Dr Dixon participates in the party and assists in the ward after the delivery of Mrs Purefoy's baby. Dixon

[229]

D'Olier Street and Westmoreland Street may be seen to the left and right of this richly animated postcard. In 'Lestrygonians' Mr Bloom notices that the timeball on the Ballast Office is down. This device, on the top right side of this picture, was linked directly to Dunsink Observatory and when the ball dropped it was precisely 1 p.m. Greenwich Mean Time.

once treated Mr Bloom for a bee sting and invites him to participate in the students' joviality.

Vincent Lynch, the mildly dissipated medical student, is a friend of Stephen Dedalus and guest at the students' party. Lynch joins Stephen in a visit to Bella Cohen's brothel but leaves the scene of an altercation between Stephen and Private Carr. For this desertion, Lynch is branded a Judas by Stephen.

William Madden is a medical student and friend of Stephen Dedalus. Madden whinges about his losses on Sceptre in the Gold Cup and drowns his sorrows at the party and at Burke's.

National Library of Ireland

The director's room of the National Library provides an ideal venue for the intellectual discussion on the nuances

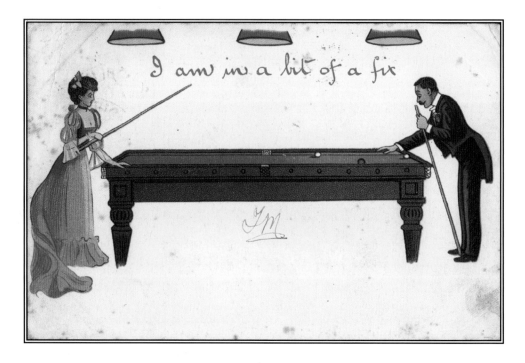

I am in a bit of a fix

of Shakespeare's life and plays. James Joyce spent many hours of his life in the National Library and this is the setting for the entire 'Scylla and Charybdis' episode. Several of the real-life employees of the National Library appear as themselves in this episode which features seven characters: Richard Best, Leopold Paula Bloom, Stephen Dedalus, Lyster, William K. Magee, Malachi Mulligan and George Russell.

Richard Best is the tall young librarian who poses difficult questions and comments as Stephen propounds his theories of Shakespeare's private life and plays.

Lyster is referred to as a Quaker librarian and by his surname, Lyster. While he joins in the discussions, Lyster is called away several times to assist visitors, most notably Mr Bloom, who wishes to inspect the files of *The Kilkenny People*.

William K. Magee, the librarian author and bachelor of

[230]

Surprisingly, the popular pastime of billiards is not mentioned in *Ulysses*. Private and public billiard rooms were a feature of Edwardian Dublin life, not least the Empire Billiard Rooms, 16 Crampton Court, a possible location for the Lenehan and M'Coy story in 'Wandering Rocks'.

"FORE!"

Tom. B.

COPYRIGHT ENTD AT STAT HALL

[231]

It would appear that the characters of *Ulysses* neither play or talk about the game of golf. However, in 'Eumaeus' Mr Bloom conjures to mind a hypothetical case of a woman running away with a professional golfer, to exemplify the exaggerated press sensationalism in the Parnell and Kitty O'Shea affair.

arts, is more often than not described under his pseudonym, John Eglinton. Magee presses some hard questions on Stephen Dedalus and is critical that Stephen is the only writer who demands money for articles in *Dana*. Magee has an uncouth peasant father who visits him periodically, much to Magee's embarrassment.

George Russell is the prominent literary figure, who writes under the pen name 'A.E.' Russell makes the point that Shakespeare's art is paramount and his private life irrelevant. Russell is presently compiling an anthology of the younger Irish poets from which Stephen Dedalus is excluded. Before he leaves, Russell undertakes to deliver Garrett Deasy's letter to the offices of the *Irish Homestead*.

The Cabman's Shelter

The interesting setting for the 'Eumaeus' episode is the cabman's shelter at Butt Bridge under the Loop Line

Bridge, adjacent to the Custom House. These shelters were wooden structures scattered about Dublin where food and drink was served at cheap prices. Among the characters associated with the cabman's shelter are Leopold Paula Bloom, Lord John Corley, Stephen Dedalus, James Fitzharris, Gumley and W.B. Murphy.

Lord John Corley is a casual acquaintance of Stephen Dedalus, encountered under the arches of the Loop Line Bridge. Corley is much the worse for drink and scrounges a loan from Stephen. Corley acquired his unmerited title through a rumour that his grandmother, a Talbot, was related to the Lords Talbot of Malahide. As a result, the debauched and down-and-out Corley is jokingly called Lord John Corley.

James Fitzharris, alias Skin-the-Goat, was a member of the Invincibles who perpetrated the political murders in the Phoenix Park. At his trial Fitzharris escaped execution on the grounds that he was merely a decoy driver. Now Fitzharris is the keeper of the cabman's shelter that, at night time at least, is the haunt of doubtful characters.

Gumley is another Invincible who works as a nightwatchman for the Dublin Corporation in a box under the Loop Line Bridge. Gumley is an erstwhile friend of Simon Dedalus and comes from a respectable family. Like many of Simon's middle-class friends, Gumley is ruined through drink.

W.B. Murphy, born in Carrigloe, Queenstown, County Cork, is a freshly returned sailor who regales the denizens of the cabman's shelter with a series of stories about his adventures throughout the world. Most of Murphy's tales are barefaced lies, perhaps even the remark that he has a wife in Cork waiting seven years for his return.

[232]

The entire episode of 'Scylla and Charybdis' is set in the National Library of Ireland. Mr Bloom passes out the main door between Stephen and Buck Mulligan at the end of the episode to symbolize the Homeric dilemma of the dangerous passage between Scylla the monster and Charybdis the whirlpool, on opposite sides of the Straits of Messina.

[233]

Love in all its many forms features throughout the pages of *Ulysses*. Gerty MacDowell dreams of true love leading to marriage with Reggy Wylie and has already experienced many of the pitfalls and emotions to be found in the upper reaches of Truelove River.

Dublin. National Library *Park Lodge. Sandycove. Kingstown. Ireland.*

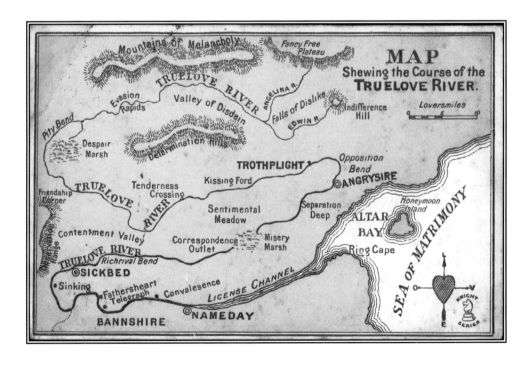

MAP
Shewing the Course of the
TRUE LOVE RIVER.

Butler's Musical Instruments / O'Connell Bridge, Dublin.

Bella Cohen's Brothel and Environs

The 'Circe' episode is set in the red-light district of Dublin, encompassing Bella Cohen's brothel at 82 Lower Tyrone Street. The narrative of this episode lurches randomly between reality and fantasy. Almost every character named in *Ulysses* makes an appearance in fantasy, while a relatively small number seem to be associated with the reality of 'Circe'.

The following appear to be part of the reality: Leopold Paula Bloom, Cissy Caffrey, Private Carr, Bella Cohen, Private Compton, Stephen Dedalus, Zoe Higgins, Cornelius Kelleher, Vincent Lynch, Kitty Ricketts and Florry Talbot.

Some of the more interesting characters, who do not feature on lists, events and locations already dealt with, do make memorable appearances in the hilarious fantasy antics: Martha Clifford, Myles Crawford, Garrett Deasy, Reuben J. Dodd, Mary Driscoll, Sir Frederick Falkiner, Councillor Joseph P. Nannetti MP, Mrs Riordan, and Drum Major Brian Cooper Tweedy.

[234]

Butler's Monument House is situated at the junction of Bachelor's Walk and O'Connell Street. In 'Lestrygonians' Mr Bloom halts at the corner of Butler's Monument House and glances down Bachelor's Walk to see one of the Dedalus girls waiting outside Dillon's auction rooms.

The theme of reciprocal love between a mother and child is constantly explored in *Ulysses*. In 'Nestor' Stephen inwardly reflects that a mother's love may well be the only true aspect in life.

Cissy Caffrey is a prostitute who plies her trade in the precincts of Bella Cohen's brothel and is not the Cissy Caffrey of Sandymount Strand. Quite early in the reality of 'Circe' Cissy solicits two British soldiers, privates Carr and Compton. Later in the night Stephen Dedalus accosts her in Beaver Street, but Cissy has principles and stays with Private Carr, who seems to have paid a shilling for her services.

Private Carr is a British soldier on the prowl for company in the brothel area with his friend, Private Compton. Carr knocks Stephen unconscious with one blow, over an alleged insult against King Edward.

DUBLIN SKETCHES.

Polo—Phoenix Park Designed and Printed in Ireland. (Copyright) B. & N., Ltd., Dublin

Bella Cohen is the keeper of a relatively upmarket, ten shillings brothel at 82 Lower Tyrone Street, as opposed to the one shilling a trick on the streets by the likes of Cissy Caffrey. She employs three girls in her establishment, Zoe Higgins, Kitty Ricketts and Florry Talbot. On the night she is working herself, entertaining a vet who finances the education of her son at Oxford University. Later she greets the new arrivals in the music room and settles the financial arrangements.

Private Compton accompanies Private Carr on their quest for paid female company in the red-light district of Dublin described in the narrative of *Ulysses* as Nighttown.

Zoe Higgins is a Yorkshire-born prostitute who touts for business at the door of Bella Cohen's brothel and eventually entices Mr Bloom to the music room.

Kitty Ricketts is a bony, pale-faced prostitute with dyed red hair who teams up with Vincent Lynch. Kitty and

[236]

Polo and cricket were played in the Phoenix Park and Gaelic games were forbidden, much to the annoyance of the characters in *Ulysses*.

Lynch leave together from the scene of the altercation between Stephen Dedalus and Private Carr.

Florry Talbot is a blonde, fat prostitute with a heavy stye on one eyelid.

Martha Clifford, whose pet name is Mady, uses the post office at Dolphin's Barn Lane to collect her secret correspondence from Mr Bloom. Martha got involved with Mr Bloom through answering his advertisement in the *Irish Times* seeking a smart young lady typist to assist a gentleman in literary work. She is aware that Mr Bloom is married, yet wishes to meet him.

Myles Crawford is the acerbic editor of the *Evening Telegraph* who publishes Garrett Deasy's letter on foot-and-mouth disease at the request of Stephen Dedalus. Crawford is interested in Stephen and encourages him to write something that will mention everybody. Mr Bloom presses Crawford too hard on the issue of the Keyes advertisement, driving the enraged Crawford to tell Bloom, a number of times, that Keyes can kiss his arse. Like most newspaper editors, Crawford is only too willing to partake in the early drinking session at Mooney's.

Garrett Deasy is the headmaster of a private school in Dalkey for well-off Protestant boys, where Stephen Dedalus works as a part-time teacher. Deasy is a misogynist, a loyal Ulster Unionist and an anti-Semite. Deasy is separated from his wife, a woman infamous for throwing soup in the face of a waiter at the Star and Garter Hotel.

Reuben J. Dodd, the unpopular Jewish solicitor, is also a money-lender and agent for the Patriotic Insurance Company. Dodd has taken cases against Father Bob Cowley and Gumley but, to the delight of most, has been foiled on both issues. The story of the rescue of Dodd's son from the Liffey is recounted in the 'Hades' episode.

R.M.S. "MUNSTER"

From your affectionate sister D Mc M

Custom House and Quays, Dublin

Two Irish members of the British
parliament, Field and Nannetti,
travel on the night sailing of 16
June 1904 by the Royal Mail
Service to ask questions in
Westminster about the issues
of foot-and-mouth disease and
the ban on the playing of Gaelic
games in the Phoenix Park.

[238]

This view of the Custom House
and Dublin quays demonstrates
that W.B. Murphy was not a total
liar when he told the occupants
of the cabman's shelter that he
arrived in Dublin on board a
three-masted sailing ship. The
shelter to the forefront is not the
cabman's shelter of 'Eumaeus',
which is under the Loop Line
Bridge, from where this
photograph was taken.

Mary Driscoll is the servant girl employed by the Blooms
when they lived in Ontario Terrace. Molly suspects that
Mr Bloom had some kind of sexual relationship with
Mary because he took Mary's side on the issues of stolen
potatoes and oysters. Molly disliked the way Mary
padded out her bottom to entice her husband and finding
garters in Mary's bedroom was the final straw leading to
one week's notice of dismissal.

Sir Frederick Falkiner probably smiled each time he
gave a verdict in favour of the downtrodden. The chief
judicial officer of Dublin, knight of the realm, and old-
boy of the 'Bluecoat School' (King's Hospital School,
Blackhall Place, Dublin, so-called after the blue uniform),
is an unlikely candidate for one of the most admired characters in *Ulysses*.

Councillor Joseph P. Nannetti MP also works as a
foreman for the *Freeman's Journal* and assists Mr Bloom
with the Keyes advertisement. Nannetti travels to London
on the night mailboat with William Field MP to raise
the issues in the British parliament of foot-and-mouth
disease and the ban against the playing of Irish games in
the Phoenix Park.

Mrs Riordan, a widow of independent means, died in
Our Lady's Hospice and left all her money to the Catholic
Church so that masses could be said for the repose of her
soul. She lived with the Dedalus family for a few years and
later at the City Arms Hotel when the Blooms resided
there. Mr Bloom is alleged to have played up to Mrs
Riordan in the hope of being included in her will.

Drum Major Brian Cooper Tweedy was proud of the
fact that he had risen from the ranks to become an officer
in the Royal Dublin Fusiliers. It is not quite clear
whether Molly Bloom's deceased father was in fact married to her mother, Lunita Laredo. Tweedy made money

PADDY AN' HIS PIG.
Arrah! don't be wastin' yer eddicashun readin milestones! jist thry a sate, an'be aisy. Paix! it's nez to the Fair at all ye're goin' me purty Boneen!

[239]

Mr Bloom makes a hilarious, fantasy appearance in court during the 'Circe' episode, dressed like the stage Irishman pictured here. Buck Mulligan habitually lampoons the Irish Literary Revivalists by imitating this type of exaggerated conversation between Paddy and his pig.

from investing in stamps and was partial to a drop of spirits. He was stationed for a time in Gibraltar and later lived in Dolphin's Barn, Dublin.

To conclude this summary, it may be useful to speculate on the main characters and their counterparts in Homer's *Odyssey* and in real life. Ever since the publication of *Ulysses* controversy has raged on this issue, and opinions are still divided. The following table reflects a personal opinion on counterparts and is based largely on the consensus of more informed authorities.

Character in *Ulysses*	Counterpart in Homer's *Odyssey*	Counterpart in real life
Leopold Bloom	Ulysses *King of Ithaca*	James Joyce *A middle-aged man*
Molly Bloom	Penelope *Wife of Ulysses*	Nora Barnacle *Wife of James Joyce*
Blazes Boylan	Eurymachus *A leading suitor of Penelope*	Oliver St John Gogarty *Surgeon and writer Erstwhile friend of Joyce*
Citizen	Polyphemus *One-eyed giant*	Michael Cusack *Prominent personality in the Gaelic Athletic Association*
Martha Clifford	Calypso *A sea-nymph*	Marthe Fleischmann *A young Swiss girl and paramour of Joyce*
Bella Cohen	Circe *Sorceress and temptress*	Mrs Cohen *Dublin brothel-keeper*
Myles Crawford	Aeolus *God of the Winds*	Morris Cosgrave *Editor,* Evening Telegraph
Garrett Deasy	Nestor *Eldest and wisest of the Greek leaders*	Francis Irwin *Headmaster, Clifton School, Dalkey, County Dublin*
May Dedalus	Anticlea *Deceased mother of Ulysses*	Mary Joyce *Deceased mother of James Joyce*
Simon Dedalus	Laertes *Father of Ulysses*	John Joyce *Father of James Joyce*

Stephen Dedalus	Telemachus *Son of Ulysses*	James Joyce *A younger man*
Patrick Dignam	Elpenor *Deceased follower of* *Ulysses*	Matthew Kane *Deceased friend of* *John Joyce*
Gerty MacDowell	Nausicaa *A young princess,* *in love with Ulysses*	Amalia Popper *A student of Joyce in* *Trieste, with whom he* *was enamoured*
Buck Mulligan	Antinous *A leading suitor of* *Penelope*	Oliver St John Gogarty
Charles Stewart Parnell	Agamemnon *Famous Greek leader,* *slain by his unfaithful wife*	Charles Stewart Parnell *Famous Irish political* *leader, ruined by his* *liaison with Kitty O'Shea*
Skin-the-Goat	Eumaeus *Faithful swine-herd*	Skin-the-Goat Fitzharris *One of the Invincibles*

[240]

Trinity College is pivotal to the comings and goings of characters in *Ulysses*. Mr Bloom saunters past in the early afternoon, Stephen meets Almidano Artifoni outside its gates, and the viceregal cavalcade executes a right turn just after the statue of Henry Grattan that points the way to Grafton Street.

[241]

This young lady, like Molly Bloom, has a soldier and sailor as admiring suitors. Lieutenant Harry Mulvey, the sailor, gave Molly her first kiss under the Moorish Wall in Gibraltar, while her soldier boy, Lieutenant Stanley Gardner, could not resist her beautiful smiling mouth.

[242]

Professor Goodwin is a professional piano accompanist, famous for his outlandish performances on stage when under the influence of alcohol. He has performed in concert with Ben Dollard and Molly Bloom, and appears on the list of Molly's suitors.

[243]

Gerty MacDowell believes she can ask any man to marry her because it is a leap year. Mr Bloom wryly observes that Davy Byrne is not over-generous to his customers, standing a free drink for customers only in leap years.

[244]

Singing is the paramount musical
attribute in *Ulysses*, with a song
likely to burst out at any moment.
The leading characters have
their own favourite songs,
usually admired and requested
by others: Molly Bloom, 'Love's
Old Sweet Song', Ben Dollard,
'The Croppy Boy', Simon
Dedalus, 'M'appari' and
Stephen Dedalus, 'Who
Goes with Fergus'.

[245]

The village of Ballsbridge in
Pembroke township is on the
road to Kingstown, two miles
from the General Post Office.
The fine buildings on the right
of the picture belong to the
Royal Dublin Society and are the
venue for the Mirus Bazaar.

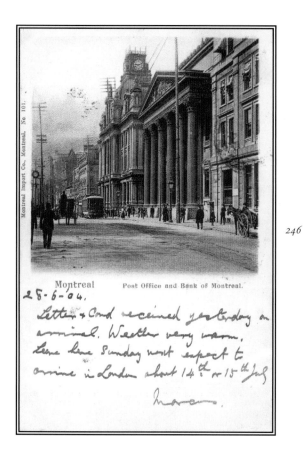

Montreal · Post Office and Bank of Montreal.

28·6·04.

Letter & Card received yesterday on arrival. Weather very warm. Leave here Sunday next expect to arrive in London about 14th or 15th July

Marcus.

We are putting in some hard work

246

247

The widely discussed Canada swindle case was heard before Sir Frederick Falkiner at Green Street Court and the accused remanded without bail. The fraud involved a newspaper advertisement offering passage to Canada for £1.00. Among Mr Bloom's assets, revealed in the 'Ithaca' episode, is a Canadian Government stock certificate for £900 with interest at 4 per cent payable twice yearly at the Bank of Montreal.

[247]

The postcard sent to Denis Breen is one of the mysteries of *Ulysses* because the names of the perpetrators and the meaning of the four-letter coded message are not revealed. This zany madness of frogs playing football would have ideally suited the purpose of the postcard pranksters, thought by Mr Bloom to be Alf Bergan and Richie Goulding.

[248]

Killiney Railway Station, with the steam engine train puffing its way to Dublin. Killiney Hill, with the Mapas Obelisk faintly visible atop, was a popular venue for picnics, although Molly Bloom found the walk difficult in Edwardian attire. Mr Bloom knew a Miss Dubedat from Killiney.

[249]

There are grounds to suspect, both in fact and fantasy, that Mr Bloom had an unhealthy interest in the family maid, Mary Driscoll.

248

249

Cabby's Smile.

9287.
DRIVER.

11·6·04.
The two men
who broke into
Graften St got
"one year hard labour."

The Cabby said, "A single fare
Of Quaker Oats, I do declare,
Is quite enough to make me wear
The smile that won't come off!"

"QUAKER OATS SMILES," consisting of ten different designs, post paid
for 8d., and three white squares cut from fronts of "Quaker Oats" packets.
Apply to Dept. P.C., Quaker Oats, Limited, London, E.C.

250

"Gone but not forgotten" Howth Harbour & Ireland's Eye.
In memory of a "departed day", passed away here, Oct 1903.

251

Licensed cabmen, like this smiling gentleman, plied their trade in Edwardian Dublin. Shelters for their rest and refreshment were in operation throughout the city, two of which are mentioned in *Ulysses*, one in Brunswick Street and the other, near the Custom House, under the Loop Line Bridge. Contemporary crime and punishment is evident in the sender's message: 'The two men who broke into Grafton St got "one year hard labour".'

[251]

The day of love in Howth between Leopold and Molly Bloom is eerily mirrored by this postcard. The message reads: '"Gone but not forgotten". Howth Harbour & Ireland's Eye. In memory of a "departed day", passed away here, Oct 1903. Are there no pens, ink or paper to be had at Inchicore? or have you lost the use of all 10 fingers together! Please relieve anxiety, if able to put in an appearance even at Grangegorman tomorrow (Sunday) at 11.15.'

[252]

A young girl arrives home, probably for Christmas, to be lovingly greeted by her mother and father. Death is one of the main themes in *Ulysses* and is uppermost in the thoughts of two leading characters, Mr Bloom and Stephen Dedalus. The sad message to her girlfriend, Rita O'Brian, 7 North Great Georges Street, Dublin reads: 'Glad to get your note this morning. But sorry I can not meet you, as Mother is sinking rapidly & I may say there is no hope now. Yours in haste. Effie.'

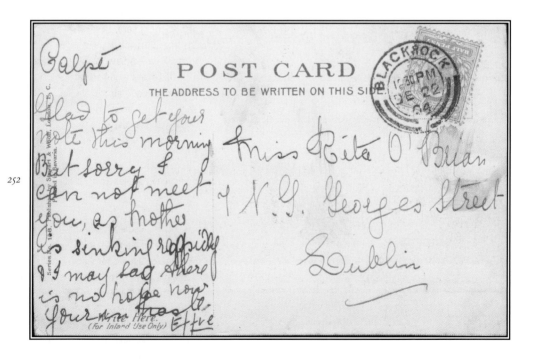

252

The end of the Journey.

252

Postcards: A Descriptive List

The index lists five different categories of information about each postcard: title, publisher, postmark, front message and back message. For reasons of space, transcripts of those five categories appear in block fashion, each category separated by a dash. Some punctuation has been standardized. The following is a guide to the categories, postal abbreviations and other extraneous matter.

Five Categories of the Index

Title	The title on front of the postcard, as indicated by the publisher. Subjective opinion is sometimes necessary, where the title is unclear, unknown or otherwise nebulous.
Publisher	The name of the publisher, as indicated in writing, trademark or inference.
Postmark	Post office name, time and date imprinted on or near the stamp. All other postmarks follow.
Front messages	Publishers' and senders' messages on the pictorial side of each postcard.
Back messages	Publishers' and senders' messages on the reverse side of each postcard. In each case the name of the addressee is listed first.

Postal Abbreviations and Special Cancellations

D.O.	District Office.
H. & K. Packet	Holyhead and Kingstown Packet. The term 'Packet' was applied to a boat or a ship, specifically employed to carry mail, passengers and cargo on a regular basis from one port to another. This maritime postmark was used to cancel mail posted on board ships that plied the route between Holyhead and Kingstown.

Paquebot	A French word meaning packet-boat. *Paquebot* was a maritime postmark used on board ships of all nations.
S.O.	Sorting Office.
T.P.O.	Travelling Post Office. Used to cancel mail being sorted aboard a moving train.
Month abbreviations	In the main, two letters were used to indicate the month of the year on postmarks. They are, beginning January: Ja, Fe, Mr, Ap, My, Ju, Jy, Au, Se, Oc, No and De.

Extraneous Words and Punctuation Marks Used in the Index

(Back)	To introduce a reverse message.
(Front)	To introduce messages on the pictorial side.
(None)	Used when there is no message on the pictorial side.
(Publisher unknown)	All efforts have failed to establish the name of the publisher.
(Readdressed to)	Used where the original address has been deleted.
(Translation)	Used for translations and the deciphering of codes.
(Untitled)	The title is not apparent.
(…)	Illegibility.

1. (On cover) James Joyce, Ulysse – (Publisher unknown) – (No postmark) – (Front) *James Joyce, Ulysse. Traduction Française Intégrale par M. Auguste Morel, assisté par M. Stuart Gilbert entièrement revue par M. Valery Larbaud et l'auteur* – (Back) (none). (Translation) James Joyce, *Ulysses*. Complete French translation by M. Auguste Morel, assisted by M. Stuart Gilbert. Entirely reviewed by M. Valery Larbaud and the author.

2. Map of Dublin and Environs – John Walker & Co. Ltd – Dublin, 4 pm, Au 10, 04 – (Front) Engraved by J. Bartholomew & Co., No 510 Geographical Series, John Walker & Co Ltd, The Liffey at Strawberry Beds, Dublin – (Back) Mr Foster, Postmaster, Castle Rickard, Enfield, Co. Meath. Rathmoylan N. School Reopens (D.V.) on Monday 12th next. Please let G. bring 1 stone of white flour cannot get it. So good Aug. is here. Bye. M. Fogarty.

3. Rathgar – Stewart & Woolf, London – Dublin, 5.30 am, Ap 27, 04 – (Front) (none) – (Back) Miss L. Norton, 53 Mountjoy Square, Dublin. 12 Kenilworth Square, Saturday. Dear L. be sure and get your part off well for the coming concert. I hear you are one of the leading members. Tom.

4. St Joseph's R.C. Church, Terenure – Hely's Limited, Dublin – Dublin, 4 pm, Ju 11, 04 – (Front) (none) – (Back) Miss B. Hurley, Pembroke Street, Tralee. Hoping you are well. Yours J.R.

5. Rathmines Road – Stewart & Woolf, London – Dublin, 6.30 pm, Au 15, 04 – (Front) August 14th 1904 – (Back) Miss Lane, 'Holmhurst', Ordnance Rd, Southampton, England. Dearest Evie, sorry cannot accept of kind invitation will explain when meet. Glad your Father is enjoying better health, I hope I shall meet your Father & Mother in London. Nelly.

6. (Untitled) – B. Killick, Bray – Bray, (…), De 23, 04 – (Front) (none) – (Back) F.J. Chute Esq., 24 Gloucester Road, Newton Abbot, South Devon. With all good wishes for Xmas 1904 & The New Year 1905. From Molly.

7. Front Avenue from the Castle, Clongowes Wood College, Co. Kildare – Lawrence Limited, Dublin – Clongowes Wood, (…), Ju 1, 04 – (Front, ctd from back) will stay like this till I go home. Union Day is on the 4th June all the past Clongonions come down and we will have a good day. B – (Back) Miss H. Ennis, Oulartard, Ferns, Co. Wexford. How do you like to have Kathleen Bolger coming? How long is she going to stay. Were you in for your music exam yet? I hope the weather

8. Sugar Loaf Mountain, (from Terrace, Powerscourt House.) Co. Wicklow – Lawrence Limited, Dublin – Dublin, 11 am, Ap 11, 04 – (Front) (none) – (Back) Miss Gwynedd Elmslie, 7 Upper Tooting Park Mansions, Marius Road, Balham, London S.W. 10-4-04 I hope you had better weather in England than we had here at Easter it was simply rotten, cold wet & muddy, enough to kill a black. With Love Uncle Dick.

9. Patrick Street, Cork – Hely's Limited, Dublin – Dublin, 5 pm, Ap 27, 04 – (Front) (none) – (Back) C.K. Taylor Esq., 280 New Cross Rd, London S.E. I don't know whether you have this card or not am sending it on chance. It is lovely here in the Park but I am all alone.

10. Kingstown Harbour – Valentine – Dublin, 6.30 pm, Au 22, 04 – (Front) (none) – (Back) Miss Pickford, Durham Rd, Manor Park, London E. Dear Mary saw a woman fall in here this morning & a man jumped in & saved her. Quite an experience. Will write a letter soon. Best love from all. Your affectionate Brother Percy.

11. Howth – Wrench Limited, London – Dublin, 11.45 am, Ju 13, 04 – (Front) We have an electric tram service from Dublin to Howth which is a lovely drive & the view from the top of the hill is beautiful. So do come & see for yourself I know you would enjoy it – (Back) Miss Lily Law, Victoria Cottage, Neptune Street, Lipton, Staffs, England. 13-6-04 My Dear Friend, We had so much sunshine of late that all our time has been spent out of doors & the correspondence has been left. Do not think dear that we have forgotten you but often wish you were here to join us. Now the school must close for the summer holiday & why not spend it in Our Green Isle. Yours with Love Mysie.

12.   H.E. Cardinal Vannutelli – Eason & Son Limited, Dublin & Belfast – Dublin, 6.30 pm, Au 3, 04 – (Front) (none) – (Back) Sr M. Michael, Dom. Convent, Wicklow. He was here yesterday executing a graceful & gracious glide for about ten minutes. U. Drumcondra.

13.   Dalkey – Chas. Cook, Kingstown – Dalkey, 5.30 pm, Se 29, 04 – (Front) (none) – (Back) Mr H.W. Whister, Scotch St, Downpatrick, Co. Down. We are having a good time here & getting good weather.

14.   Dublin Horse Show, 1904. Making for the Enclosure – Eason & Son Limited, Dublin & Belfast – Dublin, 5.30 am, Se 11, 04 – (Front) (none) – (Back) Miss Cox, Wilkinstown, Navan, Co. Meath. 10-9-04 Dearest E. This is the view of the H. Show. I hope you are quite well, I will write soon. Of course one heard the "latest". Joined by all in fondest love. *Mille baisers.* Yours L. (Translation) A thousand kisses.

15.   Kingstown Pavilion – Chas. Cook, Kingstown – Kingstown 7.45 pm, Au 14, 04 – (Front) August 9th 1904 – (Back) Miss U. Hayes, Altona, Howth Road, Clontarf. Laurie Wylie & his mannikin are here this week. Stratton, Dan Leno & C. Stanley.

16.   Dublin, Grafton Street – Raphael Tuck & Sons – Dublin, 6.40 pm, No 19, 04 – (Front) (none) – (Back) Miss R.B. O'Brian, 7 N.G. George's St., Dublin, Ireland. Yrs. as ever Bob.

17.   Stephens Green West, Dublin – Stewart & Woolf, London – Dublin, 6.30 pm. Au 21, 04 – (Front) (none) – (Back) Miss Bessie Howley, 3 Cecil Place, Paisley Road N., Glasgow. If the day is fine. Been working hard since coming here. "Cookie fights" every night finishing abt. 12 pm. Kindest regards C.

18.   Lynch Memorial Stone, Galway – Valentine – Dublin, 11.45 am, Oc 7, 04 – (Front) (none) – (Back) Mrs Bowden, 7 Pretoria Terrace, Beaconsfield Rd, Southall – Arrived here about 9 am, will write later.

19.   Cathair Luimnighe – Cuideachta na gCártai Posta Gaedhealach, Átha Cliath – Dublin, 11.45 am, De 23, 04 – (Front) Cloch na Síothchána; Droichead Tuath-Mhumhan; Caisleán ríogh Seaghán; árd-teampall Mhuire; an tSionainn. This is not Greek: it is the language which no one speaks. over – (Back) Miss Blagg, 121 Station Road, Church End, Finchley, London W. The picture represents the Treaty Stone Limerick. Having been there I know otherwise. I might be at a loss. Happy Xmas To You Percy. 1904. (Translation) Limerick City – The Gaelic Postcard Company, Dublin. Treaty Stone; Thomond Bridge; King John's Castle; Mary's Cathedral; The Shannon.

20.   Miss Dora Barton – Rotary Photo Co. Ltd – Dublin, 11.45 am, Ju 16, 04 – (Front) Best love to Tim. Hope all at home are well. I'm sorry I couldn't get a few more like this, Moll. How is T. Kelly – (Back) Miss B. Hurley, Pembroke St, Tralee, Co. Kerry. Dear Bridge I received your P.C. I suppose I will go home the 1st week in July "D.V." My brother is coming down from Belfast so I will wait to see him. I sent a P.C. to Tim. I suppose he will take my life for doing it. Yours Mollie.

21.   (Untitled) – S. Hildesheimer & Co. Ltd, London & Manchester – Blackrock, 6.45 pm, Ju 16, 04 – (Front) I got some songs which I did not pay for but it is time enough when I am writing I will tell you they will come to four shillings. I have not heard the song. Your Mother and Tom called today but I was out so he did not wait to see me as he was going to Bray. I sent Jack word to say how surprised you were at his silence. Girtie Keegan was here today & all will try and go down soon. I must say goodbye to dear (...) yourself. From your Fond Sister Mai – (Back) Miss C. Stewart, The Hotel, Cashel, Co. Tipp. My Dearest Cis, I received your welcome postcard & I am praying hard for J.B. since. We got result of singing exams which were successful. I got a pass. We got our photos taken today several groups Tennis Hockey etc. and also the Orchestra & drill class which turned out splendid. I hope we will be able to procure some copies I know you would like them.

22.   Bray Head and Parade – Raphael Tuck & Sons – Dublin, 11.45 am, Ja 16, 04 – (Front) Dear H. I am sending you particulars of Bagatelle table by this post. This is rather a good view of Bray, only it should be the Esplanade & not Parade. Yrs. Willie – (Back) J.C.H. O'Reilly Esq., 43 Eglinton St, Belfast.

23. Football Incidents. Nearly In (Rugby) – Raphael Tuck & Sons – Rathmines D.O. Dublin, 5.45 pm, Fe 22, 04 – (Front) Feb, 22th, 04. Safer to say Wed. at 12. o'c. With love to yr Mother yrs. J. Lawless – (Back) Miss Brodie, 18 Coulson Ave, Off Rathgar Ave, Rathgar. I was so sorry to see you in such pain fr. yr. teeth. I hope you are quite well by this. Miss Smith is a little better, T.G. I had four P.C.'s fr. Mollie & two fr. Agatha but fr. no other member of the family. Perhaps I may be going to see the A. de C. tomorrow, or perhaps. J.L.

24. Iona Bazaar – (Publisher unknown) – Dublin, 6.30 pm, Oc 8, 04 – (Front) Iona Bazaar in aid of the New Church of St. Columba, Drumcondra, will be held in the Rotunda, Dublin on the 3rd, 4th, 5th, 6th, 7th & 8th October 1904 – (Back) Miss M. (…) Phibsborough. Thanks for 2/– with duplicates J.C. for Iona Bazaar Committee.

25. We Had A Merry Time – Raphael Tuck & Sons – Dublin, 11.45 am, Oc 11, 04 – (Front) We had a Merry Time during the holidays. I hope you enjoyed yours. I was glad to hear that you got such good (ctd on back) – (Back) Miss Gill, Loreto Convent, Balbriggan, Co. Dublin. marks at the Inter. You must get a prize this year. How are all the nuns, I'm sure you miss Sr Alphonsus. I saw her & also Sr J. Brand. Both looked well but are busy. The latter is having her kitchen fitted up. Write soon & give all the news. (…) L.B.

26. Old Howth Village, Howth – Stewart & Woolf, London – Dublin, 4.45 pm, Se 27, 04 – Toulon sur Allier, Allier, Se 31, 04 – (Front) 27-9-04 How nice your card of Mouliers is. Thank you so much. Excuse a hurried card again Millicent – (Back) Monsieur Francisque de Boissieu, Château de la Forêt, Toulon sur Allier, Allier, France.

27. The University, Dublin – Raphael Tuck & Sons – Dublin, 5.30 am, No 18, 04 – (Front) Margery had tea with us on Thursday aft. W. is having a great time with her small cousins but we go home D-morrow. Hope you have a good place this week. P.U.D. Terenure 17-11-04 – (Back) N.J. Dickson, Campbell College, Belfast.

28. The National Library, Dublin – Hely's Limited, Dublin – Dublin, 6.30 am, Se 11, 04 – (Front) (none) – (Back) Miss Brinkley, C/o Mrs Duffy, 126 Boleyn Road, Forest Gate, London E. 36 Dawson St, Dublin, 10-9-04. Had you any P.C.'s from the Isle of Man? (…) Have not heard from you for some time. Expect long letter tomorrow. When replying shall enclose some "Mountain" and other photos. Love to All D.O.D.

29. Bárr na maidne duit – (Publisher unknown) – Dublin, 2 pm, Se 6, 04 – (Front) "The top of the morning to ye." Two of Irish & "a split". 6-9-04 – (Back) Miss P. Lenehan, Amberwood, Court Hill, Swanage, Dorset, England. Dear Lot I received your P.C. this morning & will get a table cloth for you the real collars are 7/6 & I have not enough £.S.D. for all things. I am sending Tom a Blarney Stone Card. Hope the Homes are all well. Love to all the Boys & Yourself. Your Loving Sister Nancy.

30. Nassau Street, Dublin – (Publisher unknown) – Dublin, 11.45 am, My 17, 04 – (Front) Arrived here safe 7.30 am this morning O.C.R. – (Back) Miss Smith C/o Mr Roberts, Yg Croes, St. George, Nt Abergele, North Wales. Beautiful Morning the sail was delightful no splashing & C Cyril.

31. A Galway Girl – Fergus O'Connor – Dublin, 5.30 am, De 28, 04 – (Front) (none) – (Back) A.T. Taylor Esq., 280 New Cross Rd, London S.E. Thank you very much for parcel received yesterday. It is very kind of you to think of me. Glad to hear you are all well. Tell Mother I had her letter. I hope to be able to write to her soon. Robin is not very well. The rest of us are well. With love wishing you a very Happy New Year. E. Wardlow 27-12-04.

32. The Piazza of St. Peter's – Misch & Stock's – Dublin, 2 pm, Ap 3, 04 – (Front) (none) – (Back) Miss M.K. Tighe, 31 Victoria Avenue, Donnybrook. Will see you tonight.

33. Sackville Street, Dublin – Raphael Tuck & Sons – Dublin, 6.15 am, Ja 23, 04 – (Front) Dear Jennie, I am just starting for a shop window stroll to see the latest Paris fashion; hope to be home at 8.30. Ready for T.P. Ta Ta for the present. Yours &C. Alf. – (Back) Mrs R.H. Williams, 6 Water Street, Holyhead.

34. (Untitled) – City of Dublin Steam Packet Co. – Dublin, 6.30 pm, Au 23, 04 – (Front) A cabin (double) for Mrs R. Shorter reserved with pleasure on Royal Mail Steamer leaving Kingstown on Friday morning (…) – (Back) Mr Walter Fleming, Lyndhurst, Harcourt Terrace, Dublin. Royal Mail Service, City of Dublin Steam Packet Co., 15, Eden Quay, Dublin. Two services each way daily between Kingstown & Holyhead in connection with the Mail Trains from all parts of England & Ireland. Best and Fastest Route. Telegrams "Eden", Dublin.

35. *Gruss vom Pilatus* – Frey & Sohme, Zurich – Pilatus, Kulm, Se 3, 04. Rathmines D.O. Dublin, Se 5, 04 – (Front) Just had snowballing. We are thinking of remaining longer & sleeping (…) top of mountain. (…) – (Back) Miss Johnson, 5 Rathmines Road, Dublin, Ireland. (Readdressed to) 8, Shanaganagh Tce, Killiney, Co. Dublin. L.B. (Translation) Greetings from Pilatus.

36. King's Visit, Leinster Lawn – Hely's Limited, Dublin – Dublin, 6.30 pm, My 6, 04 – (Front) His Majesty leaving Leinster Lawn after laying the Foundation Stone of The Royal College of Science – (Back) Mrs M.C. Connor, Swinford, Co. Mayo. King's Visit. We have just issued a series of six different views Picture Post Cards in connection with above embracing:
Punchestown Races
Phoenix Park Races
Leinster Lawn
Kingsbridge
Kilkenny
House Party, Vice-Regal Lodge
Put up in sixpenny Packets 3/– per Dozen
Postage 2d. extra. To be had only from Hely's Limited, Dublin.

37. George's Street, Kingstown – (Publisher unknown) – Dublin, 11.45 am, Oc 14, 04 – (Front) (none) – (Back) Miss Clanchy, Cambridge Rd, Gt Marlow, Bucks, England. Dear N. Thanks for such a lovely postcard. It was so pretty & not a duplicate. I will be going down to K. the end of this month & if you tell me what views of K. you have I will send you some you have not. Write soon. I am going shopping on Saturday shoes & collars. Your loving cousin M (…) C (…)

38. Rathmines, Dublin – Hely's Limited, Dublin – Dublin, 5.30 am, Oc 29, 04 – (Front) (none) – (Back) Miss P. Brennan, 111 Upton Pk Rd, Forest Gate, London E. Look out for Miss Zena Dare in "Catch of Season" on P. Cards.

39. Miss Gabrielle Ray – Rapid – Dublin, 2 pm, Au 30, 04 – (Front) ("Nora"). The usual question:– who does this remind you of? especially the right eye (…) – (Back) Miss A. Mooney, 43 Londonbridge Road, Sandymount. How are you after the Tom-T-S on Saturday (…)

40. The Boat Slip, Howth – Stewart & Woolf, London – Dublin, 4.45 pm, Se 27, 04. Toulon sur Allier, Allier, 04. – (Front) 27-9-04 When I came down stairs this morning your two very nice cards, my dear friend were waiting to say "good morning" to me. Thank you so much for them. Millicent – (Back) Monsieur Francisque de Boissieu, Château de la Forêt, Toulon sur Allier, Allier, France.

41. The Beach, Malahide – Wrench Limited, London – Malahide, Dublin, 6.45 pm, Ju 3, 04 – (Front) (none) – (Back) Mrs Ellis, Bank House, Omagh. Many thanks for kind letter. We are here for Summer. Did you get Hop's photo taken. I'll post 'Our Dogs' which you might please return when finished with. How heavy is Hop now. Trusting all are well & kind regards. E. Christen.

42. Greystones Railway Station – E. Greer, Greystones – Greystones, 3 pm, Jy 12, 04 – (Front) (none) – (Back) Miss D. Brinkley, 11 Carlisle Avenue, Marlborough Rd, Donnybrook, Dublin. We are having a lovely time. Were at the Cherry Orchard yesterday. Have just had a lovely dip. Dollie & I are going into the same room with May today. Love from Pollie.

43. Kate Kearney's Cottage, Killarney – Lawrence, Dublin – Kingstown, 4 pm, No 2, 04 – (Front) (none) – (Back) John MacGregor Esq., 21 Ireton Street, Botanic Avenue, Belfast. Knaht uoy os hcum tseraed rof eht owt lufituaeb sdrac. Eht A. si yllaiceps ytterp. I ma reve os hcum retteb yadot. Lliw etirw nehw I teg sruoy dna llet uoy lla eht swen. Llit neht. Reve ruoy gnilrad, Ani. (Translation) Thank you so much dearest for the two beautiful cards. The A. is specially pretty. I am ever so much better today. Will write when I get yours and tell you all the news. Till then. Ever your darling, Ina.

44. (Untitled) – (Publisher unknown) – Dublin, 5.30 am, No 12, 04 – (Front) 10-11-04 Do you recognise anybody here? Expect you think we look dangerous. Hope you are pleased with your new career – (Back) J.G. Beatty Esq., 35 Orsett Rd, Grays, Essex. Am collecting p.p.c. Thanks! you might write a decent letter. N. Mulcahy.

45. Dan Leno – Rotary Photo Co. Ltd, London – Dublin, 4.45 pm, No 16, 04 – (Front) Poor old Dan (…) – (Back) Miss Clark, 3 Beechwood Rd, Ranelagh. Gone but not forgotten (…)

46. The Castle, Dublin – E. & J. Burke's Bottling – Dublin, 4.45 pm, Oc 20, 04 - (Front) Dublin 20th Octo '04. Guinness' Dublin Stout maintains health and vitality. E. & J. Burke's Bottling is guaranteed genuine. See the label. Beware of imitations. Boston Office, 7 Water Street – (Back) Mrs J.A. Gladden, 356 Tappom St, Boston, Mass.

47. Alphabet "I" – Rotary Photo Co. Ltd – Dublin, 4.45 pm, Oc 18, 04 – (Front) (none) – (Back) Miss Ita Ennis, Oulartard House, Ferns, Co. Wexford. My dearest Ita, I was delighted to receive your grand long letter. I trust you are better by this. Indeed I do remember my sojourn on the sofa in dear old Wicklow especially English class. What do you think of the changes. Fancy I've mother entered. With love Kat.

48. Balscadden Bay, Howth – W.H. Berlin – Dublin, 5.30 am, Oc 23, 04 – (Front) Pray hold this card up to the light and you shall see a charming sight. Does this remind you of anything G.B.H. P.S. Hold this up to the light. Dear Joe am so sorry I missed you on Tuesday. I went (ctd on back) – (Back) Master J.B. O'Brien, 14 Baytown Gardens, Sheppards Bush Rd, West Kensington, London W. England. to Trinity College at 5 o'c & waited until 5 o'5. Then I went up to your house & your sister told me you were gone down to meet so that is how I missed you. When are you coming home. I hope you are enjoying your stay. I suppose you have been to the Hippodrome, if not you should go. Always yours G.B.H.

49. O'Connell Bridge, Dublin – W.H. Berlin – Dublin, 11.45 am, Au 30, 04 – (Front) (none) – (Back) Miss M. James, Sand Rd, Wedmore, Somerset, England. Dear Sister, Just arrived in Dublin. Had a nice journey from Wales. Nice weather here. with love from yrs. Affec. Bro. Charlie.

50. (Half size) Miss Marie Studholme – Giesen's – Dublin, 5.30 am, Fe 15, 04 – (Front) To Dear Rozie with love and kisses. Nellie – (Back) Miss Rozie Shinkwin, Nt, Main Street, Cork.

51. (Half size) E.S. Willard – Rotary Photo Co. Ltd – Dublin, 3.15 pm, No 11, 04 – (Front) 7-1-04 – (Back) Miss M. Broderick, (…), Co. Roscommon. Sender's name and address only allowed here. Signature on Picture Side. From Robby Ashton, Paris.

52. (Half size) Miss Topsy Sinden – Giesen's – Dublin, 5.30 am, My 17, 04 – (Front) (none) – (Back) Miss M. Moore, 25 Fair Street, Drogheda. Use picture side for sender's name and address only. Won't attempt to talk of "settling". M.S.

53. (Half size) Oh! Where's Nurse – Rotary Photo Co. Ltd – Dublin, 5.30 am, No 4, 04 – (Front) (none) – (Back) Miss Moran, Saint James, Howth Road, Clontarf. For Halfpenny Postage sender's name and address only allowed here. Signature on Picture side. From Lena to Dear Daisy with love.

54. (Diamond) (Half size) Miss Marie Studholme – Rotary Photo Co. Ltd – Dublin, 2 pm, Se 21, 04 – (Front) (none) – (Back) Miss G. Waker, 44 Blessington St, Dublin.

55. (Half size) Knitters – Rotary Photo Co. Ltd – Dublin, 2 pm, Ap 8, 04 – (Front) (none) – (Back) Miss Kellie, 27 Brooklyn Terr., South Circular Rd, Dublin. Heartiest Congratulations on your release. Best Wishes for safe Journey Home. D.

56. (Half size) Miss Marie Studholme – Philco Publishing Co. – Blackrock, 5.30 pm, Ju 17, 04 – (Front) (none) – (Back) Master A.R. Mallet, Lucerne, Albert Rd, Kingstown. B.B.B.E. 16-6-04.

57. Christmas Greetings – (Publisher unknown) – Dublin, 5.30 am, De 18, 04. Springfield Mass. Rec'd. 4 pm, Ja 3, 05 – (Front) Paper made from Irish Peat at the Celbridge Peat Paper Mills, Co. Kildare.

A Bit of Old Ireland "In fortune and in fame we're bound
by stronger links than steel."
Good luck to all our Kith and Kin this happy Xmas time.

I was a sod of turf
But now am paper brown;
And used for wrapping Parcels up
In every house in town.

– (Back) Mrs R. Brooks, 141 Johnson St, Springfield, Mass., U.S. America.

58. Christmas Greetings – (Publisher unknown) – Dublin, 4.45 pm, De 21, 04 – (Front) Paper made from Irish Peat at the Celbridge Peat Paper Mills, Co. Kildare.

O talam glar na hÉireann ag guide,
gó mbeid Nodlaig Séan-mar agat.

From the Land of Eire to wish you a happy Xmas.

I was a sod of turf
But now am paper brown;
And used for wrapping Parcels up
In every house in town.

– (Back) Miss Robinson, Russell Street, Mobeern Lands, Beds. R.L.G. Hard times come again no more. A.L.R.

59. Loading Strawberries for the London Market – Wrench Limited, London – Dublin, 5 pm, Fe 16, 04. St-Jean de-Monts, Vendée, 18 Fe, 04 – (Front) Some of the Indigenes of our country. I would it were the straw-berry season again. (…) – (Back) Monsieur E. Dibor, Instituteur, À Saint Jean de Mont, Vendée, France.

60. Irish Lion Cubs – Zoological Gardens, Dublin – Dublin, 5.30 am, Au 5, 04 – (Front) (none) – (Back) Francis Jacob Esq, Rock Villa, Newtown, Waterford. Dear Uncle Frank, This picture is of the three cubs which we saw the time Queen Victoria was in Dublin. We had a grand morning at the zoo yesterday. The keepers were most agreeable showing off their charges. The monkeys were not particularly entertaining but the elephant was just splendid, she is young only eleven years old. The keeper says they go on growing till they are 25. One kangaroo had a child and just as we were coming up it jumped into her pouch and then after a while put it's little head out. Yesterday afternoon we were at Killiney, it is 17 years since I was there last. Willie and I looked for the spot where we then stood to get a view of the Duke of Clarence & Prince George, as it was the Jubilee. Your Loving Niece Mabel Elizabeth.

61. R.M.S. Majestic – (Publisher unknown) – Dublin & Queenstown T.P.O., 1, De 23, 04. Paquebot, Philadelphia PA, Jan 5, 1.30 am, 1905. Box 1 division, Philadelphia PA Regd., Jan 5, 1 am, 05 – (Front) 3 pm. Dec 27-04. Dear Will, nearing the Irish coast – had a calm voyage all the way. Took 2nd cabin after leaving N.Y. food fine etc. Am well this sea voyage doing me good. Writing Frank and Nellie, Your brother Arthur – (Back) Mr William B. Bray, Philadelphia Inquirer, Philadelphia Pa, USA.

62.   (Untitled) – (Publisher unknown) – Dublin, 6.30 pm, Ap 22, 04 – (Front) One more for your album, with beauty and flowers; Good fortune come with it, and bright, happy hours – (Back) Miss M.M. Harvey, 41 Arran Quay, City. P.M.

63.   The White Pass, Yukon, in Winter – Colonial and Continental Church Society, 9 Serjeants' Inn, Fleet Street, London – Blackrock, 11 pm, Fe 9, 04 – (Front) 1 Clifton Place. Tuesday. Tomorrow Wed. 10 is my day do come and see us if you can & also Mr Sinclair – (Back) Mrs Cox, 53 Morehampton Road, Dublin. Mother is with me came on Monday so you will see her too! If W.C. can come too we'd be delighted. Hope you are all well. Yours L.H. Hayes. I've changed my day's at home to 10th 20th 30th.

64.   Russo-Japanese War – Cardinal – Hendon N.W., 4 pm, Ju 13, 04. H. & K. Packet, C3, 2.30 am, Ju 14, 04 – (Front) Russo-Japanese War – No 2. – Port-Arthur: 8th Feb. 1904. Naval Combat. Immediate reply by the Russian Fleet – (Back) H.V. Fleming, Lyndhurst, Harcourt Terrace, Dublin, Ireland.

65.   Russian outrage on Hull Fishing Fleet, 22-10-1904 – Valentine – Kingstown, 4 pm, No 24, 1904 – (Front) (none) – (Back) John MacGregor Esq., 21 Ireton Street, Botanic Avenue, Belfast. Nov 1904. This is the only card I have so am sending it though I cannot say I like it. Skanht os hcum rof sruoy. I ekil ti dna I ekil retteb ssik gnilrad tahw uoy etorw fo ti. It is only a little more than a week now. I ma llits *avec tout mon coeur à toi mon cher toujours. Ton* Ina. (Translation) Thanks so much for yours. I like it and I like better kiss darling what you wrote of it. I am still with all my heart to you my dear always. Your Ina.

66.   Motor Races, Portmarnock – Hely's Limited, Dublin – Raheny S.O. Dublin, 5.45 pm, De 16, 04 – (Front) Motor Races, Portmarnock. Automobile Club 200 Guinea Challenge Cup. A. Lee Guinness and J.W. Stocks starting – (Back) Miss Barker, 6 Weston Terrace, N.C. Road, Dublin. I sent you some cake yesterday hope you will get it in time. Hope Mother is better so sorry to hear of her having to stay quiet again. Write soon. V.M.C. (…)

67.   Miss Marie Studholme – Rotary Photo Co. Ltd – Dublin, 5 pm, My 4, 04 – (Front) (none) – (Back) Miss H. Thompson, Heathcot, North Parade, Belfast. Dear Lil, have you got this P.C. I was hearing Marie Studholme made £2000 by her photos alone. Will write some day soon. Love to All Evelyn.

68.   It's really too bad – Raphael Tuck & Sons – Dublin, 4.45 pm, Au 19, 04 – (Front) It's really too bad, from Auntie – (Back) Master Arthur Little, St. Michael's, Bettystown, Near Drogheda.

69.   I don't think I can – Hely's Limited, Dublin – Dublin, 5.30 am, De 8, 04 – (Front) (none) – (Back) Mr P. Gordon, 3 Dunedin, Connaught Avenue, Cork. Dear Percy I suppose you have been too busy to write. If you are writing next tell me whether you will send the fare to me. Scripture examination on Friday. We had a great time at the Girls' school. Write soon. Your affectionate Brother Cecil. 15 more days.

70.   World's Fair, St Louis 1904 – (Publisher unknown) – Dublin, 5.30 am, Se 30, 04 – (Front) Official Souvenir World's Fair, St Louis 1904. Bridge over Lagoon. Hold card to Light. Love from Emilie – (Back) Master Kennedy, Railway Hotel, Athenry.

71.   Bertie Says The Pier Is Good Enough for Him – Davidson Bros – Dublin, 11.45 am, No 17, 04 – (Front) (none) – (Back) Miss Lodge, 8 Moyne Road, Rathmines. Will you and Mrs Lodge come over on Friday afternoon for tea and fun? H.

72.   Roadside Butter Market – Hartmann – Dublin, 4.45 pm, Au 18, 04 – (Front) (none) – (Back) Miss Henderson, Public School, Redgorton, Nt. Perth, Scotland. Many many thanks for your very welcome letter received this morning. Shall write soon. Mary.

73. Irish Fair – Hartmann – Dublin, 5.30 am, De (…), 04 – (Front) (none) – (Back) Mr E. Campbell, 1 Merton Villas, Inchicore, Dublin. I have just received your P.C. I thought Mother told you the Holidays or I would have written you before. The Holidays begin on the 20th and end on the 18th of Jan. I hope you are well. I am dying for the holidays. The music exam is on Saturday next. I'm dreading it. Remind Mother to send my fare as soon as possible. Best love Eileen. Going by 9.15 train on Tuesday. I am not sure as to the exact time about nine. Please let me know. Write soon and tell me about the ticket.

74. Peasant & Turf Stack – Hartmann – Dublin, 2 pm, Se 8, 04 – (Front) (none) – (Back) Miss Burns, 74 Curzon St, Derby, England. Thursday am leaving here by the boat arrive tonight 7.30 pm and arrive Heysham Friday morning. Derby about 10 pm Friday night. All well.

75. Irish Piper – Fergus O'Connor – Blackrock, 5.45 pm, Ap 29, 04 – (Front) 4-29-04 – (Back) Miss Doris Pearson, Kylemore, Blackrock, Co. Dublin. Saw King & Queen yesterday passing through Westmoreland St going to lay stone at College of Science. Grannie.

76. Barney O'Hea – Fergus O'Connor – Clongowes Wood, (…) am, De 25, 04 – (Front) With Every Good Wish for a Happy New Year. You'd better behave yourself Barney O'Hea – (Back) Miss Ennis, Oulartard House, Ferns, Co. Wexford. Why don't you answer my letters. Bernard.

77. I know a bank – C.W. Faulkner & Co. – Dublin, 5.30 am, My 17, 04 – (Front) Please send a message by Jack if you can come Portmarnock on Tuesday instead of Wednesday. I can call about 3.30. W. Anderson – (Back) H.H. Poole Esq., 93 St Lawrence Road, Clontarf.

78. Luxor – F.M.K. – Dublin, 11.45 am, Jy 1, 04 – (Front) Not quite sure whether I can get to Bray tonight, if I do I will catch the 6.45 – (Back) Miss Maude Tighe, c/o Mrs Barnett, Duncairn Parade, Bray.

79. In the Spring a Young Man's Fancy – Valentine – Dublin, 6.30 am, De 24, 04 – (Front) Valentine's "Coon" series. With Best Wishes (…) – (Back) Miss Mary Bowler, Macroom, Co. Cork.

80. Riksha Boys – Sallo Epstein & Co., Durban – Dublin, 5.30 am, Oc 14, 04– (Front) Thursday I'm sure you hav'nt the match of this in your collection! I no longer own a bazaar. Thought you might have ventured in? Will you be over this side soon or when may I see you? Remembrance to Nora. Yours D.M. 6d. a mile and very comfortable – (Back) Miss Mary Bowler, 15 Upper Pembroke St, City.

81. *Laitières flamandes* – A L'Aiglon, Brussels – Dublin, 11.45 am, De 6, 04 – (Front) Friday eve. The Hague's No. is 35. Joe does not know Gabbie's No. & it is not in our directory as it is an old one. Raglan Rd is sure to find him. C.S. Kirwan – (Back) Mrs Magennis, 3 Herbert St, Dublin. (Translation) Flemish milksellers.

82. This bears out the "New Idea" – W.H. Berlin – Dublin, 6.30 pm, My 2, 04 – (Front) (none) – (Back) Mrs Seymour, Ravenscourt, Blackrock, Co. Cork. Of all Liquid Coffees "The New Idea" is the best. It is refreshing, delicious & convenient. May be had in large and small bottles in all Leading Grocers. Manufactured by Woods, Webb & Co., Ltd, Temple Lane, Dublin. Free Sample on application.

83. Quaker Oats Smiles – Quaker Oats Limited – Dublin, 6.30 pm, Ju 10, 04 – (Front) Willie's Smile. "Oho!" said Willie, "I should smile, This Quaker Oats is just my style;" He ate it wearing all the while The smile that won't come off! "Quaker Oats Smiles," consisting of ten different designs, post paid for 3d. and three white squares cut from fronts of "Quaker Oats" packets. Apply to Dept. P.C., Quaker Oats, Limited, London, E.C. 10.6.04 How are you all in Hendon? Love to all. H – (Back) Miss Fleming, c/o Mrs R.D. Shorter, Kingsweston, Sunny Gardens, Hendon, London N.W.

84. Irish Spinning Wheel – Lawrence, Dublin – Dublin, 11.45 am, Oc 12, 04 – (Front) Shelbourne Hotel, Dublin – (Back) Miss E.L. Worth, The Avenue, Sutton Bridge, Lincolnshire. I came over here on Sunday for a fortnight with my Auntie. I am having a very good time. Dublin is a grand town & this Hotel is full of awfully nice people. M.E. West. 11-10-04.

85. For Galway Fair. Connemara – Fergus O'Connor – Dublin, 11.45 am, Jy 26, 04 – (Front) (none) – (Back) Miss M.K. Tighe, 31 Victoria Avenue, Donnybrook. I may see you tonight.

86. A Happy Christmas – Raphael Tuck & Sons – Dublin, 11.45 am, De 24, 04 – (Front) Harry – (Back) H. Tighe Esq., 31 Victoria Ave, Donnybrook.

87. Leap Year "A two to one Chance" – Raphael Tuck & Sons – Dublin, 6.30 pm, Ju 17, 04 – (Front) 16-6-04. Does it rain much over in Hendon. It is awfully showery over here. Love to all at Kingsweston. Yrs. Herbert – (Back) Miss Fleming, Kingsweston, Sunny Gardens, Hendon, London. N.W.

88. Légendes – (Publisher unknown) – Rathmines D.O. Dublin, 5.45 pm, Oc 14, 04 – (Front) (none) – (Back) Miss Hennessy, Johnstown, Inchicore, Co. Dublin. Hope you will soon come in again to have a ride on the tram free. Do come soon again and call for me at the Loretto to come out with you. Dearest Love to All N.K. Fletcher.

89. A Gibson Girl – (Publisher unknown) – Dublin, 5.30 am, Se 26, 04 – (Front) Am looking for a girl similar to this lady. The first one I meet, I intend to marry, whether she likes it or not – (Back) Miss B. Hurley, 24 Pembroke St, Tralee, Kerry. Dear B. your letter to hand. Glad to know Boss & J. are on good terms again. Will write to Joe shortly & give her a lecture illustrated with lantern views. Have written to Mollie & C. When you see her give my "Love". Hope all are well. Tim.

90. S.S. Scotia – L. & N.W.R – Dublin, 11.45 pm, Se 3, 04 – (Front) Running between England & Ireland via Holyhead & Dublin – (Back) Miss K.M. Pasley, 22 Pembroke Park, Clyde Road, Dublin. Sloan's Hotel, Geo. St. Missed connection with Mail had to come by North Wall, stop night and go on by Mail leaving at 6.5. This is boat we came over on, rough crossing and was seasick. Had a good time and saw Llandudno, Bangor and Menai Bridge. Dont forget Wednesday and dont confine yourself to two sheets. Have you started collecting Picture Post Cards.

91. Evening, Kingstown Harbour – B. & N. Ltd, Dublin – Kingstown, 5.15 pm, Se 29, 04 – (Front) (none) – (Back) Miss A. Lee, Stepney Towers, Auckland Towers, Southsea, Hants., England. Dear Annie just a line to say we might arrive at Portsmouth Town on Saturday instead of Sunday if I can get away on Friday night we shall arrive about 12 or half past. So ta ta till we meet. With love from both. We remain your Loving Brother & Sister Charlie & Fanny.

92. A happy Christmas to you – Raphael Tuck & Sons – Dublin, 5.30 am, De 25, 04 – (Front) Are you – (Back) W. Lanigan Esq., c/o Mrs Byrne, 17 Bath Avenue, Sandymount. With best wishes for a Happy Christmas & a Bright & Prosperous New Year. From Lillie.

93. Christmas Greetings – Raphael Tuck & Sons – Dublin, 4.45 pm, De 21, 04 – (Front) from Irene with love – (Back) Miss I. Costello, 27 Morehampton Road, Donnybrook.

94. Milkmaid Brand Milk – Raphael Tuck & Sons – Dublin, 5 pm, Jy 9, 04 – (Front) Milkmaid Brand Milk. Milk arriving at one of our factories. The milk of 60,000 cows is condensed daily at our eleven factories. An old Swiss condensed milk co. 9-7-04 – (Back) Miss Fleming, c/o Mrs Shorter, Kingsweston, Sunny Gardens, Hendon, London N.W.

95. With Best Christmas Wishes – Raphael Tuck & Sons – James's Street D.O. Dublin, 5.45 pm, De 21, 04. Vlissingen, De 23, 04 – (Front) from Nelly – (Back) T.J. Flood Esq., Flushing, Holland.

96. Football Incidents, Charged Through (Association) – Raphael Tuck & Sons – Dublin, 6.30 pm, Fe 21, 04 – (Front) with love 21-2-04 to yr. Mother with Iolanthe's love – (Back) Miss Brodie, 18 Coulson Ave, off Rathgar Ave, Rathgar. Thanks very much for yr. P.C. I may not be in tomorrow at 1 as our friend Miss Katie Smith is very ill & her plans are very uncertain? I had a P.C. from Nell O'C. today. Her brother Eugene's boy died aged a few years and they are in great grief. It is very sad. You must say a prayer for poor Mrs Smith as we are all so fond of her. T.L.

97.   Linden, Convalescent Home, Blackrock, Co. Dublin – Gerrard Brothers, Dublin – Blackrock, 11 pm, No 21, 04 – (Front) M. Potter Monday. My Dear, So sorry to hear you got ill, hope you are better now. having a long chat with S. write to me when you are better. Love from S & self. Maggie – (Back) Miss Perry, 4 St Bridgets Ward, St Vincents Hospital, Dublin.

98.   John Knox's House – Valentine – Dublin, 11.45 am, Ju 16, 04 – (Front) (none) – (Back) Miss Lister, 29 Upr Temple St, Dublin. Dear Mary I will not be able to call to see you till Friday afternoon about 4.30. If that day does not suit you kindly drop me a line. L.E. French, 8 Palmerston Villas, Palmerston, P.R.

99.   Pier, Kingstown – Chas. Cook, Kingstown – Kingstown, 7.45 pm, Au 14, 04 – (Front) Tuesday August 1904 – (Back) Miss A. Harvey, Altona, Howth Road, Clontarf. The mail boat just after coming in at the Harbour from Bridge near pavilion. S.G.L.

100.   Bray, Co. Wicklow – Lawrence, Dublin – Dublin, 11.45 am, Ap 13, 04 – (Front) (none) – (Back) Mrs Elmslie, 7 Upper Tooting Park Mansions, Marius Road, Balham, London S.W. 12-4-04 Still not a line from any of you. I should very much like to know if you are all right. Love and Best wishes from Dick.

101.   Higher Line Library, Clongowes Wood College, Co. Kildare – Lawrence, Dublin – Clongowes Wood, (…) Se 29, 04 – (Front) (none) – (Back) Miss Julian Belmont, Montenotte, Cork. Dear Gladys just a P.C. to add to your collection send me some more like the last. Your fond brother Dick.

102.   Storm at Bathing Place, Sandycove – Chas. Cook, Kingstown – Dublin, 4.45 pm, Se 27, 04. Toulon sur Allier, Allier, (…), 04 – (Front) 27-9-04. I was here yesterday but had not time to post this. The sea was not like this, quite calm. Affectionately Millicent – (Back) Monsieur Francisque de Boissieu, Château de la Forêt, Toulon sur Allier, Allier, France.

103.   Dalkey Island, Dublin. (Rave Flora) – Richardson, Leinster Restaurant, Dalkey – Dublin, 6.30 pm, Ap 17, 04 – (Front) (none) – (Back) Miss W. Harold, 23 Chesnut Grove, (…), Birkenhead, England. View of chapel sent last eve. from Dalkey is one on Island very early Christian. I am sorry you saw none of Dalkey we enjoyed it very much in semi darkness M. & L. sailed over to islands to see it. As far as we know today Breakfast Service Chapel Royal, Parish Cemetery, perhaps service's St Patrick's or Magdalene's Chapels to hear Dr C. (…) sends love. Letter & enclosures just come.

104.   Sorrento Terrace and Dalkey Island – Wrench Limited, London – Dublin, 5 pm, Ap 3, 04 – (Front) There is a most delightful Band Promenade here every Saturday during summer. R.B. – (Back) Miss Bella Higgins, Somerville, Military Road, Waterford.

105.   The East Pier, Kingstown – Stewart & Woolf, London – Dublin, 4.45 pm, Se 27, 04. Toulon sur Allier, Allier, (…), 04 – (Front) My dear Friend, I wrote you so hurriedly yesterday I spelled Shillelagh (this is right this time) wrong, so you would not know what I meant. I had not time to send you this from Kingstown either, so now you have a lot to excuse. From your friend Millicent. 27-9-04 – (Back) Monsieur Francisque de Boissieu, Château de la Forêt, Toulon sur Allier, Allier, France.

106.   *Amor Materno* – N.R.M. – Dublin, 11.45 am, Au 26, 04 – (Front) (none) – (Back) Mrs Taylor, Military Hotel, Buttevant. Rec'd your card at 9.45 pm thought I would drop you one, part of today was rather wet but cleared up well. Hope everybody are well (…). (Translation) Mother Love.

107.   Owed to the Landlady – Ode to Spring – Hely's Limited, Dublin – Dublin, 9.30 am, Mr 24, 04 – (Front) I am inclined to think you will begin to imagine I am very forgetful. I hope the weather will keep like this for another fortnight as it is just the sort that will suit me as I intend to take a spin D.V. (…) – (Back) Miss Montgomery, Kilbeggan, Co. Westmeath. I hope this will find you quite well and enjoying the beautiful weather we are getting this few days. Best Wishes from your bone crusher. (…)

108. Higher Line Playroom, Clongowes Wood College, Co. Kildare – Lawrence, Dublin – Clongowes Wood, (…), Ja 25, 04 – (Front) (none) – (Back) Miss K. Ennis, Oulartard House, Ferns, Co. Wexford. Write soon and tell the children to write to me. Bernard.

109. Main Street, Malahide – Wrench Ltd, London – Donabate, (…) 04 – (Front) (none) – (Back) W. Bray Esq., Treve Cottage, Ebbw Vale, Monmouth, England. H.M. CoastGuard, Portrane, Dear W. & M., very glad to hear that nothing serious had happened. The weather is bad and disagreeable almost approaching to a hurricane still we live & move. I have been extra busy since my return. Had a run home during the cruise. Aunt R. was much better than I expected. How is Walrus Villa, Sectarian strife as usual. Yours &C. John H.

110. H.M. The King at Kilkenny Agricultural Show – Hely's Limited, Dublin – Dublin, 5.30 pm, My 20, 04 – (Front) (none) – (Back) Mrs Woodward, 22 Palatine Sq., Burnley, Lancs. Taken here a fortnight ago. Jess.

111. Dalkey Island, Dalkey, Co. Dublin – Stewart & Woolf, London – Dublin, 6.30 pm, Se 10, 04. Toulon sur Allier, Allier, Se 12, 04 – (Front) 10-9-04. In Dublin again to-day. I have been hunting up a few post cards and hope you have not already had any of these. The heartiest of hearty hand shakes. Millicent – (Back) Monsieur F. de Boissieu, Château de la Forêt, Toulon sur Allier, Allier, France.

112. River Liffey, Dublin – Wrench Limited, London – Ballsbridge D.O. Dublin, 6 pm, Jy 8, 04. London S.W. 7.45 am, Jy 9, 04 – (Front) The entire family retire there for a month or more. Tomorrow I shut up this house – we will live on the sea!! House on shore & wildish mountains. Will write soon. E.S. – (Back) W. (…) Esq., Wilfred, 41 (…), Streatham Common, London S.W. 53 Morehampton Sqe, July 8 Your hasty Mother owes me a letter!! I am anxious to know how your exams got on. Do write to Garryowen c/o (…) Kilcoole, Wicklow. Love to all.

113. Russo-Japanese War – Cardinal – Dublin, 6.40 pm, No 6, 04 – (Front) Russo-Japanese War. No. 8, Talien-Wan 11th Feb. 1904. Landing of six hundred Japanese near Talien-Wan. Charge of Cossacks – (Back) H.V. Fleming, Lyndhurst, Harcourt Tce, Dublin. I hope you are all very well at home. Give my love to them all. Maudie.

114. Guinan Bros – Guinan Bros, 1 Harolds Cross – Dublin, 2 pm, Ap 12, 04 – (Front) (none) – (Back) Miss Murray, Floral Cottage, Dunleer. Dear Lillie Expecting a letter daily or am I past forgiveness for not writing. Hope all are well, all here splendid. Best love from Miss C. and Self to all. E.J.G.

115. Nautical Terms "Taking in the Sheet" – Valentine – Dublin, 5 pm, Fe 12, 04 – (Front) (none) – (Back) Miss Ida Duncan, Grand View, Hutchison Square, Douglas, Isle of Man. I don't know what you mean by the "business letter" but "<u>he</u> usually is a boy" and <u>she</u> is generally a girl.

116. St George's Church, Dublin – Lawrence, Dublin – Blackrock, 2.30 pm, De 29, 04 – (Front) (none) – (Back) Miss K. Callaghan, Kingswood, Clondalkin. New Year with kind remembrances and every good wish for a Bright New Year. From your brother always R.D. Hoping you feel well to-day.

117. The Palm House, Botanic Gardens, Dublin – E. & S., Ltd, Dublin – Bray, 12 pm, De 28, 04 – (Front) 28-12-04 – (Back) Mrs Greer, Bridge St, Newry. Just to say I arr. safely last night. Had company all the way to Bray. I had mild weather. Writing soon. Yrs. G.

118. The Grosvenor Hotel, Dublin opposite Westland Row Railway Station – (Publisher unknown) – Dublin, 6.15 pm, Fe 24, 04 – (Front) (none) – (Back) Miss Sadie McDonogh, Prospect Ho., Dunmore.

119. St. Andrew's, Westland Row – Stewart & Woolf, London – Dublin, 6.30 pm, De 24, 04 – (Front) (none) – (Back) Miss Cecil, Medop Hall, Camolin, Co. Wexford. With Love and best wishes for a Merry Xmas. From Polly.

120. Westland Row, Dublin – Stewart & Woolf, London – Dublin, 4.45 pm, De 7, 04 – (Front) (none) – (Back) Miss C.E. Stirling, Northdene, Castlecomer, Co. Kilkenny. Have you already one of this place? I think it's such a good one & so well coloured. Damp again so we can't get out. Your packing is immensely admired in both parcels. Write when you can to yrs. Cis.

121. King's Hospital and Cricket Ground, Dublin – Lawrence, Dublin – Blackrock, 11 pm, Se 11, 04 – (Front) (none) – (Back) Mrs Adams, Glasthule Hse, Glenageary. Art and I will be down tomorrow Sat. afternoon, if possible. Sophie is away on a visit to her sister in Galway. We will drive down if it is fine and provided Art comes home early from business. Walter.

122. Grand Hotel, Greystones – E. Greer, Greystones – Greystones, 6 pm, Ju 28, 04 – (Front) (none) – (Back) Miss Byrnes, Bank House, Skibbereen, Co. Cork. Very glad to hear from you. All well here. W.M.S., 4, Sidmonton Place, Greystones. June 28.

123. O'Connell's Statue, Dublin – (Publisher unknown) – Dublin, 2 pm, De 17, 04 – (Front) (none) – (Back) Master 'Jock' Horne, 6, Hawthorne Place, College Road, Cork.

124. Mater Misericordiae Hospital, Dublin – (Publisher unknown) – Dublin, 2 pm, Jy 11, 04 – (Front) Just like it. – (Back) Miss McKenna, Sacred Heart Convent, Roscrea, Co. Tipp. Dearest Cousin, Mother asked me to write you to thank you for your last letter to her. I told you cousin Mike called to see me but of course I was out & he could not wait. I had a card last night from him & I thought to run down to see him tomorrow but I don't think I shall for I got two teeth out today & I'd be afraid to go out in the cold tomorrow. I hope you like this card though you cannot see all "The Mater". The right wing cannot be seen, but it's the same size as the left wing. When you can, write to your loving Cousin and Sister. J.J.

125. O'Connell Monument, Glasnevin, Dublin – Wrench Limited, London – Dublin, 7.15 pm, Fe 13, 04 – (Front) From Dick – (Back) Miss E. Euens, Caerleon House School, Aberystwyth, Wales.

126. Parnell's Grave, Dublin – Hartmann – Dublin, 6.30 pm, Au 24, 04 – (Front) (none) – (Back) Miss E. Bagshaw, Wood View, Totley Brook Rd, Totley Rise, Sheffield. Mrs Oates, Kenilworth House, Central Prom., Douglas. Have just been to see spot on the picture. Love to all. H.E.

127. Palmerston Park, Rathmines – Stewart & Woolf, London – Dublin, 6.30 pm, Ap 1, 04 – (Front) (none) – (Back) The Rev. James George, (…), Norfolk, England. Thanks for kind letter, will write later on. Hope you have received a little parcel from me and the good wishes of the dear wife. Yrs. E.A.G.

128. Dublin Horse Show. The arriving crowd – Eason & Son Ltd., Dublin & Belfast – Dublin, 5.30 am, Se 24, 04 – (Front) (none) – (Back) Miss Delany, Liberty Hall, Armagh. Dear B. You will be surprised to see Mrs Dignam & I tomorrow. We are really going by 2.45. Mrs D. will wait for you to meet her. In haste. M.F. I did not know until now.

129. A Telephone Tragedy – Raphael Tuck & Sons – Dublin, 5.30 am, Au 10, 04 – (Front) A Telephone Tragedy. (in 6 Acts.) Act. 1. Jubilation! ("Ringing up") August 9th 04 – (Back) Miss Fleming, Elephant & Castle Hotel, Knaresbro, Yorkshire. August 9th 04. I cannot find my P.P.C. Albums. Do you know if you took them in mistake & if so could you send them to me. How are you all? Thank Father for the P.P.C. they are splendid. Love to Father & yourself, Uncle & Aunt & all in Knaresbro. Yrs. Herly.

130. Great Storm, February 27, 1903 – Lawrence, Dublin – Bray, 6.30 pm, Fe 26, 04 – (Front) Great Storm, February 27, 1903. Phoenix Park – 2,948 Trees blown down (1,242 Forest Trees, 1,706 Thorns). Am sending you this as a little reminder of the Great Storm of last year – (Back) Miss L.M. Greer, Bridge St, Newry. Hoping all quite well at home. All well here. Such terrible wet weather. I wish it would clear up. G.L.S.

131. Rathmines, Dublin – Hartmann – Dublin, 6.30 pm, Au 15, 04 – (Front) (none) – (Back) Miss Lane, "Holmhurst", Ordnance Rd, Southampton. Dear Evie, Phil leaves London on Wednesday for home by long sea. He is sure to be in Southampton on Thursday or Friday. Try to meet the boat. Kelly.

132.   Dublin, O'Connell Bridge and Sackville Street – E. & J. Burke's Bottling – Dublin, 2 pm, Se 21, 04 – (Front) Dublin 20th Sept. '04. Guinness' Dublin Stout creates strength and energy. It is bottled in Dublin by E. & J. Burke, (see label) Boston Office, 7, Water Street. Beware of imitations – (Back) Mrs Joe Armstrong, 191, Huntington Ave, Boston, Mass.

133.   Dublin, Stephen's Green from Shelbourne Hotel – Pictorial Stationery Co. Ltd, London – Rathmines D.O. Dublin, 5.45 pm, Se 17, 04 – (Front) Where will you find its like? – (Back) J. MacGregor Esq., 21, Ireton Street, Botanic Avenue, Belfast. *Mes sentiments sur le sujet de ta dernière post-carte sont trop profonds que des mots les exprimeraient. Mais attends, tu les entendras le samedi prochain! Tout à toi B.* (Translation) My feelings on the subject of your last postcard are so deep that words could not express them. But wait, and you will hear them next Saturday. All to you. B.

134.   The Royal Visit, Dublin, July, 1903. Westmoreland Street decorated – Lawrence, Dublin – Dublin, 11.45 am, Se 30, 04 – (Front) (none) – (Back) Miss A. Philipson, Blackdown, (…), England. Very fit this morning & just going out. Raining hard.

135.   Combridge & Co., Booksellers, Stationers, Picture Framers, Printsellers, 18 & 20 Grafton Street, Dublin – (Publisher unknown) – Dublin, 1.15 pm, Ju 22, 04 – (Front) To Mrs Fowler, Combridge & Co. beg respectfully to acknowledge receipt of kind order, which is having their best attention and has been forwarded today by mail, with exception of 3 books which are being sent direct from Publisher – (Back) Mrs Fowler, Robinstown, Enfield, Co. Meath.

136.   King's Hospital, Dublin – Lawrence, Dublin – Dublin, 3.30 am, Ju 30, 04 – (Front) (none) – (Back) Miss E. F. Devenish, Glendair, Ilkley, Yorkshire. King's Hospital, Dublin. My Dear Fairy, I hope you are quite well. I am sending you two postcards, one of the back & front of the school, with the cupola. I remain your loving brother Tommy.

137.   The National Library, Dublin – Wrench Limited, London – Castleknock, 5.45 pm, Mr 29, 04 – (Front) – My Dearest Mother, I will write long letter to you on Wednesday. I got (…) letter today. Your loving son Anthony. – (Back) Mrs McDonogh, Prospect, Dunmore, Tuam.

138.   Mr Wilson Barrett as Hamlet – S. Hildesheimer & Co. Ltd, London & Manchester – Dublin, 5 pm, Ju 3, 04 – (Front) Dear May, why have you not written to me. I have not had a letter for over a week & send me my collars. With love from Clare – (Back) Miss Grew, Burbrae House, Portadown, Co. Armagh. I got leave to go out today so Mona Campbell & Irene Nolan came with me & we all went to see Annie Perry. She looks much better than I thought she would & very pretty. I think she will have to go out of the hospital on 1st July & is delighted. She says she does not care where she goes so long as she gets out. She walks with two sticks & seems to have suffered very much. Would'nt it be lovely if she could come home with me. I will be going about Wednesday fortnight. She was asking for all.

139.   Camden Street, Dublin – (Publisher unknown) – Rathmines D.O. Dublin, 4.15 pm, Oc 13, 04 – (Front) Dear B, thanks for card. Am glad to hear you are looking so well. M. is grand. My cold still sticks but it is all right again. Love from all (…) – (Back) Miss Greville, Three Castles, Manor Kilbride, via Dublin.

140.   National Library of Ireland, Kildare St, Dublin – The "National" Series – Dublin, 11.45 am, Au 19, 04 – (Front) (none) – (Back) Miss M.K. Tighe, 31, Victoria Avenue, Donnybrook.

141.   Co. Dublin. Malahide Castle – M. Hall, Malahide – Malahide Dublin, 6.45 pm, De 21, 04 – (Front) (none) – (Back) Mrs Kinch, Heynestown Rectory, Dundalk. To wish you all a very Happy Xmas & New Year. J.H.

142.   Custom House, Dublin – (Publisher unknown) – Dublin, (…), 04. Birmingham, 9.20 pm, Jy 29, 04 – (Front) (none) – (Back) Miss May Whithorne, 3 Preastley Place, Main Street, (…), Birmingham. With love from Aunt Lizzie.

143. Miss Connie Ediss – Rotary Photo Co. Ltd – Dublin, 5.30 am, Ja 21, 04 – (Front) I typed this all by my little self. (…) – (Back) Miss Carnegie, 28, Grosvenor Square, Rathmines.

144. The Scalp, Co. Wicklow – Hely's Limited, Dublin – Dublin, 2 pm, Au 11, 04 – (Front) (none) – (Back) Miss M.K. Tighe, 31, Victoria Avenue, Donnybrook.

145. The City Hall, Dublin – Hartmann – Dublin, 5.30 am, Se 22, 04 – (Front) This is our one. I dare say it is dirty but antique so what matter? Of course it can't hold a candle to your magnificent building – (Back) J. MacGregor Esq., 21 Ireton Street, Botanic Avenue, Belfast. Many thanks for yours this morning it looks a very pretty place and would I am sure make a nice walk. Isn't the weather lovely? I hope it may continue for this week anyway. *Tout á Toi.* B. (Translation) All to you.

146. Leinster Lawn and Merrion Square, Dublin – Valentine – James's Street D.O. Dublin, 5.45 pm, Mr 1, 04 – (Front) (none) – (Back) Mrs Burrow, 45 Merton Hall Rd, Wimbledon, London. Have just been to Torrey's P. meeting. Very few there but not bad considering the weather! A perfect blizzard is raging as I write – talk about pigeons! Nice prospect for the Curragh this afternoon. Love to all. Dom.

147. Dublin, Grafton Street – Pictorial Stationery Co. Ltd, London – Dublin, 5.30 am, De 13, 04 – (Front) (none) – (Back) Miss M.K. Tighe, 31 Victoria Ave, Donnybrook. Was very bad with my cold this morning. Had to give in and see a doctor. He has ordered me to bed, so I am afraid I cannot see you tonight.

148. House Party at the Vice-Regal Lodge, April, 1904 – Hely's Limited, Dublin – Dublin, 6.15 pm, My 13, 04 – (Front) (none) – (Back) Miss Bella Higgins, Somerville, Military Road, Waterford.

149. Their Majesties' Departure from Kingsbridge for Kilkenny, April, 1904 – Hely's Limited, Dublin – Dublin 11.45 am, My 9, 04 – (Front) (none) – (Back) Miss M.M.I. Bolton, (…) Pembroke Park, Dublin. With love & best wishes from J.W.B. May 9th 1904.

150. Her Excellency Countess Dudley – Hely's Limited, Dublin – Dublin, 4 pm, My 16, 04 – (Front) Do you see the resemblance – (Back) Miss Liston, 3, Ardilaun Ter., Nth Cir. Rd, Dublin. To Dearest Zoe, from an ardent admirer. (…)

151. Their Majesties at Ballsbridge, about to receive Address from Citizens' Committee – Hely's Limited, Dublin – Ballsbridge D.O. Dublin, 6 pm, Jy 30, 04 – (Front) (none) – (Back) Cyril Leeper Esq., 16, Waterloo Rd, Dublin. Quite well thank you!

152. Grattan Bridge, Dublin – Lawrence, Dublin – Dublin, 11.45 am, Au 12, 04 – (Front) (none) – (Back) Miss Julia Ward, Corbetstown, Co. Westmeath. Picture me turning the corner Sunday morning. You can imagine what I will say. Don't do too much.

153. Weather Reports. Illustrated. "Glass falling. Storms expected!" – Raphael Tuck & Sons – Dublin, 4.45 pm, Se 6, 04 – (Front) (none) – (Back) Miss M. (…), Fairy Mount, Kingscourt, Co. Cavan. Quite well. Best wishes. W.

154. Father Matthew Statue, Dublin – Lawrence, Dublin – Dublin, 11.45 am, Oc 18, 04 – (Front) It affords me pleasure to send you the picture of the monument of Ireland's Temperance apostle. Cecil – (Back) Mr Bunoz Francois, 64, Rue de la Chaussée, (…), Paris, France.

155. Dublin – B. & N. Ltd, Dublin – Dublin, 5.30 am, My 5, 04 – (Front) (none) – (Back) Miss G. Grey Bentley, 9, Sefton Street, Southport, Lancashire. Dear Gert., Thanks for card. Our neighbour's cats don't sit on the gate but the backyard wall makes a very good substitute. You may be pleased to hear that I'm suffering no ill effects from the "pun". The weather (same old subject) is very unsettled. Yesterday was a lovely summer's day while today is East – Windy & Rainy. I hope you & my S'port Mamma are quite well. Give my love to Ma. We are all delighted with our new house & wouldn't go back to the R.H. for anything. Lots of love to yourself from the Tobins.

156. Guinness Brewery. Locomotive Malt Waggon – Wrench Limited, London – Dublin, 6.15 pm, My 20, 04. Toulon sur Allier, Allier, My 22, 04 – (Front) Dear Mr de Boissieu, Thanks for the card this morning also the pretty flower cards the rose is like a real one. Yours truly Louie (…) Just fancy I have not been through this great brewery yet – (Back) Mons. F. de Boissieu, Château de la Forêt, Toulon sur Allier, Allier, France. (Readdressed to) Rue Marbeuf 39, Paris.

157. Evicted tenant & his family – Hartmann – Dublin, 5.30 am, No 17, 04 – (Front) (none) – (Back) Mrs Hall, 9 Albert St, Sligo. Owing to a very bad bicycle cut happened yesterday but could not be helped. Many thanks for your nice offer but could not find the paper here. Believe one of my play books (…) Are you going to write it, it might alter design. With fond love excuse writing (…)

158. St. Lawrence Gate, Drogheda, Co. Louth – Lawrence, Dublin – Dublin, 6.30 pm, Au 24, 04 – (Front) (none) – (Back) Miss Nellie Strahan, 45, Northumberland Ave, Kingstown. If you go up to the left as I have marked you will meet the Christian Bros. Schools. Pres. Rev. Bro. Strahan. We saw it last month. Kiss Georgie. Tom.

159. Irish Terrier – C.W. Faulkner & Co. – Dublin, 5.30 am, No 28, 04 – (Front) "Lest you forget"!! – (Back) Miss M.K. (…), c/o Mrs B. Jones, (…), Wexford Road, (…), Cheshire, England. Was glad to hear you are having a good time. How do you like the weather? Had a letter from (…) They did not seem to know that you would be in D. for Xmas, rather hazy about your movements in general!! When do you return! With love J.S.

160. Star of the Sea Church, Sandymount – Hely's Limited, Dublin – Dublin, 6.30 pm, Ap (…), 04 – (Front) (none) – (Back) Miss Nichols, 85 Ranelagh Road, Dublin. For your collection. J.

161. Martin Harvey – Rotary Photo Co. Ltd – Dublin, 5.30 am, No 18, 04 – (Front) (none) – (Back) Miss R.B. O'Brien, 7 N.G. Georges St, Dublin. W.S.H.

162. Leap Year. Buttonholed – Raphael Tuck & Sons – Rathmines D.O. Dublin, 5.45 pm, Mr 14, 04 – (Front) (none) – (Back) Miss Brodie, 18, Coulson Ave, Rathgar. Will expect you tomorrow Tuesday at 2 o'c. without fail. Hope yr cold has quite recovered! With thanks for good wishes & love from Iolanthe Lawless. March 1904.

163. The Obelisk, Victoria Hill, near Dalkey – Stewart & Woolf, London – Dublin, 5.30. am, Au 25, 04 – (Front) (none) – (Back) Miss D. Brinkley, c/o George Brinkley Esq., Orwell Villas, Burnham-on-Crouch, Essex, England. Got your letter, will write tomorrow. Weather fine hope it is fine with you. Channel fleet in Kingstown but have not seen them yet. Willie borrowed Wm. Gunn's camera and took the family of the lodge at camp, turned out very well. Mrs Rose coming home, have been to Douglas I.O.M. Gym has not opened yet, have not heard when it will. Dad says to gather up every bit of news for budget this week. Hope Uncle George, Emily, Polly and yourself fare well. A kitten we have caught a rat on Monday. The slips Miss Gibbon sent are doing very well. Joined by Father in love to Uncle George, Polly and Emily. I remain, your loving Sister, Dolly.

164. Bailey Lighthouse, Howth Head – W.H. Berlin – Dublin, 5.30 am, Au 24, 04 – (Front) Pray hold this card up to the light, And you shall see a charming sight – (Back) Miss D. Brinkley, Orwell Villas, Burnham-on-Crouch, Essex, England. Thanks for the p.p. cards for my collection. Only came home on Friday. Spent Saturday afternoon at the camp. Had a great time, the boys are getting along in great style. Hope you are having a good time on your holidays. Yours Alice.

165. The Vatican Gardens, The Pope and Cardinals – Misch & Stock's – Dublin, 11.45 am, Au 5, 04 – (Front) (none) – (Back) Miss M.K. Tighe, 31, Victoria Avenue, Donnybrook.

166. Liverpool, Landing Stage – Raphael Tuck & Sons – Dublin, 5.30 am, Au 26, 04 – (Front) (none) – (Back) Miss M.K. Tighe, 31 Victoria Avenue, Donnybrook. Am mad I can't see you tonight can't get off. Going to have a row in the office and give in resignation.

167. Castle from the Lawn, Clongowes Wood College, Co. Kildare – Lawrence, Dublin – Clongowes Wood (…) Ju 10, 04 – (Front, ctd from back) -ing finished yet. I am counting the days till the 21st June. The exams commence next week. Bernard – (Back) Miss K. Ennis, Oulartard, Ferns, Co. Wexford. I was delighted to get your letter. I think you have six C-W-C post cards now. Is the new build-

168. The Castle, Dublin – Lawrence, Dublin – Dublin, 2 pm, Se 27, 04. Toulon sur Allier, Allier, (…), 04 – (Front) Dear M. de Boissieu Would you please post your cards so that they would reach me on Sunday when I get the post myself as sometimes my cards get lost or mislaid if they come when I am not in. You will be thinking I am a great bother. This is a different view from what I sent before. Yours Louie – (Back) Mons. F. de Boissieu, Château de la Forêt, Toulon sur Allier, Allier, France.

169. (Untitled) – C.W. Faulkner & Co. – Dublin, 5.30 pm, Se 24, 04 – (Front) Dear D. I hope I shant inconvenience you by this scrawl; My holidays are all over, we are back from Camp. Hope you have good weather (…) – (Back) Miss D. Brinkley, c/o Mrs Duffy, 126 Boleyn Road, Forest Gate, London E. Have you heard that Robinson is dead, Yes, poor chap, cut off in the prime of his manhood. Alas, Jack says he doesn't smoke but never mind he will soon enough.

170. A Telephone Tragedy – Raphael Tuck & Sons – Dublin, 6.30 pm, Au 15, 04 – (Front) A Telephone Tragedy. (in 6 Acts.) Act. VI. (5 minutes later) Realisation! ("Cut off!") August 15th 04 – (Back) Miss Fleming, Elephant & Castle Hotel, Knaresbro, Yorkshire. This should be the sixth which makes the comp. set. Have you got six? Love to all. Send some P.P. yrs. H.

171. In Coourt – Lawrence, Dublin – Dublin, 2 pm, My 4, 04 – (Front) In Coourt. Counsel: "What's your name?" Witness: "The same as me Father's." Counsel: "And what is your Father's name?" Witness: "The same as mine." Counsel: "But what is both your names?" Witness: "Sure there both alike" – (Back) Master Gerald Burns, 6 Rosetta Avenue, Ormeau Road, Belfast. Dear Gerald, we will be home tonight by the 1.45 train so hope to see you & Clare. Best love to all. Auntie Belle.

172. Vesta Tilley – Rotary Photo Co. Ltd – Rathmines D.O. Dublin, 5.45 pm, Se 14, 04 – (Front) Doing best with collar – (Back) Miss M. Donogh, Prospect House, Dunmore, Co. Galway. How are your getting on without the job. Hope you are keeping good. Had a real nice time going through Guinness's B.

173. An Port Gaedealac – An cead Ceim Súbailte. The Irish Jig – Leading off Double – Lawrence, Dublin – Dublin, 5.30 am, De 23, 04 – (Front) (none) – (Back) Miss D. Coombes, 7 Princes St, N., St Thomas, Exeter, Devon. 1 Geraldine St, Dublin. 23-12-04. Dear Dorothy, Just a few lines to wish you a very Merry Xmas and Prosperous New year. With kind regards from your friend Adelaide Dawson.

174. Irish Piper – Fergus O'Connor – Dublin, 5 pm, Ap 5, 04 – (Front) With best wishes & kind remembrances from (…) – (Back) Mrs Spratt, Drayton House, Westcliff Rd, Birkdale, Southport, Lancs.

175. The Irish Emigrant – Fergus O'Connor – Dublin, 5.30 am, Au 16, 04 – (Front) I'm sitting on the stile Mary. – (Back) Mrs Brent, c/o Mrs Carpenter, 34 The Waldrons, Croydon, Surrey, England. Dear N. I hope you are getting on alright. We are enjoying ourselves very much. With love from E.

176. Blanche Miroir – (Publisher unknown) – James's Street D.O. Dublin, 4.45 pm, Oc 12, 04 – (Front) Dear Miss K. I hope you are getting stronger. I saw Dr H. yesterday. He is sending me to Stillorgan for a fortnight. Kind love from yours Mary Nolan – (Back) Miss M. Kellie, No. 5 Ward, Stevens' Hospital, Dublin.

177. Clyde Road, Ballsbridge – Stewart & Woolf, London – Dublin, 6.40 pm, No 9, 04 – (Front) (…) – (Back) Monsieur (…), Paris, France.

178. Quaker Oats Smiles – Quaker Oats Limited – Dublin, 6.30 pm, Jy 25, 04 – (Front) Cook's Smile. "I must," exclaimed the country cook, "Get Quaker Oats by hook or crook;" She did; now see her happy look, <u>The smile</u>

that won't come off!" "Quaker Oats Smiles," consisting of ten different designs, post paid for 3d., and three white squares cut from fronts of "Quaker Oats" packets. Apply to Dept. P.C., Quaker Oats, Limited, London, E.C. 25.7.04 will send P.P. cards to morrow. Love to all. H. – (Back) Miss Fleming, c/o Miss Williams, The Lindens, Church Walk, Llandudno, N. Wales.

179. His Majesty's arrival at Punchestown, April, 1904 – Hely's Limited, Dublin – Dublin, 5.30 am, De 26, 04 – (Front) (none) – (Back) Mrs Stivey, 3 Coleman's Terr., S. Circular Rd, Dolphin's Barn, Dublin. A merry Xmas and a happy New Year. From Father and Mother and Myself. From E. Jones.

180. Injustice to Ireland – Lawrence, Dublin – Dublin, (…), Se 6, 04. Vlissingen, Se (…), 04 – (Front) Injustice to Ireland. Is it there, yez are, ye two-faced Lyin' Blaguard wid yer mane Blarney about the Sun; no Sun ivir riz anywhere, afore it did in Ould Ireland! England afore Ireland! nivir! Hurroo!!! – (Back) T.J. Flood Esq., Flushing, Holland.

181. Great Northern Railway Terminus, Dublin – Stewart & Woolf, London – Dublin, 2 pm, Fe 23, 04 – (Front) was at P.rush on Saturday meeting a cousin. Saw a friend of yours. I expect you had a big day at B.castle. I didn't write. My cycle was away on Monday. Cannot have it so much now. I could meet you any day this week. Would Thursday do? Have you been to P.rush yet. Could you not go down some day. Thanks very much for invitation. I am sure it will be good. I will do you something. (…) – (Back) Miss Hamilton, Ballyrobin House, (…)

182. Custom House and Quays, Dublin – Lawrence, Dublin – Dublin, (…), 04 – (Front) (none) – (Back) Mrs Crowley, 60, Hibernia Gds, Cork. Glad A. is keeping well. Hope all the rest are A.1.

183. Skerries, The Harbour – Wrench Limited, London – Rush, 6 pm, Se 8, 04 – (Front) The Shanty, Rush, Nr Dublin. Awfully windy & showery, so we are settling down to sew & to read for the day. Teresa – (Back) Mrs G. Graham, 234 Primrose Rd, Bootle near Liverpool. Do not sell any of yr coloured clothes as if you want to dispose of any, we might buy them off you & give a better price than the old woman. Teresa.

184. Bridges & Custom House, Dublin – Stewart & Woolf, London – Dublin, 4.45 pm, No 5, 04 – (Front) Maire, I have heard thee in thy soliloquy; May I cross the Bridge – (Back) Miss Maire O'Donnell, Gordon Place, Clonmel, Co. Tipp. Hello who is this? Well hasn't he a nerve, I wonder who can it be, at all? Ah this is a joke & yet maybe not, but we shall see.

185. Baile Átha Cliath. Museum Stáire Nádúrdha & Íomhaigh Tighearna Pluncoet – Cuideachta na gCártaí Posta Gaedhealach, Átha Cliath – Dublin, 11.45 am, Oc 5, 04 – (Front) (none) – (Back) Miss M.K. Tighe, 31, Victoria Avenue, Donnybrook. Could not get round to see you last night. Was expecting a wee note from you. Am afraid you are forgetting me. Will do my best to see you tonight. Sorry I can't write a letter. (Translation) Dublin. National Museum and Baron Plunket's statue. The Gaelic Postcard Company, Dublin.

186. The Low-Backed Car – Lawrence, Dublin – Dublin, 1.15 am, Au 28, 04 – (Front) The Low-Backed Car. Oh, I'd rather own that car, sir, With Peggy by my side, Than a coach and four, and gold galore And a lady for my bride; For the lady would sit fornenst me – (Back) Miss Ita Ennis, Dominican Convent, Wicklow. Got home. All safe. Will write later on. Your loving Mother and Brother.

187. The Birth of an Heir – Lawrence, Dublin – Fairview D.O. Dublin, 6 pm, My 13, 04. Roundwood, My 13, 04 – (Front) The Birth of an Heir. Och! Paddy, wake up, don't be dhramin' Joy, agrah, from your eye should be sthramin' Arrah, whist, to the SMALL STRANGER schramin' "I'M HEIR to the BYRNES and O'TOOLES." So am I. Are you – (Back) Mrs Gilbert, P.O. Roundwood, Co. Wicklow. Still no news. Hope you all are well. Lovely weather now. Best love. Was in the City yesterday, going to the park tomorrow.

188. St. John's Church, Sydney Parade – (Publisher unknown) – Dublin, 5.30 am, Jy 27, 04. Newcastle, Co. Down, 11.15 am, Jy 27, 04 – (Front) (none) – (Back) Miss Brewster, Sea Cape, Newcastle, Co. Down. Very many thanks for roses, they arrived perfectly fresh. We are going on all right. Baby is getting so fat. B.R.

189. Rotunda Hospital. Dublin – The National Series – Dublin, 2 pm, Ap 26, 04 – (Front) (none) – (Back) Dr J.L. Nevin, Main Street, Ballymoney, Co. Antrim.

190. Irish Farmyard – (Publisher unknown) – Dublin, 6.30 pm, Jy 3, 04 – (Front) Irish Farmyard, "The Decent cot that tops the neighbouring hill." – (Back) Miss May Pickford, 56 Durham Road, Manor Park, Essex, London. Dear May, Ask Percy to bring you over when he is coming. Love and Kisses from Uncle, Auntie & Georgie to all.

191. Interior of Royal Hospital, Kilmainham, Co. Dublin – (Publisher unknown) – Dublin, 5.30 am, Ap 17, 04. Brooklyn, 2.30 pm, Ap 27, 04 – (Front) 16-4-04. My Dear Ada, Thanks very much for your last letter & P.C. this will remind you of the Sundays we came here. How is your collection. I have 716 now. Mrs (…) had a baby girl last week. They are back in Dawson St. Alice will write you soon. love Edie – (Back) Miss Ada Llaute, c/o Mrs V. Price, Hotel St George, Brooklyn Heights, Brooklyn, U.S.A.

192. He won't be happy till he gets it – Cynicus Publishing Co. Ltd, Tayport, Fife – Dublin, 4.45 pm, De 31, 04 – (Front) He won't be happy till he gets it. Oh be careful and always get there first what price this "Pussy" – (Back) P. Kidd Esq., Mount Sherlock, Donadea, Kilcock, Co. Kildare. Wishing you a Happy New Year.

193. Mrs Langtry – Raphael Tuck & Sons – Dublin, 6.15 pm, Ap 6, 04 – (Front) Mrs Langtry. "What honour to be born on Fortune's Hill? The merit is to climb it." Yours sincerely Paula Hughes – (Back) Miss Cassie (…), King Lake St, Edge Hill.

194. Lithographic Department, Hely's Limited, Acme Works, Dame Court, Dublin – Hely's Limited, Dublin – Dublin, 6.30 pm, Oc 26, 04 – (Front) Lithographic Department, Hely's Limited, Acme Works, Dame Court, Dublin. Lithographic and Letterpress Printing, Designing, Engraving. Account Book Manufacture, Letterpress Bookbinding, Ruling, Etc. – (Back) Mrs B. Conway, Portlaw, Co. Waterford. From Hely's Limited, Stationers, Printers & Bookbinders, 27–30 Dame Street, Dublin. We desire to acknowledge and thank you for your kind order, which is having our careful attention. We shall forward same in due course.

195. Strawberry Beds. Dublin – Wrench Limited, London – Ballsbridge D.O. Dublin, 6 pm, Mr 5, 04 – (Front) Mar 5/04. This is a picture of the Strawberry Beds in Phoenix Park, where we once went & had strawberries & cream. Love Jonnie – (Back) Miss (…), Glen Iveagh, Church Hill, Whitby, Yorkshire. Hope you are keeping well & that Hilda is good. Jonnie.

196. Mr Beerbohm Tree – (Publisher unknown) – Dublin, 6.30 pm, Ja 1, 04 – (Front) How do you like this old chap? – (Back) Miss Moira Cosgrave, 174, James's St, Dublin. Dearest Moira, Just a card to wish many happy returns of the day also a Happy & Prosperous New Year. Hope to see you all early next week. Yr. fond Cousin Ellie. 1-1-04.

197. Dodder Bridge, Rathfarnham – W.H. Berlin – Dublin, 6.40 pm, De 31, 04 – (Front) Pray hold this card up to the light, And you shall see a charming sight. Best of wishes for the New Year 1905 – (Back) Miss Ingram, 8, Adelaide Terrace, Kilmainham, S.C. Road, Dublin. Dear L. Many thanks for nice card. You are smart to be first to see Mr P. Mrs Bailey was in office seeing Molly yesterday and said Mr P. is going out to (…) tomorrow (Sunday). She will bring him to see us so I am writing to ask her to drop a card when arriving. Ina.

198. Rhododendrons. Howth Castle, Demesne. Co. Dublin – (Publisher unknown) – Howth, 6 pm, My 19, 04 – (Front) Expect you home. yours David – (Back) Samuel Bell Esq., B.A., Farnworth, Nr Widnes, Lancs., England. Unless you have written don't do so until you hear from me further as I expect to go to new lodgings on Saturday. Had a letter from home yesterday, they (…)

199. House Party at Lismore Castle, May 1904 – Hely's Limited, Dublin – Rathmines D.O. Dublin, 5.45 pm, My 17, 04. Farnham, 11 am, My 18, 04 – (Front) (none) – (Back) Miss D.E. Robinson, c/o Mrs Julius, Claremont, Gilford, Farnham, Surrey. May 17, 1904. Another King. River Dale, Terenure, Co. Dublin. Your P.C. of 14th came last night. Princess V. is in House Party Vice Regal Lodge, sitting down on left with dark fur boa. Hope

you keep out of way of motors. Better learn to drive our's so you won't be frightened. I think you have all the King series. Yrs. (…)

200. Fisher Folk. Howth. Co. Dublin – (Publisher unknown) – Dublin, 4.45 pm, Se 27, 04. Toulon sur Allier, Allier, Se 29, 04 – (Front) My dear Friend I like so much the new series of Parisian cards, with plenty of room for a kind message from you. Best of hand shakes from your friend by the sea. Millicent. 27-9-04 – (Back) Monsieur Francisque de Boissieu, Château de la Forêt, Toulon sur Allier, Allier, France.

201. Dublin. O'Connell's Monument – Pictorial Stationery Co. Ltd, London – Booterstown, 5.30 pm, Jy 8, 04 – (Front) July 8 1904. My dear Mrs George I am sending you these cards & I hope you will like them. I am very sorry that I could (ctd on back) – (Back) Mrs A. George, Baker Arms, Blandford, Dorset, England. not get them all like these but will try again. We arrived here quite safe. We had a lovely passage. Indeed we are having lovely weather here. Hope this will find you all quite well. With love to you all from yours F.E.

202. Fionnglaise, sráid-bhaile i n-aice Baile Átha Cliath – Cuideachta na gCártaí Posta Gaedhealach, Átha Cliath – Dublin, 6.40 am, No 1, 04 – (Front) (none) – (Back) Mrs Phelan, 50 Beresford Street, Waterford. 21 Belvidere Avenue, Nth S.R. Dear Mr & Mrs Phelan the silver arrived safely. A thousand thanks it is simply lovely. Tom & I are most grateful. Excuse card will write in a day or two. Agnes Ennis. (Translation) Finglas, a small village near Dublin. The Gaelic Postcard Company, Dublin.

203. A City Jaunting Car, Dublin – Valentine – Dublin, 11.45 am, Ju 19, 04 – (Front) Last lap, old Reg. Hope to be with you all tomorrow afternoon about 6 or half-past. This is not a bad photo is it? The place is the library. A.E.C.D. – (Back) Reginald E. Dickenson Esq, Grove House School, Highgate, London.

204. Castle Street, Dalkey, Dublin – Richardson, Leinster Restaurant, Dalkey – Dalkey, 10.45 pm, Au 10, 04 – (Front) Hope you & your Mother have enjoyed your holidays. The weather was nice wasn't it? V.H.H.P. is coming Dalkey 10-8-04 – (Back) Miss D. Allwright, c/o Mrs Cleeve, Oxford Wood, Godalming, Surrey, England. Ever so many thanks for your sweet letter which I received in London when we arrived at 5.30 Monday evening. We had a lovely 4 hours passage from Ostend to Dover. The moment we got to the Metropole Muddie & Bunnie scrambled into evening dress, dined & off to the theatre to see the (…) Not worth while writing letters now as I hope to see you. Home tomorrow. (…) V.

205. St Matthew's National Schools, Irishtown – Hely's Limited, Dublin – Ballsbridge D.O. Dublin, 6 pm, No 14, 04 – (Front) (none) – (Back) Miss Annie Evans, Harbour House, Skerries, Co. Dublin. My Dear Annie I am sending you this postcard and I hope you will like it. Hoping all are well. Please give my love to Miss Sheils and the Girls. I remain your loving friend. Y.H.

206. View of Salthill Hotel, Monkstown, Co. Dublin – Gerrard Brothers, Dublin – Blackrock, 11 pm, Au 13, 04 – (Front) 13-8-04 Trust you feel rested by now. We drove into Dublin after luncheon and have just returned. It rained of course. Let me know when you reach Lancs. Hope you put my name on the bike. J. – (Back) Miss Wright, c/o Mrs Kilminster, Chalford Vale, Stroud, Gloucester.

207. Phoenix Park Races, April, 1904 – Hely's Limited, Dublin – Dublin, 6.30 pm, My 6, 04 – (Front) Phoenix Park Races, April, 1904. The Duke of Devonshire. H.R.H. The Duke of Connaught. The Marquis of Londonderry. H.M. The King. His Excellency The Lord Lieutenant – (Back) Miss Mollie Morton, 44 Derby Street, Leck, Staffs, England. With love from Uncle Jack.

208. Procession on the Way to the Cathedral – Eason & Son Ltd, Dublin & Belfast – Dublin, 5.30 am, Au 4, 04 – (Front) Procession on the Way to the Cathedral, H.E. Cardinal Vannutelli, His Grace The Archbishop of Dublin – (Back) Miss Shiels, Green Hills, Drogheda. *Tempus Fugit* looking back how time appears but a myth and happenings after all a nothing. Monday finds me on the ocean again. Had a nice drive Friday last. Kind regards E. Maritivsovich. (Translation) Time Flies.

209. Sackville St. Dublin – W.H. Berlin – Dublin, 11.45 am, Jy 26, 04 – (Front) (none) – (Back) Master Bob Akers, Kirby Underdale, York, England. Mother hopes you are a good boy. We shall soon be coming to see you. Are you growing fat? Mother.

210. Pro Cathedral Marlborough Street – Hely's Limited, Dublin – Dublin, 5.30 am, Se 8, 04 – (Front) (none) – (Back) Miss Brinkley, c/o Mrs Duffy, 126 Boleyn Road, Forest Gate, London. 11 Carlisle Ave, Marlboro Road, Dublin. 7 Sept 1904. P.C. to hand. Shall write fuller on receipt of (…) Sunday. Call to 11 Finsbury Square when in neighbourhood and get your "Quaker Oats" pot which was purchased at Rink Exhibition. Please send solution of conundrum on card. i.e. Why should "Romford Road have to make another leg for Forest Gate" is the latter shaky?

211. Guinness Brewery – Wrench Limited, London – Dublin, 6.15 pm, My 20, 04. Toulon sur Allier, Allier, My 22, 04 – (Front) Guinness Brewery, Loading Wharf, River Liffey. I suppose you have seen these barges on the Liffey when you were in Dublin. Splendid weather for the race (human). Well, were you elected Mayor? 19th May Louie – (Back) Mons. F. de Boissieu, Château de la Forêt, Toulon sur Allier, Allier, France. (Readdressed to) Rue Marbeuf 39, Paris.

212. Skerries – Mealley, Fancy Depot, Skerries – Skerries Co. Dublin, 8 pm, Se 9, 04 – (Front) How do you stand Lizzie? I can't know. She is the greatest little Piggie I ever met. Don't mind her if she says she is enjoying herself. She tells the most awful lies I ever heard. What do you think of the view? It is one of the principal views in the whole place. Joined in love by "Our Sister". Yours very sincerely. Gretta C. – (Back) Miss B. McArdle, 17, Cabra Park, Phibsboro, Dublin. Dear B. I shall go up tomorrow evg. To meet Agnes. Liz.

213. Hely's Limited, Printers and Bookbinders, Dame Street, Dublin – Hely's Limited, Dublin – Dublin, 6.30 am, Ja 6, 04 – (Front) In our "Acme" works – a corner of Binding Room, No. 1. Hely's Limited, Printers and Bookbinders, Dame Street, Dublin – (Back) W.B. Hill, Esq., Mullacroghan, Drogheda, Co. Louth. From Hely's Limited, Stationers, Printers & Bookbinders, 27–30 Dame Street, Dublin. We desire to acknowledge and thank you for your kind order, which is having our careful attention. We shall forward same in due course.

214. St James's Bazaar and Fete – (Publisher unknown) – Dublin, 6.40 pm, De 31, 04 – (Front) St James's Bazaar and Fete. Shamrock Souvenir. Amusements Stall, December, 1904. Rev. R.B. Bryan M.A., Rev. J.C. Irwin B.D., Rev. G.S. Eves M.A. "Tis theirs to pluck the amaranthine flower Of faith, and round the Sufferer's temples bind Wreaths that endure affliction's heaviest shower, And do not shrink from sorrow's keenest wind." Wordsworth – (Back) Miss M.J. Kelly, 14 Main St, Trim, Co. Meath.

215. Carmelite Church, Clarendon Street – (Publisher unknown) – Dublin, 6.30 pm, Au 1, 04 – (Front) (none) – (Back) Miss Howley, 18 Pembroke Road, Dublin. A long, cheerful letter from Newcastle. Shall call Wednesday evening. (…) J.P.R. 1 Au 04.

216. Map of Wicklow – John Walker & Co. Ltd – Dublin, 6.15 pm, Mr 16, 04. Tours, Indre et Loire, 4.45 am, Mr 16, 04 – (Front) Engraved by J. Bartholomew & Co., No. 508 Geographical Series, John Walker & Co. Ltd, Poul a Phouca Waterfall, Dublin – (Back) Miss P. Gubbins, Villa La Pierre, Tours, France.

217. Rotunda, Dublin – (Publisher unknown) – James's Street D.O. Dublin, 4.15 pm, Oc 3, 04 – (Front) (none) – (Back) Miss Wiseborough, 16 Palace Gdns Terrace, Kensington, London W.

218. Miss Mabel Love – Stereoscopic Company – Dublin, 4.45 pm, Au 3, 04 – (Front) Kathleen S. – (Back) Miss M.J. O'Neill, Hazeldean, Sydney Parade. 1-VIII-04. Do you like this one of Mabel Love? I suppose you were too grand to come in & see me today. Did you write to "J." yet? Love from H.

219. Dublin. The Museum – Raphael Tuck & Sons – Dublin, 6.30 pm, Au 20, 04 – (Front) (none) – (Back) Miss Sheils, Green Hills, Drogheda. Thanks for card, hope you enjoyed yourself at Dundalk. The weather being so fine there is a good stir for Horseshow Week. Trusting you and all are well. Kind Regards. M.J.G.

220. Dublin Horse Show, 1904 – Hely's Limited, Dublin – Dundrum Dublin, 6.30 pm, Se 17, 04 – (Front) Dublin Horse Show, 1904. His Excellency The Lord Lieutenant in the Enclosure. September, 17th 1904. Hope you had a good passage and arrived safely. Yrs. Jim – (Back) To Miss Edith Horne, 23, Kensington Sq., London W., England.

221. King Edward VII at Punchestown, April, 1904 – Hely's Limited, Dublin – Fairview D.O. Dublin, 4.40 pm, Ap 30, 04 – (Front) King Edward VII at Punchestown, April, 1904 – (Back) Miss L. Hammell, 47 Melrose Bank, Culcheth Lane, Newton Heath, Manchester. Dear Leah, We are quite loyal here this week. I suppose you have heard we are entertaining Royalty. With love to all. Ada.

222. The Castle Dublin – Hely's Limited, Dublin – Dublin, 5.30 am, Ja 16, 04 – (Front) 15-1-04. Dear J. Dont forget to-morrow – (Back) Master J.M.B. O'Brien, 7 Nth Great Georges St, Dublin Nth City. I will be up at your place about 2.15 p.m. sharp and if Willie is up with you, we could go to Bioscope Pictures. I remain Yrs. etc. B.

223. Sorrento Terrace and Dalkey Island. Co. Dublin – (Publisher unknown) – Dalkey, 10 am, Ju 16, 04 – (Front) (none) – (Back) Mrs Fisher, 95 Sinclair Rd, West Kensington, London W. I have put a dot over No 3. The island is the place with the tower on it.

224. Dublin Sketches, Howth Harbour – B. & N. Ltd, Dublin – Dundrum, 10.30 pm, No 8, 04 – (Front) M.F. – (Back) Miss M. Brodrick, Tarmon, Castlereagh, Co. Roscommon. I am sorry I have not a nice card. Thanks for yours. Love from Mary.

225. Vendor of Eggs – Hartmann – Dublin, 5.30 am, No 17, 04 – (Front) (none) – (Back) Miss Hall, 9 Albert St, Sligo. (…)

226. Quaker Oats Smiles – Quaker Oats Limited – Dublin, 6.30 pm, Ju 14, 04 – (Front) Judge's Smile. "We cannot," says the judge, "dispense With wholesome grains of common sense; we find for Quaker Oats," and hence The smile that won't come off!" "Quaker Oats Smiles," consisting of ten different designs, post paid for 3d., and three white squares cut from fronts of "Quaker Oats" packets. Apply to Dept. P.C., Quaker Oats, Limited, London, E.C. 13.6.04. Dear M. I have had enough of Judges last week at the commission. I will get 25/– for being there – (Back) Miss Fleming, Kingsweston, Sunny Gardens, Hendon, London N.W.

227. Weather Reports. Illustrated – Raphael Tuck & Sons – Dublin, 5.30 am, Jy 16, 04 – (Front) Weather Reports. Illustrated. "Dull and Gloomy!" – (Back) W. Smith Esq., C/o J.R. Taylor, Church Street, Skerries. Hope you got out all right. Nan.

228. (Untitled) – (Publisher unknown) – Dublin, 5.30 am, Ja 10, 04 – (Front) If this had been the fashion when some people I know were at Skerries, there would have been more bathing. (…) – (Back) Miss Violet Lefroy (Victoria), 174 Rathgar Road, Rathgar, Dublin.

229. O'Connell Bridge & D'olier Street, Dublin – Stewart & Woolf, London – Dublin, 4.45 pm, Au 17, 04 – (Front) (none) – (Back) Miss Brinkley, c/o Mr Geo. Brinkley, Marmick Villas, Burnham on Couch, Essex, England. Have not heard from you for some time, don't forget usual weekly. Do your "rainbows" turn out like this? Sent packet of "very rapid" to take views at Regatta. Hope you will have fine weather. Love to all.

230. (Untitled) – Stewart & Woolf, London – James's Street D.O. Dublin, 4.15 pm, De 16, 04. Vlissingen De 19, 04 – (Front) I am in a bit of a fix. T.M. – (Back) T.H. Flood Esq., Flushing, Holland.

231. "Fore!" – Davidson Bros – Dublin, 4.45 pm, Oc 24, 04 – (Front) "Fore" – (Back) Miss Muriel Mellor, Victoria High School, Londonderry. From Dot to Auntie, How's your poor foot.

232. Dublin. National Library – Pictorial Stationery Co. Ltd, London – Kingstown, 12.15 pm, Au 2, 04 – (Front) Park Lodge, Sandycove, Kingstown, Ireland – (Back) Miss Holland, 14 Raleigh Gardens, Brixton, London. I heard from Mother this morning that you have returned home. How is Cook? I do hope better. I wrote Mother

asking news but she was uncertain. I hope you and Mr Holland are the better for your change. Love to kiddies. Yrs. Affec. (…)

233. Map Truelove River – Knight – Dublin, 11.45 am, Oc 7, 04 – (Front) Map Shewing the Course of the Truelove River – (Back) Miss M. Kelly, Main Street, Trim, Co. Meath.

234. Butler's Musical Instruments, O'Connell Bridge, Dublin – (Publisher unknown) – Dublin, 6.30 pm, Mr 22, 04 – (Front) (none) – (Back) Sr M. Agnes, Dominican Convent, Galway. Your esteemed order will be forwarded in 2 days time. We have not the Eternelle but a string we think better.

235. (Untitled) – Meissner & Buch, Leipzig – Balbriggan, (…), De 24, 04 – (Front) With all good wishes for a very Happy Xmas. Kate. 1904 – (Back) "Nurse", c/o Mrs Cumiskey, Drogheda Street, Balbriggan.

236. Dublin Sketches, Polo, Phoenix Park – B. & N. Ltd, Dublin – Killiney D.O. Co. Dublin, 10.15 pm, Oc 3, 04 – (Front) (none) – (Back) Miss L. Monaghan, Glenageary, Kingstown, Co. Dublin. Your letter rec. glad all are so well. Same here T.G. Would write more only the nasty King's postman reads cards I hear. Hope pears went down well. No visitors that you know this week. I gave the message about the St I think the nights are so cold it would be better for to send me a fur for Sat. night by F.P. Please. M. is doing the B. it faded a little she says, also send me a pocket handkerchief with fur & any books you have.

237. R.M.S. "Munster" – City of Dublin Steam Packet Co. – Kingstown, 1 pm, No 29, 04 – (Front) From your affectionate sister D. McM. – (Back) Mr B. McMahon, Killaloe, St Marys, Maynooth. Royal Mail Service. City of Dublin Steam Packet Co. 15, Eden Quay, Dublin. Two services each way daily between Kingstown & Holyhead in connection with the Mail Trains from all parts of England & Ireland. Best and Fastest route. Telegrams "Eden, Dublin".

238. Custom House and Quays, Dublin – Lawrence, Dublin – Dublin, 5.30 am, Oc 8, 04 – (Front) (none) – (Back) Mrs Dobbie, 42 Afton Crescent, Cliffow Street, Ibrox, Glasgow. Hope you are all well & that you received my letter. I forgot the correct address until finding it today. E.H.

239. Paddy an' His Pig – Lawrence, Dublin – Dalkey, 10 am, Jy 13, 04 – (Front) Paddy an' His Pig. Arrah! don't be wastin' yer eddicashun readin milestones! jist thry a sate, an' be aisy. Faix! it's not to the Fair at all ye're goin' me purty Boneen! Smoile a big one! – (Back) Mr J. Thomson, 12 Seedley View Rd, Pendleton, Nr Manchester. 4 girls & Jack at Killiney and we all miss another Jack. It would just be perfect Jack dear if you were here, what we have said a 100 times today. Oh why are you not here? I won't tell you what Lois & Jack were doing, I'm not a gooseberry. But I wish, guess what I wish? May & Aggie are now rambling Bessie's. Love from all of us. Francis. X. Thats Lois. XXXX This is Jack.

240. Trinity College and College Green Dublin – Raphael Tuck & Sons – Dublin, 5.40 am, No 1, 04 – (Front) (none) – (Back) Miss Cochrane, 84 Moyne Rd, Rathmines, Dublin. May you live long & die happy.

241. A Lucky Xmas – Weiners Ltd, London – James's Street D.O. Dublin, 4.15 pm, De 23, 04 – (Front) (none) – (Back) Miss E. Turton, c/o Mrs E. Willis, No 5 Church Alm House, Newtown Road, Newbury, Berks, England. Dear E. Hoping you will have a Merry Xmas and that you received the box quite safe. Shall go out and get a card or two and send. With love Bill. XXXXX.

242. "Bridge" Expressions Illustrated – Davidson Bros – Rathmines D.O. Dublin, 4.15 pm, No 5, 04 – (Front) "Shall I play?" Lena, May, Faithful One, Bert, G., T.P.C. – (Back) Miss May Symes, 87 St Lawrence Rd, Clontarf, Dublin. Many thanks for the sticky back. We are just off to Monkstown on our bikes. Hope to see you before you go. Love from E.E.S.

243. Leap Year Goods – Raphael Tuck & Sons – Dublin, 4.45 pm, Au 23, 04 – (Front) Leap Year Goods. "Will Keep its Color" – (Back) Miss P. Campbell, c/o Mrs F. Kelly, 14 Main St, Trim, Co. Meath. Hope you & all are

quite alive again. I am only (…) way, nearly did a die on Saturday night and am in blanket since. What is the idea of H.R. appearing in court. Please tell me as you excited my "curo". Mae declares he goes up Switzers side, he's "too ould". How is K's heel hope quite healed. "Mind your jaw". Now Poppie Dear do not excite too much in Trim for I'm afraid you are a wee bit giddy E.P.P. as I can only get a "bare Glimpse" at this P.C. I'll say (…) with love to May, K.K. and self, not forgetting all swimming friends. D. Mr K. is this like Miss Doyle? Wow she has a tooth ache.

244. (Untitled) – S. Hildesheimer & Co. Ltd – Blackrock, 11 pm, Ju 18, 04 – (Front) I enjoyed Father B. greatly, he seemed to be struck on your colour. Fr Gorman is the name of your friend. He is Chaplin to the Carmelite Nun's so now I must say goodbye hoping to see you on 24th. I hope you are thinking of sending me P.O. for songs 6^s and oblige your fond Sister Mai. Love to Mother & Marcus. Have not seen Jack for ages – (Back) Miss C. Stewart, The Hotel, Cashel, Co. Tipp. 18-6-1904. My Dearest Cis, I had a visit from your friend Father Bridge and also from J.H. who is looking splendid not withstanding all he went through he settled all about the Mass. I hope you intend to come. You will have a letter on Monday with all news.

245. Ballsbridge – Stewart & Woolf, London – Dublin, 6.30 am, Fe 14, 04 – (Front) (none) – (Back) Miss Murphy, Rathgoury, Southcliff, Eastbourne, England.

246. Montreal, Post Office and Bank of Montreal – Montreal Import Co., Montreal – Montreal Canada, 3 pm, Ju 28, 04. Rathmines D.O. Dublin, 7 am, Jy 9, 04. Dublin, 11.45 am, Jy (…), 04 – (Front) 28-6-04. Letter & card received yesterday on arrival. Weather very warm. Leave here Sunday next expect to arrive in London about 14th or 15th July. (…) – (Back) Miss Johnston, 5 Rathmines Road, Dublin, Ireland. (Readdressed to) 8 Shanaganagh Tce, Killiney, Co. Dublin.

247. We are putting in some hard work – Davidson Bros – Dublin, 4.45 pm, De 22, 04 – (Front) (none) – (Back) Master Gerald Burns, 6 Rosetta Avenue, Ormeau Rd, Belfast. Wishing dear Gerald a very Merry Xmas & a Happy New year. From Yours Sincerely J.E. Lauden.

248. Killiney – Chas. Cook, Kingstown – Dublin, 5 pm, Jy 20, 04 – (Front) (none) – (Back) Mr J. Thomson, 12 Sudley View Rd, Pendleton, Nr Manchester. My Dear Don, This is where we were enjoying ourselves. We walked this lovely woods, & had a delightful scramble up to the Obelisk on the Hill. The view from there is simply beyond description, Jack said he had not seen anything grander & May said she had never seen anything more beautiful in her life. It was an ideal day, bluest of skies and the water! Well see P.C. but this only gives a faint idea. They say the Bay is another Bay of Naples. I would go into raptures but I must not on a P.C. must I? Monday morning Jack took us down on a jaunting car, Lor' did enjoy it she had been on before but the driver or jarvey was young, nearly drove them into the Liffey. Agnes, May & she had a great (…) however we went (…) They had a delightful passage home Agnes & May are enjoying their little selves. It is a great city (…) but there are the meetings too, ours is drawing nearer Jack. Very pleased to have your letter this AM & yesterday AM too. Hope you keep improving and perhaps rest at home will do you good. My love & best wishes that you may be quite well. Bessie had a pretty P.C. from Scotland "Larg's Country, Ayr". Have you been? It looks very fine.

249. The Lady's Maid – Davidson Bros – Dublin, 5.30 am, Mr 29, 04 – (Front) (none) – (Back) Miss Brodie, 18 Coulson Ave, Rathgar, Co. Dublin. Will expect you at any hour you like tomorrow evg. No particular news. Any resemblance to Ernest on the other side? I saw Milly C. & Aggie M. & a man drive into Haddens this after noon with Mrs Hadden for the Hockey Match, I was surprised. With love to yr. Mother. Yrs I.L. March 28th 04.

250. Quaker Oats Smiles – Quaker Oats Limited – Dublin, 6.30 pm, Ju 12, 04 – (Front) Cabby's Smile. The Cabby said, "A single fare Of Quaker Oats, I do declare, Is quite enough to make me wear <u>The smile that won't come off.</u>" "Quaker Oats Smiles," consisting of ten different designs, post paid for 3d., and three white squares cut from fronts of "Quaker Oats" packets. Apply to Dept. P.C., Quaker Oats, Limited, London, E.C. 11.6.04. The two men who broke into Grafton St got "one year hard labour". Love to all. Yrs H. – (Back) Miss Fleming, c/o Mrs Shorter, Kingsweston, Sunny Gardens, Hendon, London N.W.

251.   Howth Harbour & Ireland's Eye – Hartmann – Dublin, 5.30 am, Mr 20, 04 – (Front) "Gone but not forgotten". In memory of a "departed day", passed away here, Oct 1903 – (Back) F.H. Doggett Esq., 8 St Patrick's Terrace, Inchicore. 19th March 1904, Saturday. Are there no pens, ink or paper to be had at Inchicore? or have you lost the use of all 10 fingers together! Please relieve anxiety, if able to put in an appearance even at Grangegorman Tomorrow (Sunday) at 11.15.

252.   The end of the Journey – Stewart & Woolf, London – Blackrock, 12.30 pm, De 22, 04 – (Front) (none) – (Back) Miss Rita O'Brian, 7 N.G. Georges Street, Dublin. Calpé, Glad to get your note this morning. But sorry I can not meet you, as Mother is sinking rapidly & I may say there is no hope now. Yours in haste. Effie.